S0-BWR-912

ERAU-PRESCOTT LIBRARY

MANNOCK

MANNOCK

THE LIFE AND DEATH OF MAJOR EDWARD MANNOCK
VC DSO MC RAF

Norman Franks and Andy Saunders

Amazon 10/08

Grub Street • London and Philadelphia

Published by
Grub Street
4 Rainham Close
London
SW11 6SS

Copyright © 2008 Grub Street, London
Text copyright © 2008 Norman Franks and Andy Saunders

British Library Cataloguing in Publication Data
Franks, Norman L. R.
     Mannock : the life and death of Major Edward Mannock,
     VC, DSO, MC, RAF
     1. Mannock, Edward, 1887-1918 2. Great Britain.
     Royal Flying Corps – Officers – Biography 3. Great Britain.
     Royal Air Force – Officers – Biography 4.
     World War, 1914-1918 – Aerial operations, British 5.
     Fighter pilots – Great Britain – Biography
     I. Title II. Saunders, Andy
     940.4'4941'092

ISBN-13: 9781906502126

All rights reserved. No part of this publication may be reproduced, stored in a retrieval
system, or transmitted in any form or by any means electronic, mechanical, photocopying,
recording, or otherwise, without the prior permission of the copyright owner.

Cover design by Lizzie B Design

Book design and formatting by:
Roy Platten, Eclipse – roy.eclipse@btopenworld.com

Printed and bound by MPG Ltd, Bodmin, Cornwall

Grub Street Publishing uses only FSC (Forest Stewardship Council) paper for its books.

CONTENTS

ACKNOWLEDGEMENTS

The following people and institutions all have our sincere thanks for their help in piecing together the story of Edward Mannock. In no particular order they are: Lord Ashcroft KCMG, Mike O'Connor, Stuart Leslie, Tony Mellor-Ellis, the late Frank Cheesman, Andrew W Walker BA, Graham Day (Air Historical Branch, MoD, Bentley Priory), Gordon Leith (RAF Museum, Hendon), David Tonks (Wellingborough Library), Nicholas Andrews (Commonwealth War Graves Commission), David Amos, Peter Burden, the staff at the Public Archives, Kew, the staff of the Imperial War Museum's reading room, Lambeth, London, Guy Smith, Brad King and Air Chief Marshal Sir Peter Squire GCB DFC AFC DSO.

PROLOGUE

THE LAST DAY

Major Edward Mannock DSO and two Bars, MC and Bar, was awoken as dawn broke and just as he had been countless times over the last two years or more, was instantly alert and pulling on his flying clothes. After a quick splash of cold water on his face from the jug and basin in his room, he left the hut and crossed to the squadron office. The airfield was St Omer, not only an operational base but the home of a pilot pool and an Air Depot. For many flyers St Omer was their first landing spot on coming across the Channel from England. Here they would wait for a posting to a squadron, filling dead men's shoes.

Within a few moments a second airman arrived, Lieutenant D C Inglis DCM, who had travelled from New Zealand to fight in this great war. Mannock acknowledged the other man's presence and then both headed out across to where the four squadron Bessonneau canvas aircraft hangars stood. In front of them the mechanics had already rolled out, primed and tested, two SE5a fighters, Mannock's E1295 and Inglis's E1294, interestingly but quite co-incidentally, numbered in sequence. Both machines had arrived on the squadron on consecutive days, 16 and 17 June. E1294 had been flown on a number of sorties over the last several weeks but Mannock in E1295 had achieved seven victories with it since his arrival to take command of 85 Squadron on 18 June. Soon after he arrived he had test flown it, liked it, and was now comfortable in it.

Students of WW1 flying will know the famous picture of 85 Squadron's SE5 line-up in front of these same hangars, taken on 21 June 1918, with Captain S B Horn MC seated in Billy Bishop's old C1904 'Z'. It was here that Mannock and Inglis prepared to climb into their machines on this fateful July morning in 1918. Visitors today to St Omer airfield can easily locate the spot, it is just to the right of the British Air Services Memorial stone, where a WW2 hangar now stands. 85 Squadron's buildings would have been further along.

Mannock had already studied the morning sky. Despite it being July, all he could see were lowish grey clouds. From his experience he felt sure it would rain later but at least going out on patrol with these clouds he would not have the glaring rays of the rising sun to contend with as they headed east. They would of course need to fly lower than was comfortable, but so too would any German aircraft they encountered. They could expect German two-seaters, either making a dawn reconnaissance, or trench strafing.

In the front line trenches just south of Pacault Wood [1], by the La Bassée Canal, near where Mannock would have his last air battle, British troops were viewing a grey sky too. Not thick or heavy, but the sort of greyness that soon disperses when the sun rises. Visibility was

[1] On British trench maps and in all official correspondence referred to in this book, Pacault is spelt without an 'l', ie: Pacaut. The authors have followed the correct spelling although this demonstration alone is a good illustration of variations of interpretation on maps and documents, given that such anomalies are a crucial element of issues discussed in chapters 11 and 12.

good and they could see the Nieppe Forest, some seven miles to the north-west, quite clearly.

The two airmen's flying boots were wet with dew as they arrived at their aircraft. Each said the customary few words with their ground crews before climbing into the tiny cockpits to begin the routine checks. It is sometimes assumed that Donald Inglis was a new boy, but in fact he had been with the squadron longer than his SE5a had. His first CO had been the Canadian, Billy Bishop. This belief has come about because Mannock was, this July morning, taking him out to try and help him down his first Hun. Mannock, ever the leader and teacher, was always concerned that pilots be blooded as soon as possible. It would give them heart, encouragement and hopefully and equally necessary, that killing instinct which fighter pilots had to have if the war was ever to be won.

Up to this moment as they started their engines, it had been virtually the same ritual as had occurred just 24-hours earlier. On the evening of the 24th, Mannock had casually asked Inglis if he had succeeded in shooting down a German yet. Doubtless he knew already that the New Zealander hadn't, he would have already gone through all his pilots' files and noted that Inglis had yet to put in a combat report for a successful air fight. Inglis had replied that he hadn't as yet been successful. Mannock, in a matter-of-fact way, said, 'Well, we'll go out and get one.'

Donald Inglis was no new boy, nor a youngster. He was just a month past his 25th birthday, having been born in June 1893 and in 1914 he had been a motor engineer/mechanic in Christchurch. Joining the New Zealand forces he had served in the 2nd Battery of the NZ Field Artillery as a bombardier/fitter and had won the Distinguished Conduct Medal at Gallipoli, for repairing three guns despite heavy Turkish fire. Having transferred to the RFC in August 1917, he joined 85 Squadron while the unit was working-up and under training, then following further instruction he had finally returned to 85 in France on 21 May 1918. Therefore he had been with 85 in France for over two months. What is more, he would end the war with the squadron, finally leaving in December 1918, having been successful in surviving the air battles above the Western Front for six months – itself no mean achievement.

Inglis had recalled all this in an article for *Popular Flying* magazine in July 1938, edited by the creator of the famous *Biggles* – Captain W E Johns – himself a World War One pilot, but flying bombers, not single-seat fighters. No doubt Inglis had told the story often enough in the intervening twenty years, and while it may have been finely tuned, would nevertheless be approximately the same.

On the morning of the 25th both he and his CO had prepared for take-off. It was a reasonable day, promising a blue sky although the forecast predicted some possible showers as the day progressed. In the event it didn't matter for although his leader took off, Inglis's machine, much to his chagrin, had a problem. His elevator controls were jammed. The ground crew worked to try and clear the fault, but it was going to be a longer job than he hoped. Mannock's SE5 arrived back over the airfield and landed. Taxying up to the hangars, Inglis ran over to report the bad news to Mannock. Mannock grinned and said it was all right. 'We will go out tomorrow and get one.'

So here they were again, on the 26th, both seated in their machines. It was now well past 5 am, and Mannock's final instruction to Inglis was, 'Sit close on my tail and if you get too far away I will waggle my wings!'

While it may seem that Mannock and Inglis had merely flown off in order to bag a Hun for the New Zealand lad, there was also a viable reason for this early sortie. According to Captain Lance Rushbrooke, who had visited the squadron some time after the events of

26 July 1918, a front line army division on 85 Squadron's portion of the front had complained that at specific times each day two low-flying German machines flew over and 'worried' the infantry in the trenches. These were obviously aircraft of the Schlachtflieger units, whose two-seater crews' task was to ground strafe Allied front line trenches both to inflict casualties and damage morale among the soldiers. Mannock had, Captain Rushbrooke learnt, received a call – unofficially – from friends in this division and had decided to do something about it. While no doubt Inglis recalled his involvement as the suggestion of Mannock in order to get him a victory, Rushbrooke was told that Mannock had in fact asked for a volunteer to accompany him. A pilot had offered and the two had set out together. Essentially the same story, but with a little variation. [1]

The two SE5s headed for the front, Inglis recalling they were never higher than 50 feet, and then flew along the front between Nieppe Forest and Mont Kemmel, where Mannock kept mostly to the gullies. Inglis recalled:

'… suddenly he turned for home [i.e. west] and commenced climbing full out. I knew from this he must have spotted a Hun. As I climbed after Mick I kept my eyes skinned for the Hun, but could not pick him up. However, a few moments later I noticed that Mannock half-rolled and went into a power dive. But the Hun must have spotted Mick as he was attacking from the rear. Apparently he disabled the rear gunner, as when [I finally saw the German] I attacked the Hun gunner was not shooting.

'Both my guns were going full out, when suddenly the Hun's tail shot up in front of me. A chill ran through me as I pulled up, just missing his tail and wing by a fraction. Looking back I saw my first Hun going down in a mass of flames.

'We circled once and started for home. The realisation came to me we were being shot at from the ground when I saw the major was kicking his rudder. Suddenly a small flame appeared on the right of Mick's machine, and simultaneously he stopped kicking his rudder. The plane went into a slow right-hand turn, the flame growing in intensity, and as the machine hit the ground it burst into a mass of flame.

'I circled at about 20 feet hoping for the best – but Mannock had made his last flight.'

At this stage the two SE5s were at about 200 feet. In his combat report, the New Zealander wrote:

'I went into a spiral down to 50 feet and saw machine go straight into the ground and burn. I saw no one leave the machine and then [I] started for the lines climbing slightly; [and] at about 150 feet there was a bang and I was smothered in petrol, my engine cut out so I switched off and made a landing 5 yards behind our front line.'

[1] The 1930s pulp fiction writers became renowned for their embellishments to stories of the air war, and the impression has certainly become fixed that Mannock would often take out un-blooded pilots in the way Inglis described. This too led these writers to embellish the tale by saying that Mannock, in doing this, would not therefore claim any such victory achieved, but would 'give it' to the youngster. This all sounds magnanimous and gallant but in reality, there was no need. These fiction writers had obviously not understood that during WW1, fighter pilots who shared a victory were each given credit (although the same rules did not apply in the German Air Service), so while Mannock and A N Other might well down a German aircraft, both men would be able to add it to their overall score.

There is also the thought, if this logic is pursued, that Mannock's score would have been very much higher than it was, had he not 'given away' these victories, but that is just not the case. One has to remember too, that Mannock, like the majority of the more successful fighter aces, was always mindful of his personal victory score, and would not easily give a victory credit away. It is facile to assume that men such as Mannock – and many of his contemporaries – did not think so materialisticly about personal scores, yet most of them did. Mannock often wrote to friends, and in passing, mentioned his score, so we know he ran a mental total at least.

Inglis crash-landed near to British trenches and soldiers of the 24th Welsh Regiment ran out, got him out of the machine and quickly pulled him into the nearest dugout. He was quite shocked and bemoaning the fact that the Germans had shot down his major. Once he pulled himself together and was able to give an army officer details of himself and his squadron, the officer arranged for a message to be put through to St Omer and 85 Squadron.

At St Omer the squadron had no inkling of the disaster as the two SE5s were not yet overdue. Then came the devastating message from the Welsh Regiment trenches:

> 'Major Mannock down by machine-gun fire from ground between Calonne and Lestrem after bringing enemy aircraft two-seater down in flames at Lestrem. Lieutenant Inglis shot through petrol tank landed on front line at St Floris. Machine OK, pilot OK. Machine likely to be shelled, salvage to-night if possible; more later. Machine at Sheet 36a SE, or 36 NW, K.31.D.14.'

That night 85 Squadron did indeed send out a party in an endeavour to retrieve Inglis's machine, led by the equipment officer, Lieutenant Peter Rosie. He and some of his men managed to get within 600 yards of the position indicated by the Welshmen but heavy artillery fire made it impossible to get closer without endangering the salvage party. In the event the SE5 was abandoned and struck off charge on the 28th.

Mannock and Inglis's two-seater victory was a DFW CV (2216/18) piloted by Vizefeldwebel Josef Hein and his observer Leutnant Ludwig Schöpf of Feldflieger Abteilung (A) 292b, (the 'b' denoting a Bavarian unit) so not ordinarily a trench-strafer, but an artillery observation staffel. Both men, Hein, aged 24, from Dortmund, and Schöpf from Pfaffenhausen, aged 24, died in the action and are buried in Billy-Berclau German cemetery, south-east of La Bassée.

Inglis would later suffer another forced landing after being shot-up by ground fire on 31 August, and again survive. Donald Inglis finally brought down his one and only sole victory on 9 October 1918, a Fokker DVII fighter.

* *

The evening of the 26th saw a very subdued dining-in night at St Omer. Several of Mannock's friends from neighbouring squadrons came over. Keith Caldwell, Mannock's former CO with 74 Squadron was one of them and he made a short speech saying that Mick would not have wanted them to brood over his death, but this failed to raise spirits any higher. According to J I T Jones, also of 74 Squadron who also attended (he was later Mannock's biographer), even with drinks and a well used record player, it was a sombre affair.

Next day, after Inglis returned and confirmed the spot where the CO had fallen, a number of pilots flew out at low level to inspect the area – and to shoot-up any sign of German troops in nearby trenches.

The devastating, terse, telegram was despatched to Mannock's mother on the 29th, to 96 Ettington Road, Aston, Birmingham:

> 'Regret to inform you that Major E Mannock DSO MC RAF, is reported missing on July twenty sixth. Letter follows.'

Another communication was sent the same day to his brother Patrick, at 13 Albert Road, Dover, which was received by his wife Dorothy, as Patrick was in France with the Tank Corps.

Mick's cousin (also) Patrick received the news of his relative's passing, and wrote to 85 Squadron in early August. Cousin Patrick's father was J P Mannock, a famous billiard player who had taught King Edward VII the game. The squadron adjutant, Lieutenant W E W Cushing, replied:

85 Squadron,
Royal Air Force,
BEF, France

Patrick L Mannock Esq,   7/8/18

Dear Sir,

I am in receipt of your letter dated August 3rd. I have already written to Major Mannock's brother, who has answered my letter.

I think I can tell you all you wish to know, but I was not an eye-witness. Only one officer was with him at the time, Lt D C Inglis, who is at present on leave, and is due to return on the 14th August.

At all events, this is what happened. At 5.0 am on July 26th Major Mannock left the ground in company with Lieut. Inglis; they drove down a hostile machine in flames, about 5.30 am, the fight finishing at a height of 200 feet over enemy territory. They then turned towards our own line, and had covered half the distance when Inglis noticed flame coming from Major Mannock's machine, which at once fell uncontrolled to the ground. Inglis spiralled down to fifty feet hoping that he would see Major Mannock climb out of his machine, but the S.E. was so completely obscured in smoke and flame as to render it impossible to see anything. Inglis then left for our lines and was himself shot down, but landed unhurt just inside our front line.

Under the circumstances it is useless to tell you that there is a chance of Mick being alive; it is such a remote one that I would only raise false hopes. I should like to repeat what I wrote to his brother, that we all loved him, both as a friend and a chief. One could not wish for a more loveable, thoughtful or energetic leader. Please accept sincerest sympathy from 85 Squadron.

CHAPTER ONE

FROM MODEST BEGINNINGS

For years, even before starting to research Mannock's life in detail, we were always aware that his birth place and date, appeared to be uncertain. In various publications one can read that he was born in Brighton, Canterbury, Aldershot, India, and Cork. The reason for this was due to his father being in the army and having been stationed in various places during the late 1880s.

Ira Jones wrote his biography of Mannock in 1934, stating 24 May 1887, in the Preston Army Barracks, Brighton. In 1963, in their book *Ace with One Eye*, Frederick Oughton and Vernon Smyth quoted the same place and date. (Apparently this book was written by Oughton from information supplied mainly by Smyth.) However, Oughton, in his book covering the entries in Mannock's diary, in 1966, appears to have either made a typing error, or disagreed with Smyth's date, and recorded 1889 as the year of birth.

In a Canterbury newspaper in 1978, the date 21 May 1887 is recorded, and again Brighton, but the writer quotes the Ministry of Defence as showing 1888, and that they believed he was born in Aldershot. James M Dudgeon in his book *Mick*, in 1981, records 24 May 1887, with Cork as the birth place. Chaz Bowyer, in his book on Air VCs in 1992 says Brighton on 24 May 1887, while in 2001, Adrian Smith in his book *Mick Mannock Fighter Pilot*, shows 21 May 1888, Brighton.

A search at Somerset House has thus far not revealed a birth date or place. Children born to fathers in the army were often recorded separately, but there is no record of his birth there either. Perhaps Cork is the correct location, where a mention in UK records would not be made. Mannock himself confused the issue by recording both Brighton and Cork on documents.

Mannock's father, Corporal Edward Mannock, had joined the 2nd Dragoons – Royal Scot Greys – under his own mother's maiden name of Corringhame, for reasons best known to himself, and is described as being a soldier of fine physique. In 1881, the 2nd Dragoons had been stationed on the outskirts of Cork, in southern Ireland, where he had met and courted Julia O'Sullivan, then married her in 1882. Julia had lived in a suburb of Cork, the village of Ballincollig.

The couple moved with the regiment to Edinburgh, and soon afterwards Corporal Corringhame was sent to Egypt, Julia returning to Cork while he was overseas. While away fighting with the Heavy Camel Corps, a daughter Jessie (Jess) was born and upon her father's return the family moved into the West Cavalry Barracks in Aldershot, Hampshire in 1886. That same year a son Patrick J was born and in early 1887 another move came, this time to the Preston Cavalry Barracks, Brighton. This is how Mannock's birth place is deduced, but it may be that Julia again returned to Cork (her husband possibly on manoeuvres in Ireland), and it was here that a second son, Edward, came into the world, on 24 May 1887.

The young Edward Mannock does not help settle the matter of his birth, although he undoubtedly had reasons for leaving red-herrings around for future historians. When he joined the Territorials in 1915, he actually wrote on his entry form that his date of birth was 24 May 1888! In early 1914 on the occasion that Mannock applied for a passport to travel to Turkey, he again wrote in his own hand that he was 24 years of age, whereas he was actually 26. Confusion over his birth place is again due to Mannock. On the occasion he received his Royal Aero

The Mannock family c1900. Seated, Mrs Julia Mannock, with (left to right) Edward, Jess, Patrick and Nora.

Club flying licence, it records his place of birth as Cork. One might have thought that to enter an incorrect age on a passport document, then to show Cork as his birth place on his flying licence if incorrect would have been rather a stupid thing to do so perhaps Cork at least is correct. Certainly when he joined the Royal Flying Corps, they noted his birth date as 24 May 1887. According to James Dudgeon, he was told by family members that Cork was correct.

Army life for Edward senior continued, with postings to Louth, Ireland, Newbridge, near Belfast, and from the latter the corporal ended his period of army service. For a while the family lived in various places around London, but the soldier's heart was still with the military, and during a visit to Liverpool, he suddenly re-joined the army, even giving his proper name of Mannock as he did so. He became a trooper with the 5th Dragoon Guards, then stationed in India, and six months later, Julia Mannock and her three children arrived in India to join her husband, and were to remain there for almost six years.

The young Mannock appeared quiet and reserved by nature and was rarely seen charging about with other children, and was more often than not found reading or deep in thought. It was in India that he first became aware of a slight defect in his right eye. For a while he seemed totally blind in that eye, but the condition gradually returned to almost normal within a few months. He liked football and cricket, and while he enjoyed target practise with an air-rifle or even a bow and arrow, never tested his skills against living targets such as birds and animals.

His father had regained his old rank of corporal by the time the regiment went to active duty during the South African war where he saw a good deal of action, although his family naturally remained in India. By now a further daughter had arrived, Nora.

At the culmination of that war, Corporal Mannock's second period of service was again nearing the end. Returning to England he went first to Shorncliffe, then to the cavalry depot at Canterbury where his wife and children joined him. Within a few months he left the army and the family took up residence in Military Road, Canterbury. Then, quite out of the blue, Edward Mannock senior left, completely abandoning wife and family. He never saw them again, nor supported them in any way at all from that day on. [1]

Young Edward – he was often referred to as Paddy, or Eddie – was 12 years old at the time his father left. Despite this desperate turn of events, Julia dug in her heels and stoically went on undeterred, helped in part by small incomes from Jess and Patrick. The family had never been well-off, and now they existed on the bare minimum, but exist they did, and she kept them all together, long enough to have them eventually fend for themselves.

In September 1905 his sister Jess married. The Mannocks were now residing in St Peter's Street, Canterbury and the wedding took place at St Thomas's catholic church in the town. Jess's husband Edward Ainge (Ted) was in the army, his address given as Canterbury Barracks.

Another pilot who flew with Mick in 40 Squadron during 1917, was C O Rusden. He later recorded in a 1957 letter to one of Mannock's biographers (Vernon Smyth):

> 'He was very conscious of his social background and never sought the limelight for that reason more than any other.'

Meantime, Edward was making friends in Canterbury. He was a member of the St Gregory's cricket team, and with an interest in religion had joined the Church Lads Brigade, even though he was a catholic. They had a band, and Edward did good work with the kettle-drum.

Someone who recalled Mannock at this time for Vernon Smyth in 1957, was S J Powell, then living in Whitstable, Kent.

Powell had related that he had known Mick when he was living in King's Street, Canterbury, when Mick was working for the National Telephone Company, and remembered him as being '... in poor circumstances.' Powell often took Mick home for evening meals and sometimes his mother would give him a parcel of underclothes.

Powell also related how Mick later had helped form the local Territorial Army unit and played a bugle in the band, and that while others might read the occasional book, Mick always seemed to be reading and studying a dictionary! He remembers him as tall, reticent, serious-minded, and modest. Mannock would often suddenly burst out excitedly for a few seconds over something, and then quite unexpectedly

Patrick and Edward at a telephone company outing to Deal in July 1904.

[1] Mannock would have been only too aware of his and his family's status in life. In 1917, in France, he confided to a fellow pilot, C W Usher about his humble origin. Usher later wrote: 'After a discussion in the Mess one evening, during which he [Mannock] expressed himself freely on the social order, he concluded by saying, "You fellers were born with silver spoons in your mouths. I had an iron shovel."'

revert to his normal quiet manner. So, whether kettle-drum or bugle, Mannock had some musical talent at least, and was improving himself by reading.

** **

Edward was going to St Thomas's School, but he needed to earn money at the earliest opportunity. Brother Patrick had got himself employment as a clerk with the National Telephone Company in the town, and he contemplated joining his brother with this firm. However, Edward did not fancy being a clerk, preferring outside work, so he become a messenger boy to a local greengrocer but after a few months moved to become a barber's assistant. This did not suit him either, so he managed to join Patrick as a clerk, but although better paid and with shorter hours, the job was not to his liking. Still longing for outside work he succeeded in getting himself accepted to fill a vacancy as a linesman, assisting the engineers. Scrambling up telephone poles had some appeal apparently. The downside to this was that the vacancy was in Wellingborough, so he had to leave the family home and Canterbury, and find himself digs in the Northamptonshire town.

Luck was with him and he fell firmly on his feet. He found lodgings with Mr and Mrs A E Eyles, 64 Melton Road, Wellingborough. (They later resided in Mill Road.) Their meeting was quite by chance, for Edward had started to play for the local Wesleyan cricket team, and Jim Eyles was also a member. Obviously living accommodation came up in conversation and Jim suggested he come and live with them, which he did. Jim Eyles and his wife 'May' (they had married in September 1908) became a second father and mother to

Edward expounding on his political theories to a group of YMCA friends in 1911.

him and remained so for the rest of his life. Eyles was the manager of the Highfield Foundry and Engineering Company in Wellingborough, and he liked Edward a lot, and took him under his wing. They too knew him as Paddy.

Later Jim Eyles was to record that Paddy was a keen cricketer and in the Wesleyan club played as wicket-keeper: '… a position needing a keen eye.' (So much for a serious eye problem!) He recalled too, Edward joining the local parliamentary debating society as well as becoming the secretary of the local branch of the labour party. He remembered also his infectious laughter, and the fact that he taught himself to play the violin.

All in all he is described as quiet and reserved, in many ways self-educated and a profound reader. He was also fond of music. One thing he abhorred was snobbery and sham. Mick also decided to join the Home Counties (Territorial) RAMC – Royal Army Medical Corps – so that despite moving up north, he would be certain to meet up with his old TA mates each year at summer camp. He achieved the rank of sergeant shortly before 1914.

With a few shillings in his pocket he opened a bank account. This was in 1912 but he quickly fell foul of the bank manager. A letter survives written by Mannock to the manager.

> 64 Melton Road,
> Wellingborough.
> 15 April 1912

Dear Mr Cook,

I enclose herewith postal order value 10/- which please credit to my account. This will leave a debt still outstanding amounting to 9/- which I will send you later.

I rather regret that you should adopt such a tone in your letters regarding this matter, more so in view of the fact that the account itself has only been contracted since September last, and you may have known that money was safe.

> Yours faithfully,
> Edward Mannock

One has to smile on reading this, for it seems that the young Edward Mannock thought he must be doing the bank a service by having an account with them.

**

Life might have easily jogged along had it not been for Mannock's desire for some form of promotion. The job of assistant to an outside telephone engineer did not excite him especially with no immediate prospect of advancement. With so many young men of the age heading for varied foreign climes – Canada, South America, South Africa to name a few – Mannock suddenly decided that telephone engineers might be eagerly sought after in some developing countries. Why exactly he chose Turkey is unclear, but shortly after Christmas 1913, he informed Mr and Mrs Eyles that he planned to head away from England. At that stage he was happy to contemplate not only an extension of the job he knew, but again, like so many others, had tea planting or cattle ranching in his mind.

He applied for a passport, and this document survives to this day in the RAF Museum, Hendon. Unlike the passport documents we know now, this is a large 11″ x 8″ (29cm x 20cm) sheet of white paper, that feels like those old £5 notes that went out in the 1950s, folding to make four sides. A small snap-shot of the holder was glued to the front page, and on the back of the last page are the stamp impressions of the various countries he travelled through. This passport paper is dated 10 January 1914 and Mannock describes himself as a telephone and telegraph mechanic.

Borrowing money from Jim Eyles and brother Patrick, Mannock boarded a tramp steamer in February 1914 and worked his passage to Constantinople. After his arrival, he sought an interview with the manager of the English Telephone Company, and got a job as an outside engineer. He worked for this company during the spring and summer of that fateful year even rising to the position of district inspector, but when war was declared in

August, and Turkey looked as though it would come down on the side of Germany, Mannock, along with other foreign workers, became aware of anti-European feelings, especially against the British. Work consequently dried up, as did wages and access to food that could be afforded. By October some work had started again but the following month, with sides finally taken, Mannock became interned, as a prisoner of war.

Silence followed, no letters being received from him, and finally Jim Eyles contacted the American embassy in Turkey for news. They managed to discover that Mannock was well and still in Constantinople, but the telephone company had been taken over by the Turks. Apparently he had tried several times to escape so had been put into a prison camp. He remained a constant irritation to his captors and in so doing became something of a hero to his fellow detainees. When guards told him England was finished, his invariable reply included thumbing his nose at them.

Finally, through diplomatic reasoning, the detainees were gradually selected for exchange, and it is believed that Mannock had begun conveying to his captors that he was virtually blind in one eye, and that this, together with his vast age – he was now approaching 28 – convinced them that he would be of little value as a soldier. This, and the fact that he was such a nuisance, made it easier to release him than keep him, so at the beginning of April 1915 he regained his freedom and returned to England.

In some cuttings that Mannock's first biographer Ira Jones stuck into a large RAF book, there is a loose one referring to the occasion Mannock was a best man at a chum's wedding. He signed himself A Wyler (although in correspondence to Vernon Smyth, his name appears as R Wyles), who after the war was living in Penshurst, Kent. He wrote that he had known Mannock in the Territorials pre-war and that when the war came along he had gone into the infantry while Edward went into the Royal Engineers. 'He was my "best man" and the last souvenir he gave to my wife and me was a photograph – duly signed – and bearing these words. "The path of glory leads ...."'

When writing to Smyth in the 1950s, Wyles recalled Mannock returning from Turkey and meeting him again when Mannock decided to rejoin the

Edward Mannock's passport photograph in 1914.

Mannock in Turkey, complete with fez, 1914.

Edward in his RAMC uniform in 1915.

RAMC. Mannock had entered the orderly room to find his former friend sitting behind a desk as the OR sergeant. No sooner had the two friends got over their reunion, than Wyles got Mannock a job as transport sergeant. He also recalled that while they were at Halton camp, Tring, in Hertfordshire, Mick was the life and soul of the evening debates. Wyles was later commissioned into the Duke of Cornwall's Light Infantry.

Mannock had joined the transport section of the 3/2nd Home Counties Field Ambulance Company. Enlisted here on 25 May 1915, on the form he had to fill-in he noted his year of birth as 1888, and in answer to the question of where he would like to go, requested either the Royal Engineers, Signal Section, or the Army Service Corps, or the infantry, but mainly desired the 101st Field Company of the REs. The army was always interested in a man's ability to ride a horse at this time, and in answer to this question, Mannock confirmed: 'Yes, well.'

The problem he now faced was that in the RAMC he would be expected to attend to German wounded, not just British or French. This did not sit well with him at all, so he decided to move to a more combatant role, hence his desire for the REs. One job he thought would be good was as a tunnelling officer, so that he could '… blow the bastards up! The higher they go and the more pieces that come down, the happier I shall be.' Thus the mild-mannered telephone mechanic, soured by his time as a prisoner of the Turks, had become, if not a Hun-hater, certainly a Hun-disliker.

Mannock got his wish and turned up at the RE depot at Fenny Stratford, just outside Bletchley, Buckinghamshire, as a cadet. He was a good deal older than most of the other cadets and seemed rather insular. He was ill at ease with the training, but eager to get into the fighting. Like so many other soldiers feeling kept from the war, he moved to try and expedite matters, but it was quite a sudden change of direction – at least his CO thought so – to have him request a transfer to the Royal Flying Corps. Anyway, he had now received a commission, and his CO, despite thinking the move a foolish one, did not block his request. Suddenly Edward Mannock was about to start flying training.

**

It was now the summer of 1916 and there is little doubt that Mannock, like others, had been hearing and reading about the exploits of the airmen on the Western Front, and especially of Albert Ball, who was regularly jousting with German pilots and shooting them down. He understood too, that any eagerness to get to France would end up in the dreary and dangerous work in the trenches. Long gone were the battles in open fields and sweeping plains. Engineers and signals people would also be exposed more than most to hostile fire, when having to deal with cut telephone wires and ensuring communications between front line units and headquarters.

One obvious first hurdle would be the medical, and more especially his eyesight. Even today there are two schools of thought about his defective eye. Was it a problem or was it something that hero-worshippers could refer to, to indicate that he was a wonderful pilot and shot despite one eye. Obviously there was something amiss, but one can imagine that it was not perhaps that serious. Some of his flying chums, when asked about it, were surprised there was a problem. It might be said that some medicals in WW1 were not as thorough as later, and Ira Jones seems to suggest that the doctor merely asked Mannock if his eyesight was all right, and he had confirmed that it was, so that was that. Depth perception was really a must for pilots in order to judge distances and heights, especially when landing. Shooting might be done with one eye closed, and in any event, the fighting pilots who were to fly Nieuport Scouts and later the SE5s, generally screwed one eye to an Aldis telescopic gun-sight anyway. J W Shaw who flew with Mannock in 40 Squadron told me (Norman Franks) once that if there was any problem it must have been very intermittent. Shaw knew he had a 'cast' in the left eye but that he could see with it perfectly well. Overall, it can be said that the problem was not too great a one, and obviously did not affect his ability in the air in any way.

Mannock's transfer to the RFC came in August 1916 when he was in Bedford and, as he confided to his diary, when the depot adjutant called him in to tell him, he could have kissed the man. He had his sights firmly set on becoming a fighter pilot like Ball, and as we know he achieved his aim. What might have happened had he had been selected to be a bomber pilot, or a reconnaissance pilot can only be guessed at. Mannock might have been in Bedford at this moment, but his address he gave upon joining the RFC was: Rolvenden Layne, Rolvenden, Nr. Cranbrook, Kent. His next of kin he gave as his mother Julia, 96 Ettington Road, Aston, Birmingham.

** **

Would-be pilots often began their association with flying by a posting to No.1 School of Military Aeronautics, at Reading, Berkshire, and so it was with Edward Mannock. Yet there were no aeroplanes, just classrooms, where the new boy would be taught the theory of flight, and gain knowledge of how aero-engines work, how to rig an aeroplane, how to read a map from the air, discover the secrets of the main machine guns of the day – the Lewis, drum-fed gun, and the belt-fed Vickers – and a myriad of other subjects he would come across, not least some rudimentary history of the RFC, despite only being four years old. All military units have their traditions, and the RFC were fast establishing theirs.

Mannock was then sent for his ab initio training. However, he did not impress as a natural pilot. Training at Hendon with 9 Reserve Squadron, was far from smooth, and indeed, at one stage it was thought he might well be returned to the REs. Arthur Glendower Graves, who had been a second lieutenant in the 9th Somerset Light Infantry, passed his flying test in November 1916. He had met Mannock there, and when Vernon Smyth was researching for his book *The Ace with one Eye* in the late 1950s, Arthur Graves, who for some years had been the Clerk of the Peace for the County of Middlesex, wrote the following account of his recollections of Mannock at Hendon, and later at Joyce Green. Smyth was the researcher and Frederick Oughton, his co-author, did the writing, but they did not include all that Graves recalled of his time with Mannock:

'I knew Mannock extremely well and indeed learned to fly with him at Hendon early on in the First War.

'He was then a young man of twenty or so [actually nearing thirty] and was of a most tempestuous nature; even then nothing daunted him, and indeed, he had been at

Hendon only a very short time, some two weeks or so, when becoming restless with the "eternal situation" as he called it (we had no dual control in those days) and being impatient and wanting to fly solo on his own, he went onto the tarmac early one morning (there was no-one about, just two mechanics) jumped into a Caudron and flew around the aerodrome for ten minutes or so; on landing he was severely reprimanded by the C.O., who ordered him to remain grounded until further orders.

'In those far off days, the Royal Flying Corps having taken over Hendon, which was of course a civil aerodrome, the officer pupils and staff were billeted in the neighbourhood, mostly in Colindale Avenue, and had their meals in the then civilian restaurant on the aerodrome, which was staffed by waitresses; it did not take Mannock long to pick out the most seemly and make an appointment to take her out for a walk one evening. Unfortunately for him, however, the C.O. saw them on their return, walking down Colindale Avenue.

'In the morning he was ordered to appear in the orderly room and the C.O. gave him a proper talking to, referring to his being an officer and a gentleman and expected to behave as such, to which Mick replied with just a little politeness: "Neither you nor anyone in the British Army will prevent me from going out with the girl I love." To which the C.O. was unable to reply, or in any event he did not do so.

'Mannock, restless as ever, wanted to get to France as soon as possible, and was therefore posted to his finishing squadron in England, for further experience on the War Scout machines of those days. He was soon away in France where as we all know, he covered himself with such glory.

'He was a great humourist and was most excellent company. I did not see him again for he was soon to die doing his duty – a brave man.'

Moving on he was posted to No.10 Training Squadron at Joyce Green, near Dartford Creek, commanded by a South African, Major J G Swart MC. One of his instructors was none-other than James McCudden, as yet not famous but already a successful fighter pilot, with a Military Medal and a French Croix de Guerre. Under his tutelage he did well but he did have at least one brush with the 'grim-reaper'.

Arthur Graves had moved to Joyce Green too, and recounted this story. The pupils were out on the airfield and had watched McCudden spin a DH2 from around 3,000 feet over the aerodrome and finally pull out very low down. Mannock, according to Graves, thought it a good show, and obviously impressed by it, sought out McCudden that evening and had a long chat with him. Next morning, there was a low cloud base but a few machines were up. Suddenly those still on the ground heard the whine of wires, and looking up saw a DH2 spinning down from about 1,000 feet.

At little more than 200 feet above the ground the DH2 came out of the spin, but pointing not towards the aerodrome but at the Vickers TNT works on the other side of Dartford Creek. It disappeared from view below the dyke and everyone watching expected the noise of a crash, or even an explosion, but there was neither. Of course, it was Mannock. He had actually managed to pull up about ten feet from one of the huts where explosives were made. He returned some time later and had his leg pulled pretty badly.

He had misjudged his height but it was typical of the man, reported Graves, that he intended to succeed at something that was considered fairly difficult. As one might expect,

McCudden had more than a few words to say.

The chief flying instructor at Joyce Green was Lieutenant Edward Alexander Packe, formally with the Oxford and Bucks Light Infantry. He had been injured in France and in 1916 became an instructor, firstly with 46 TS, then with 31 RS before moving to 10 RS in November 1916. He would later go back to France with 32 Squadron before returning to instructing in 1918. He ended the war with the DFC and a Mention in Despatches. At Joyce Green, Packe made most of his students very nervous by his manner, including Mick Mannock.

Mannock was sharing a room with Meredith Thomas, another trainee pilot. Thomas would become an ace with 41 Squadron in late 1917 and would rise to the rank of air vice-marshal in the RAF. In recalling Mannock he recorded:

Captain James McCudden VC DSO MC MM CdG. He was one of Mannock's instructors in England prior to being posted to his first operational squadron.

'We shared a room and he told me many interesting stories of his pre-war life; it appeared to have been a hard one. At this time he was a staunch teetotaller and a fairly regular churchgoer, although during chats with him he professed to have no particular religion. We were great friends at Joyce Green and had many serious and amusing talks when waiting in the cold [sitting] on a petrol bin for a flight, but I cannot recall anything definite beyond our mutual disgust because of the manner in which the staff threatened the pupils, many of whom had seen pretty severe war service before transferring or being seconded to the RFC, whilst the staff had seen very, very little, and in some cases none.

'My first impression of Micky was that he was very reserved, inclined to strong temper, but very patient and somewhat difficult to arouse. On short acquaintance he became a very good conversationalist and was fond of discussions or arguments. He was prepared to be generous to everyone in thought and deed, but he had strong likes and dislikes. He was inclined to be almost too serious-minded.'

It would be of interest if any of his contemporaries had mentioned if he had any Irish accent. Considering his upbringing and the places and people he frequented during his first quarter century, it seems very unlikely he had anything resembling an Irish brogue. Yet he is often referred to as an Irishman, due simply to his birth-place being recorded as Cork. As his father was English, and Mick spent most of his early life among Englishmen, especially soldiers and their families in India, it would be difficult to have any chance of picking up an accent.

Once his training was complete, he received his Royal Aero Club certificate, No.3895 dated 28 November 1916, and the coveted RFC wings presented and sewn on his uniform,

Mannock's RAeC certificate. Note he gives his place of birth as Cork.

he awaited his first posting to a squadron. He was assessed a proficient pilot in March 1917 and posted to France, to Clairmarais near St Omer, the home of No. 1 Aircraft Depot. He began a diary now, the first entry being what would be an auspicious date in 1918, 1 April 1917, noting:

'Just a year ago since I received my commission, and a year to the day earlier I was released from a Turkish prison. Strange how this date recurs. Let's hope that a year hence the war finishes and I return for a spell to Merrie England.

'Well. Landed at Boulogne. Saw the MLO and discovered I was to be away to St Omer the following day at 3.45 pip emme [pm]. Rested and fed at the Hotel Maurice. Quite a nice place as continental hotels go. Wisher, Tyler [1] and two more strangers (RFC) kept us company. Rotten weather. Rain. I'm not prepossessed with the charm of La Belle France yet.'

Mannock arrived at St Omer on the 2nd. Once the war had settled down after the initial rush to France in the early weeks of WW1, St Omer became the major staging post for the RFC, where aircraft and airmen came prior to posting to operational units. By the end of the war it was a vast military flying base. On the 3rd he noted he met other new RFC types, Lemon, Dunlop and Kimbell. Second Lieutenant Richard Evison Kimbell, aged 19, would be sent to 60 Squadron and be killed in action in less than two weeks (16 April). Dunlop would be posted to 40 Squadron along with Mannock, but he was seriously injured in a crash on 9 April. Brian Bertie Lemon had passed his flying tests to receive his licence on 21 November, No.3849 – a week before Mannock. Andrew Crawford Dunlop, a Royal Engineers second-lieutenant had joined the RFC in October 1916.

[1] 2/Lt J V Wischer RGA. RAC Cert No.3792, 10 November 1916. R C Tyler, RAC Cert No.4059, 19 December 1916. Wischer (an Australian) went to 16 Squadron (BE2s) and with his observer was shot down and taken prisoner on 28 April 1917, by the German ace Kurt Wolff.

On 6 April Mannock received orders to report to No.40 Squadron. Mannock noted it was at Aire/Lens, although actually 40's base was known as Aire/Treizennes. This airfield was south-east of St Omer, half way between there and Béthune. He and his meagre possessions were put aboard a Crossley tender for the one and a half hour drive to the airfield. He was met by Captain McKechnie and Dunlop, the latter having preceded him a day earlier. In due course he was introduced to the squadron commander, Major L A Tilney, who told him he would be flying with C Flight, led by Lieutenant H C Todd. Pilots awaiting postings at St Omer were generally in the queue to replace dead or wounded pilots. 40 Squadron had lost a pilot on the morning of the 6th, another had been reported missing on the 3rd (prisoner of war) and they had also lost one on 30 March. Disaster had already occurred a month earlier, on 9 March. A patrol had been caught by Baron Manfred von Richthofen's Jasta 11, and had lost four pilots and had had two other FEs badly shot-up.

It is understood that Mannock actually replaced the missing lad who had been shot down on the 6th, Second Lieutenant H S Pell. Todd had led a special mission, an attack on the German balloon lines, a highly dangerous operation, for which 40 Squadron would become famous. Todd himself had been lucky to get back, the anti-aircraft fire being intense, as well as rifle fire from troops on the ground. Harry Pell had not been so lucky and his Nieuport 17 had been hit by MFlak 60 battery. The young Canadian from Toronto did not survive the crash inside the German lines.

Major Tilney was 22 years old, therefore, seven years younger than Mannock. A former officer with the Duke of Lancashire's Own Yeomanry (TF), he had become a pilot in 1915 and served in France with 11 Squadron the following year. Towards the end of 1917 he received the Military Cross for his leadership of 40 Squadron, while the Belgians awarded him their *Croix de Guerre*, then made him an *Officier de l'Ordre de la Couronne*.

The Squadron was in a high state of activity when Mannock arrived, having been on the aforementioned balloon strafe that morning. Henry Todd had flamed one gasbag and had been lucky to return home. In the Mess later that day, Mannock inadvertently sat in the chair that Pell had usually sat in and there was an awkward silence – but it passed. The next day the Squadron went on another balloon raid and Todd had again been subjected to much ground fire. These had been the unit's first operations with their new aeroplanes, French Nieuport XVII Scouts (more usually referred to in the RFC as 17s) having replaced the antiquated FE8 'pusher' type scouts at the end of March.

Mannock made no reference to these events in his diary, his first few days being totally occupied getting used to the Nieuport 17 that he would shortly be flying against the enemy. He made his first 'solo' flight in a Nieuport on the 7th – serial number A6733 – between 0950 and 1015 am. He described it as a 'Lovely 'bus', in which he 'tootled around and went as far as the lines via Béthune.' For the first time he saw the flashes of the big artillery guns, the trenches and the smoke of war.

That same afternoon he made two more practice flights, again in A6733 between 1415 and 1500, then in B1502, a short hop between 1835 and 1850 pm. The next morning he was taken on his first line patrol (LP) in B1502 (0750-0815) with Todd leading. This would not turn into a fighting sortie unless Todd spotted German machines over the front worrying the two-seater corps aircraft, which if it did occur, Mannock would have had orders to break away and fly home. No, this was just another practise flight, getting the new boy used to flying with other aircraft and adding to his knowledge of the area over which 40 Squadron operated. New pilots needed to become familiar with the locality in quick time as it was too easy to become lost, and a lost pilot was vulnerable.

The Squadron had been in France since August 1916 with their FE8s, and had moved to Treizennes that same month after a stop at St Omer. Their new aeroplanes had been well received by the Royal Flying Corps. They had been used by the French – in its earlier variants – for some time, and the type 16 (XVI) had been in service with the British for over a year, although in the early days employed just in small numbers with two-seater squadrons. By mid-1916 there were enough machines to equip whole units, and No.60 was among the first. The Nieuport type 17 (XVII) started to arrive on British squadrons in mid-July 1916, and by the time 40 Squadron began to receive them, at least three other RFC squadrons were equipped with the type; 1, 29 and 60.

The type XVII had a 110 hp Le Rhône engine and it was easily identified in the air because of its sesquiplane wing design – the lower wing being much narrower than the top wing. (In fact this was copied by the German Albatros Company later, which it used with their Albatros DIII and DV models.) Armament for the Nieuport in British service was a single drum-fed Lewis gun situated on the top wing centre section, fitted so that the bullets would pass harmlessly over the spinning propeller, to a point some way ahead of the aeroplane's line of flight. A successful interrupter gear was only just being made available but the RFC – and RNAS – used only the top wing gun with their Nieuport Scouts. Much earlier aeroplanes, such as 40's old FE8s, the other 'pusher' type scout, the DH2, and the earlier Vickers FB5 two-seater, plus the FE2b/d types, cleared their frontal field of fire by having the propeller at the rear.

The wing-mounted Lewis gun assembly had been the invention of a Sergeant R G Foster of the RFC, while with 11 Squadron. This ingenious mounting embodied a quadrantal slide which permitted the gun to be slid down rearwards so that the pilot could replace the empty drum with a full one. Naturally it did not take RFC pilots long to see that the gun, pulled down, could easily be used to fire upwards into the under-belly of an enemy aircraft. In this way, the first intimation of danger by the German pilot, was as bullets began slashing through the bottom of his machine. Each drum held 47 rounds of ammunition.

Later, once an interrupter gear became available, the French in particular began using a belt-fed Vickers gun mounted on the fuselage immediately ahead of the cockpit, so that the pilot could aim and fire directly at an opponent, and although the RFC used this Alkan mounting too, it really came at a time when the Nieuport Scout was being phased out.

CHAPTER TWO

WITH 40 SQUADRON IN FRANCE

Mannock's arrival in France at the start of April 1917 came at a time when the British army was about to begin their first major offensive of the year – the Battle of Arras. It was Easter Monday, the 9th.

The previous day, when Mannock had flown his first Line Patrol with Major Tilney, it had been a fine day although cloudy. British ground troops had, after weeks of preparation and planning, finally pushed forward in the vicinity of the Bapaume-Cambrai road along a front of 3,000 yards north of Louverval.

At around midnight the shelling of German positions had begun, a necessary and already time-honoured prelude to an attack. British artillery would pound German front line trenches and strong points, hoping too to cut the mass of barbed-wire that stretched inexorably in front of them. Between the British front line trenches and the wire, was 'no-man's-land' – the killing zone. Soldiers, with no more bodily protection than a chance cigarette case or small bible in a breast pocket, would have to face a mass of deadly machine-gun fire as they pressed forward across an already shell-crated, lunar-like landscape, cluttered with the debris of war, holes full of stagnant, cold, stinking water, but with bayonets fixed, they hurled themselves at the enemy. Their only hope was that the shelling had cut the barbed-wire sufficiently to let them through, and that the defending soldiers were either dead, wounded, or so stunned as to be unable to resist the assault. It was rarely successful, and today would be no different.

Dawn, when it came, was cold. Low clouds and strong wind blew across the landscape, which would continue all day. There had been few able to sleep. The dread of the attack made it impossible to relax. Within minutes of their officer's whistles blowing, they could be dead or badly wounded, lying out in the open with no immediate chance of help. And if they got as far as the enemy trenches, would the wire be cut, or would they be snagged up upon it, easy prey to machine-gun and rifle fire?

One major target was the high ground that constituted Vimy Ridge. The Canadians were going after that. In a land as flat as Flanders, any high ground was contested vigorously. The side that commanded the heights, any sort of heights, dominated the battle areas. At the moment, the Germans were in occupation and they had to be ousted.

Mannock's squadron was just that little bit north to be involved in the start of the battle. Nevertheless, they could hear the guns to the south and knew what was happening. The weather in any case was not conducive to flying. Even the squadrons directly involved over the battle front were restricted, and by the end of the first day, British infantry had only moved forward some 6,000 yards, but at least Vimy Ridge had been taken.

Next day the weather was little better and aerial activity was again almost non-existent. Snow and sleet had supplemented the already severe weather. On the ground the troops had to try and maintain forward momentum without support of gunfire directed by artillery observation aircraft marking and correcting the fall of shells. News came through to the Squadron that Vimy had been secured, and of course, the noise of battle remained constant in the distance. Mannock got his replacement aircraft on the 12th, testing it the following day.

The Squadron was able to put up a patrol, and Lieutenant H E O Ellis, on his first war flight, managed to stumble across a German two-seater and shoot it down over Courrières at 11.30 am. Henry Todd got back to the airfield after having an armour-piercing bullet slash through his engine plus several bullet holes punched through the Nieuport's fabric.

That same evening Mannock flew over the lines for the first time, part of a six-plane formation. Anti-aircraft fire exploded around them, Mannock's first experience of hostile fire, and one shell blew up about 100 feet from him. He put his machine into several aerobatic manoeuvres, but in doing so he lost the flight leader. He then saw some German aircraft a long way off but could do nothing about it. The next day, the 14th, Mannock flew three OPs (Offensive Patrols), again saw enemy aircraft in the distance but again had no chance to close with them.

More patrols followed but the weather again proved perverse and restricted activity along the front. Then on the 19th Mannock had some excitement. He took off for some firing practice, diving on a ground target from a height of 2,000 feet. At 700 feet his starboard bottom wing snapped off and went fluttering down, but he managed to right the machine and working diligently with stick and rudder, was able to crash land about half a mile from the airfield.

Mannock seated in his Nieuport Scout B3607, late summer 1917. Note his flight leader's streamers on the wing V-strut and the distinctive propeller boss which he had painted yellow, reminding his fellow pilots of his slow start! Lt R N Hall MC is standing in front between the mechanics, named as F/Sgt Hancock and Sgts Jackson and Mather. The two on the far right are not named.

Upon Mannock's return, he saw his rigger, Air Mechanic Geary walking towards him, looking totally crestfallen. Smiling, Mannock assured the man that it had not been his fault in any way, which brought a relieved smile to the man's face. Next day Mannock was driven to St Omer to pick up another aircraft, despite suffering from a 'good night' – a party for McKechnie who was being rested and sent home to England.

His nervous system was not improved a day or so later. Flying the Nieuport belonging to Parry, the engine cut out three times. On the 23rd he flew out with Captain F L Barwell, as escort to a BE.2. They spotted a couple of German machines but they were way too high to go after, and in any event, it would have meant leaving the BE. On the way back he and C A Brown did chase a German back over the lines but could not catch it.

Mannock was on another OP on the 24th, again led by Barwell – six pilots this time – with Mannock now flying B'1552, a machine with a large blue number 4 on the fuselage aft of the roundel, edged in white. Apart from the varnished wooden wing and inter-plane struts, the Nieuport was silver-doped. An enemy machine was encountered, and while Mannock fired 20 rounds at it, there was no effect. Two balloons were also seen south of Douai and again, firing towards them proved ineffective. Barlow also went after a German machine, then dived towards four balloons and saw the observers all bale out and descend by parachute.

The Squadron was also preparing to move bases, from Treziennes to Auchel. Auchel/Lozinghem was just to the west of the town of Béthune, so their main section of the battle front was between Laventie in the north, south via the La Bassée Canal area, to Lens and Vimy. However, within a few days, they had moved again, this time to Bruay, seven miles behind the front line, arriving on the 25th. This airfield was

Captain F L Barwell, 40 Squadron, killed in action 29 April 1917.

situated 19 miles north-west of Arras, and therefore, just a few miles south-west of Béthune. The patrol line would be roughly the same, but perhaps a little further to the south.

**

As April ended, Mannock had almost been with 40 Squadron for a month. Apparently at this time, there was something of a feeling going round that Lieutenant E Mannock was not being as aggressive as was expected and that he was perhaps shirking his duty somewhat.

How true this was is unclear for any new pilot was necessarily cautious until he found his feet. Some new pilots of course didn't live long enough even to get to this stage. It has to be said that Mannock, older than most of the others, would have been naturally more cautious, and it was easy in later years to blame some of this cautiousness on his supposed sight problem. Nevertheless, it must have been a little un-nerving to think that his comrades in arms were questioning his bravery and even his suitability as a combat pilot. However, it might be highlighted, that Mannock had survived what was about to be termed 'Bloody April', a period where casualties among the RFC and RNAS were the greatest the British flying services had sustained. That Mannock had survived this terrible month must say something for his fortitude, ability – and luck – during his first weeks in France.

In the 1930s this matter of his apparent lack of 'dash' was discussed within the pages of the well-read aviation magazine *Popular Flying*. In a letter published in the January 1935 issue, by one of Mannock's companions in 40 Squadron, G L 'Zulu' Lloyd MC AFC, a South African, he related:

> 'He was not actually called yellow, but many secret murmurings of an unsavoury nature reached my ears. He showed signs of being over careful during engagements. He was further accused of being continually in the air practising aerial gunnery as a pretence of keenness – in other words, the innuendo was that he was suffering from cold feet.'

Apparently Mannock had later confided to Lloyd:

> 'Of course, I have been very frightened against my will – nervous reaction. I have now conquered this physical defect, and want to master the tactics first. The present bald-headed ones should be replaced by well-thought-out ones. I cannot see any reason why we should not sweep the Hun right out of the sky.'

These comments by George Lloyd and Mannock himself are interesting. Lloyd had previously been flying with 60 Squadron from April to July 1917 – Mannock's early days with 40 – and had only moved to 40 Squadron in July to be a flight commander. One assumes therefore, that what Lloyd had gleaned about Mannock had been after the event, and he was, supposedly, being made aware of a problem which had by the time he arrived, been overcome. And of course, Mannock makes absolutely no reference to any eye problem, which he could easily have referred to by then being part of the reason, as he was now starting to score victories.

However, Mannock did at one point make the following comment to his old pal from Canterbury, S J Powell, at the time Mannock was transferring to the RFC. Powell wrote to Vernon Smyth, saying that he had asked him about those early days, and Mannock had replied: 'Well, I can only see out of one eye and all I want to do is to get over the other side and bring down some of those b____ Jerries.'

Of course, he could have meant that he could only see 'properly' out of one eye, or he could have been over-emphasising the case. Why Mannock, if he truly could only see out of one eye, thought that being a pilot would help negate this problem is beyond understanding. Depth perception is not only crucial in air fighting, but in actually flying and landing an aeroplane it is surely essential, as we have discussed earlier.

Another fact that is never referred to when dealing with Mannock, is that if he truly had that much of an eye problem, it says much for him that he did not use it to stay away from the fighting altogether. He surely could have made certain he failed any medical he was given.

In the same wing as 40 was 43 Squadron, commanded by Major William Sholto Douglas MC, a future air commander of some note. He met Mannock briefly and, like many others in the RFC, heard a good deal about him. In his book *Years of Combat*, Douglas gave an enlightening and apt thumb-nail sketch of Mannock as he remembered him.

'... although possessed of a lively Irish temperament, which he got from his mother, he was a lonely man. The rugged, forthright quality about his character – he was nearly ten years older than most of us – must have come from the background of his family life. It had not been an easy one because his father, who became a corporal in the Army, deserted his family while Mannock was still a child.

'Tall, slim and dark, almost saturnine, Mick Mannock walked in a somewhat ungainly fashion. But for all that, what immediately impressed one about him was his vitality, which was so well expressed in his eyes. They were clear and of a piercing blueness. He spoke clearly and decisively, and I noticed on the occasions when I visited 40 Squadron Mess as a guest that he was an excellent after-dinner speaker. There were also occasions when he expressed himself with a vehemence that was a little startling.

'It was that vehemence of Mick Mannock's, and his forthrightness of expression, that left us in no doubt about the intensity of his patriotism that drove him on, and that was coupled with his very real hatred of the Germans. And yet, because of the slowness of his start, there was at first a doubt in the minds of those with whom he flew about his ability and even his desire to fight. Being an older, more articulate, and more experienced man of the world, Mannock did not hesitate to voice his opinions, even if he had not yet proved himself; but his self-assurance, while not being in the least arrogant, was resented by some of those who thought, because they happened to be scoring, that they knew better.'

The pilots in 40 Squadron in the spring of 1917, were quite a go-getting bunch. Although Tilney, the CO, was one of those pilots who did not actually lead much in the air, and RFC HQ did not encourage squadron commanders in any event to do so, they being generally more useful as ground commanders than air fighters, his flight commanders were good. Captain Robert Gregory MC, Captain Ed Benbow MC, who had left just before Mannock arrived, had an excellent record, and Henry Todd had done well. Captain William A Bond MC and Bar was about to succeed before his untimely death in July 1917, and Robert 'Bob' Hall, from South Africa, would win the MC with the Squadron. [1]

Robert North Hall had been a farmer in South Africa, where he was born in May 1888. He had been in the Natal Carabiniers in 1909 and made sergeant in April 1915. Coming to England he had gained a commission into the Royal Field Artillery, serving with the 18th Reserve Battalion till August.

**

While J I T Jones was Mannock's first biographer, William Maclanachan wrote many articles about him during the 1930s especially following the publication of Jones's book – *King of Air Fighters* – in 1934. Maclanachan, encouraged by the enthusiasm these articles engendered, and supported by his friends, wrote his own book about his war experiences with 40 Squadron in 1917, which was published under the title of *Fighter Pilot* in 1936. His articles, and then his book, were written under the pseudonym of 'McScotch', a name given to him by Mannock himself, in order to distinguish him from another friend in 40, G E H McElroy, whom he named 'McIrish'.

[1] Others of note were D deBurgh, H E O Ellis MC, Ian P R Napier, L L Morgan MC, K MacKenzie, Charles W Cudemore, Harry A T Kennedy, Lionel Blaxland and Herbert Redler. These would be joined by men such as Captain Arthur W Keen, Albert Earl Godfrey, Gerard B Crole and William Maclanachan. All were press-on types so it is easy to see how anyone appearing to be even slightly hesitant in the air, for whatever reason, would stick out like the proverbial sore thumb. Lewis Morgan in particular, was seemingly always in the air. So much so they called him the 'Air Hog'; always up, always aggressive.

Maclanachan – also known as 'Mac' – was eight or nine years younger than Mannock but they became firm friends. Before joining the RFC he had been with the Royal Welsh Fusiliers. Maclanachan was as eager as his friend to get to grips with the enemy and was always up for any expedition that would engender contact with the Germans, and equally keen to join in any prank that would bring joy and amusement to his fellow pilots. Unfortunately, Maclanachan, so one former pilot in 40 told one of the authors [Norman Franks], and Major Tilney disliked each other almost from the start, and Maclanachan seemed always happy to snipe at anything Tilney said or did, or did not do, that he disagreed with. It was probably this tension between them that became the reason Mac never received any decoration for his successes with the Squadron. No doubt aware of the post-war comments about Mannock's early courage, Mac was eager to put his late friend's name in a better light.

One has to remember that air fighting in 1917 was still new. We later generations are so steeped in knowledge of flying and air battles that we tend to forget that Mannock and his companions were all still learning the art of fighting in the air, developing tactics, while desperately trying to stay alive in this new environment. In one of his many articles in *Popular Flying* (May 1936), Maclanachan wrote the following, which in part gives a clue to any assumed reluctance by Mannock to get to grips with the enemy during his early days at the front, and how he later used his early experience to influence the way in which he would act when in a position of command:

'During the war, when we had little or no real education in [air] fighting, having to learn our "profession" empirically at the wrong end of German machine guns, very few, even of our bravest fighters, could claim any excuse for their survival of their first fights other than the bad marksmanship of the particular Germans who got them into their sights. I have seen Mannock in his early days, burying his head in his hands and trembling from head to foot after he had to spend ten minutes of adrenal energy in keeping clear of a hail of lead that was being fired at him from four or five machines simultaneously. He, like all brave men, was the first to admit that his one and only desire was to save his life – so, if the "King of Air Fighters" could show such a terrific mental and physical upheaval, what would have been the effect on an inexperienced pilot who had lacked even a little of Mannock's will and spirit?

'The difference between the pilot who will develop into the right kind of fighter and the broken spirited pilot who avoids a patrol or combat whenever possible, is that the former uses his intelligence to analyse what did actually happen and makes up his mind to remedy the defects in his next encounter with the enemy; while the other lets his imagination play tricks with his membranes that should hold his entrails securely to his abdomen.

'[Sometimes], promising novices were retarded, if not ruined, by injudicious "safety first" attitudes on the part of senior pilots.

'In "40" after being given command of A Flight, Mannock was very quick to realise that, both in the interests of the economics of the war, and for personal liking for the pilots, it was preferable to safeguard and preserve the spirit of the junior members by looking after them, than letting them face both the physical and moral dangers alone. In doing this, he had to encourage the most backward and to retrain the more impetuous. He thus succeeded in nursing the inexperienced through the teething stage until they could bite for themselves. Of his protégés, G E H McElroy alone brought down 46 enemy machines, while Tudhope, Harrison and Learoyd each had good scores. In "74", by the application of the same method, he was even more successful – witness the achievements of J Ira Jones (Taffy) and Dolan. These fighter pilots were the first to acknowledge and pay tribute to the efficiency of Mannock's tutelage.'

Indeed, it is enlightening here to consider the background of two of Mannock's pupils. McElroy, a lot more 'Irish' than Mannock, was born in Donnybrook, near Dublin, almost exactly six years after Mannock's birth, 14 May 1893. He was the son of a schoolmaster, and had actually been born at the school (National Schools, Beaver Row, Donnybrook) where his parents, Samuel and Ellen, were resident.

No doubt due to his father's influence and position, he did well at school, firstly at Beaver Row till 1906, then at the Educational Institute, Dundalk to 1909, followed by Mountjoy School, Dublin to 1911. 1912 saw him at Rosse College, Dublin following good results with his 1910 Intermediate Education Board for Ireland Certificate. He had passes in English, Natural Philosophy, Latin, French, Trigonometry, Chemistry and Mechanics. Also passes with Honours in Arithmetic, Algebra and Geometry.

Leaving college he had become a clerk with the civil service but when war came he immediately enlisted in the army and as No.28292 became a despatch rider, serving at the front between 30 September 1914 and 8 May 1915, thereby becoming a recipient of the '1914 Star' campaign medal and making corporal. Commissioned into the 1st Battalion of the Royal Irish Regiment in May 1915, and later attached to the 4th Battalion, he served in France for six months, then in Ireland for six months on garrison duty after being badly gassed. In May 1916 he relinquished his commission to become a gentleman cadet at the Royal Military Academy. From here he took his commission into the Royal Flying Corps. He was not particularly tall, being just five foot, six inches in height.

McElroy had joined 40 Squadron in September 1917 but did not have his first victory confirmed until 28 December. He never felt comfortable in the Nieuport but quickly found his niche with the arrival of the SE5a.

If future ace George McElroy's background was interesting, so was Mannock's other pal in 40, John Tudhope. He had been born a British subject in Johannesburg in April 1891, the son of a director of Robinson's Gold Mine, and appears to have divided his life between South Africa and England. His education began at the Diocesan College in Cape Town and the St John's College in Jo'burg. By 1906 he was at Tonbridge School, Kent, where he excelled at rowing for the following few years and also in Western Transvaal in 1912. After four years in his Kent school OTC, he had spent time with the South African Militia between 1910-12, then a year with the Imperial Light Horse in South Africa, commencing in 1914 and had seen active service in the South African Rebellion and then in German South-West Africa 1914-15.

Two years spent as a fitter in the Transvaal Gold Mines and then some farming, broadened his mind even more and by the time the war started he was also a married man. In England again he joined the Dorsetshire Regiment and then moving into aviation in November 1916, received a commission into the RFC on 13 April 1917.

** *

No sooner had the Squadron settled in at Bruay than it lost two pilots, Captain F L Barwell and J A G Brewis, on 29 April. Frederick Barwell, a Berkshire man, was only 22 but had taken over from Todd as Mannock's flight commander. Brewis had been shot down and killed on a dawn show, but Barlow had been lost twelve hours later, in a fight with Jasta 5, his victor being Edmund Nathanael, the German's 13th victory. A Spad of 23 Squadron RFC would shoot him down in flames on 11 May, his score having risen to 15. The Spad pilot was Captain W J C K Cochran-Patrick MC, and Nathanael was his 9th victory of an eventual 21. Mannock described Barwell as having: 'A heart like a lion.'

Now came the period during which 40 Squadron would become famous. Attacking German observation balloons was never easy and particularly dangerous. Both sides in the war used these tethered balloons, beneath which dangled a basket in which one or two observers would study enemy positions. By using early Morse code signalling techniques, these observers could direct artillery fire on hostile gun batteries, strong-points, transport and even moving soldiers. They were generally just a few miles behind the front line trenches. Obviously needing to be near enough for the men in the baskets to view potential targets and troop movements, and hopefully just out of range of enemy ground fire.

Because of their vulnerability, they were always defended by a number of light anti-aircraft guns and machine guns not to mention rifle fire from soldiers on the ground. Some balloons even carried a light machine gun in the basket too. However, almost at the first intimation of danger from approaching aircraft, the observer(s) would rapidly prepare to jump! Unlike the airmen in their aeroplanes – at least in 1917 – balloon observers had the use of parachutes. These, due to their size and bulk, were fitted to the side of the basket, a static line being attached to a harness worn by the observer. He needed only to jump over the side, and his weight would pull the parachute canopy from its pack and provided that the man was not hit by gunfire, or have a burning balloon fall on him, he would float to the ground and safety.

Balloons were a way of life for the military on both sides and both sides were eager to preserve and protect them. Occasionally specific balloons were targeted if an offensive was about to begin, but more often than not, individual pilots tended to have a crack at them if nothing else was worth attacking. Indeed, while there were a number of pilots during the war who tended to attack them more frequently, there were many other pilots who had no intention of doing so, as they deemed it far too dangerous.

However, 40 Squadron was about to start a short period of anti-balloon missions that began on 2 May although Mannock was not among the stalwarts that went for the German balloon line *en masse*. They claimed four in flames, the successful pilots being Lieutenants W T Walder, B B Lemon, L L Morgan and K MacKenzie. They flew over at 20 feet and although all the Nieuports were damaged by ground fire, everyone returned. General Hugh Trenchard, GOC of the Royal Flying Corps, sent a telegram of congratulations to all concerned. Mannock noted in his diary that he was disgusted that he hadn't been in on it.

Brian Bertie Lemon came from Surrey, born in December 1888, so was more Mannock's age. He had joined the RFC in August 1916, and 40 Squadron from Joyce Green where he had met Mannock, in March 1917. He would survive his time with 40 and become an instructor the following year. He survived the war too and became a sheep farmer in New Zealand.

The day before this balloon 'strafe', Mannock had gone out on patrol to escort four Sopwith $1^1/_2$ Strutters of 43 Squadron, with his new flight commander, Keen, only to discover on testing his gun, that it was jammed. Nevertheless he continued on even though his only armament was a revolver. They were attacked by some Albatros Scouts, one of which Keen claimed shot down in company with a Sopwith crew. Mannock described how one '.. beautiful yellow and green "bus" attacked me from behind.' He could clearly hear the German's machine guns rattling away at him and as he made a rapid turn, saw the German pull across to attack Parry, with Mannock turning after it.

Mannock reported that he'd seen one Sopwith go down, but it was not lost. The crew, Captain D C Rutter and Air Mechanic Cant, despite serious damage to their tail, got home. It had been this pair who had shared the victory with Keen. 43 did lose a crew this same day, but it was in another engagement and another sortie.

On 5 May, Herbert Ellis gained more laurels for the Squadron. On an early evening sortie, he spotted two German Albatros Scouts south of Douai and in attacking them, they collided and fell to earth. He then went after another, ran out of ammunition, but with just his automatic pistol must have hit something vital for this too crashed. London-born Ellis had won his MC before transferring to the RFC and his successes this day brought his score to seven. Unhappily he was injured in a crash the very next day.

Things were still not going well for Mannock, for on the 6th he made what he described as a rotten landing, and turned his machine (B1552) upside down. As luck would have it, Keen did the exact same thing an hour afterwards, so no doubt little was said.

Morgan and Captain Gregory both claimed victories on the 6th, and some of Mannock's new pals left. Brown and deBurgh went home to England, and Blaxland went on leave. Blaxland was a particular friend, and he asked him to let his brother and the Eyles know where he was. Then came 40's second 'balloon strafe' and this time Mannock took part.

The line of balloons hung in the sky in the Drocourt area, beyond the front line trenches and 10 Wing Headquarters had ordered the Squadron to destroy as many as they could, and force the others down. The 3rd Battle of the Scarpe had started on 3 May and no doubt HQ wanted to blind the enemy for a while, especially as the fighting was continuing just to the south, around Bullecourt. Captain W E Nixon was another new flight commander, and he would lead the foray. Nixon had been with 24 Squadron in 1916, and earlier with the King's Own Scottish Borderers, following time at Sandhurst.

Before this event occurred, however, Mannock flew a patrol and had a fight with a German machine, along with Keen and another new pilot, who Mannock had known at Joyce Green (J B Raymond, known as 'Rastus') and drove it away east. Mannock was then engaged himself by what he described as several 'red devils'. At this period of the war, any hostile aircraft seen with any part of their empennage coloured red, were automatically thought to be Baron von Richthofen's squadron, Jasta 11, as their Albatros Scouts all had parts of their aircraft painted, or doped, red.

At this time, Jasta 11 were based at Roucourt, south-east of Douai, so it was on 40 Squadron's patch. Whether or not he had encountered Jasta 11 is unknown but with the skirmishing, Mannock became separated from the other two Nieuports and when Captain Keen landed, with no sign of Mannock, he reported that he thought he might be missing. Upon landing shortly afterward, Mannock was in receipt of much handshaking at his reappearance.

Then came the balloon attack order. Nixon selected Bobby Hall, Cudemore, Redler, Parry, Morgan and Mannock for the raid, which began at 0850. Here it has to be said that if Mannock's diary entry is correct, he had done an awful lot that morning with a combat action patrol already flown.

Once again 40's tactic was to fly fast and low in order to assail the gasbags from below, rather than dive on them from a great height. Another Flight would go over at height, which hopefully would make the balloons start to descend. In this way they hoped that an element of surprise would help the lower attacking force as they approached the descending gasbags. Also, by not attacking from above, they would be less likely to run into serious anti-aircraft fire. Low down the AA guns were somewhat hampered, but the risk from rifle and machine-gun fire was ever present. In the event the only loss was Captain Nixon (B1631), who was killed. The others all put in claims for balloons, Mannock being one of the successful pilots, and he had thereby made his first successful claim for a victory. His report read:

'Crossed the trenches at 0912 am not higher than 15 feet. Apparently not fired on whilst crossing the lines, but by machine guns afterwards. Attacked balloon south of Quiéry la Motte [east of Douai].

'The balloon was approximately 3,000 feet and was hauled down to 2,000 feet when Nieuport opened fire, and it continued to go down whilst pilot was firing. Shots were seen to enter envelope and smoke seen issuing from balloon, Nieuport kept up fire and saw top of balloon flame when it was between 20 and 30 feet from the ground.

'Nieuport was being fired on by machine guns and small arms and on the return journey by field guns, machine guns and possibly AA guns. No flaming onions were observed.

'Nieuport observed the 3rd balloon, which appeared to be north of Quiéry la Motte burst into flames. Only one parachute was seen to descend about one minute before Nieuport flew off. Parachute was not seen to land.

'No HA was seen and Nieuport returned flying at an average height of 20 feet.'

Mannock recorded too that he was the only pilot to return and land at Bruay without mishap, although his wings had been pretty well peppered with more holes through his fuselage. Hall and Cudemore both cracked up in more or less crash landings. Parry (B1541) had been shot-up and his fuel tank holed, so was forced to crash land at Camblain L'Abbé airfield south-west of Lens, situated near the Canadian HQ, at 0930. Others put down at numerous locations after destroying their assigned targets, Redler (B1640) crash-landing at Savy airfield, also south-west of Lens. Morgan's balloon was seen in flames by the La Bassée Canal, while Hall, Cudemore and Redler flamed balloons between Harnes and Hénin-Lietard. Redler reported seeing no fewer than three burning balloons north of Hénin-Lietard as he turned for home. It had been quite a morning and that afternoon Mannock went over to St Omer to fetch back a new machine. Hall (B1541) turned over on landing back and so did Walder (A6785).

Major Tilney wrote to Eric Nixon's father: 'You will be glad to know, that your son was taking part in one of the most brilliant and perilous undertakings which the Royal Flying Corps have ever been called upon to do, and that it was perfectly successful and has earned the highest praise from the higher command.' Just why Tilney thought his father – the Reverend W H Nixon, senior chaplain to the 73rd Division, would be 'glad to know', is unclear!

Captain W E Nixon, 40 Squadron, killed in action 7 May 1917, aged 19.

Nieuport B1552, taken in Egypt after it had become 'war weary' with 40 Squadron. Mannock scored his second victory in this machine on 7 June 1917.

After a quiet day on the 8th, quiet except for an afternoon foray and party in St Omer, the 9th saw Mannock with Keen and 'Rastus' Raymond chasing a German two-seater from Hénin-Lietard to Courcelles. The third pilot broke off with engine trouble and then Mannock's gun jammed once more and his Aldis sight oiled up. To add to his woes, the engine then conked out at 16,000 feet just as three German Albatros Scouts turned up. This could have been the end of his career but turning sharply he managed a dive towards the lines, kicking his rudder bar this way and that in order to avoid the machine-gun fire from the pursuing Germans. At 3,000 feet near Arras the engine picked up but by then the enemy machines, nearing the lines, had turned east. Climbing back to 12,000 feet he came across another German machine but by this time he had had enough and flew home, knees trembling and with a high state of nervous tension prevailing. Later he was once more sent over to St Omer to bring back a new machine, this time flying in the back seat of a 16 Squadron RE8, which shared the airfield with 40.

* *

Keen and Rastus Raymond engaged a two-seater on the 12th and brought it down, but the next day, on a similar sortie, Raymond did not return, ending up as a prisoner of war. On another sortie, B B Lemon was surprised by a German fighter, had his petrol tank holed but was lucky enough to get down on the Allied side of the lines. Mannock took off after a two-seater was seen over the lines and although he spotted it he only managed to chase the Hun back over the trenches.

On the 14th Mannock was again sent to St Omer to collect a new machine although this time bad weather forced an overnight stay. In his diary he reflects about losses and tired pilots, meeting a friend from another squadron who reported that they had lost four new pilots in five days. He named the man Lloyd, no doubt G L Lloyd of 60 Squadron, a unit that had had some losses recently. 'Zulu' Lloyd – a South African – would be joining 40 in a couple of months as a flight commander.

MacKenzie was about to go on leave, Mannock thinking this was a good thing as the youngster was, in his opinion, ready to break down. At this time it wasn't always appreciated or understood that the need for pilots to be rested was essential. Some began to feel the strain of constant flying and action more than others. Mannock himself reflected on his own ability to continue, wondering if he too would start feeling 'it' sooner, or later.

Some bad weather now gave everyone a break, and Mannock recorded in his diary a good party that several of them had in St Omer on the 16th – Gregory, Keen, Bond, 'Jake', Thompson and Redler. Two new pilots arrived at this time, one being A E Godfrey, a Canadian from Vancouver. Not far off his 27th birthday, he was nearer Mannock's age than to most of the youngsters in the Squadron. Albert Earl Godfrey, but generally known as 'Steve', had already been in service with 25 Squadron as an observer, and earlier in the trenches with the Canadian army. He would win a MC with 40 and eventually make group captain in WW2.

The other was Lieutenant W E Bassett, known as 'Melbourne' after his birth place. Mannock noted in his diary that Bassett had a dominant personality and imagined that he would do big things. Fate, however, had other ideas, and Bassett only lasted until 1 June, the day he was wounded in an air fight and sent back to England. He did, however, send a two-seater down 'out of control' on 28 May but that was his only success.

The few other successes in May were all by the more experienced pilots in the Squadron. Robert Gregory and Bill Bond claimed victories on the 10th, Keen another on the 12th, Gregory one more on the 26th, while Bond and Steve Godfrey shared two scouts down 'out of control' on the 28th. The 'main event', however, in May concerned Lewis Morgan – the 'Air Hog'.

On the 23rd he was notified of the award of a Military Cross, but the next day was his last with 40. While on a show the Welshman from Swansea was attacked by an Albatros flown by Max Müller of Jasta 28, who felt he had finished off the Nieuport. However, on his way down an artillery shell smashed into the Nieuport when he was at 6,000 feet. Morgan's right leg was fractured in two places below the knee and it later had to be amputated. He managed to crash-land on the right side of the lines, and some time later he was fitted with an artificial lower right leg.

In the early spring of 1918 he actually managed to return to flying, and was sent to 50 Squadron at Bekesbourne, Kent as an instructor. Sadly, on 26 April, taking off in an SE5 (C5342) his engine started to miss-fire and in attempting a turn and landing, he crashed on a railway embankment north of the airfield and was killed.

More changes occurred. Captain Gregory was sent home on rest (he would later command 66 Squadron in Italy) and Captain Keen went down with influenza, despite a welcome change to hot weather. Captain W T L Allcock arrived to take over from Gregory, the latter having just heard that the French had awarded him the *Légion d'Honneur*. With Keen absent, and a sudden shortage of experienced men around, Tilney had to ask Mannock to take temporary charge of the Flight, so obviously he had out-lived the period when his courage was in question. Mannock later had a pointed boss fitted to the hub of his propeller, designed to improve forward movement. He had it painted yellow, and it is said he chose this colour because of the earlier questioning about his inability to engage the enemy. Captain Allcock lasted until 5 June, on which date he was killed in action. Two German aircraft dived on him as he was attacking another and he failed to see them. Vizefeldwebel

Wilhelm Reiss of Jasta 3 got him. He was 21.

This 'promotion' came at a time Mannock claimed his first aeroplane victory, which occurred on 7 June. Godfrey and Bond had made claims in the first week of June, and Gregory made his own total four on the 7th while Herbert Redler had bagged an Albatros Scout 'out of control'. Mannock's claim came on an early morning escort mission, which took off before 7 am. There were seven Nieuports, led by Bond.

North of Lille, at 13,000 feet, a single enemy machine attempted to dive upon one of the FE2b machines 40 Squadron were protecting on a bomb raid, but the German pilot then saw the Nieuports and turned, then went into a dive. Mannock dived too, closed the distance and at close range opened fire with a burst of 30 rounds, which he saw splatter around the cockpit area, and engine. The Albatros turned upside-down, nosed over and begin to spin down. Mannock tried to watch its fall but was unable to do so without losing more valuable height and leaving his charges. However, Blaxland and Lemon confirmed seeing the enemy machine going down 'out of control'. Vizefeldwebel Franz Eberlein of Jasta 33 was slightly wounded in a combat on this date and in the general area of Mannock's action. Mannock confided in his diary:

> '... I brought my first dead certain Hun down this morning – over Lille – north. Have been up to 21,000 feet in the morning (3.30 am) looking for the early birds...... The push on Armentières-Ypres sector commenced this morning.[1] We escorted FEs over Lille on bomb-dropping business – and we met Huns. My man gave me an easy mark. I was only ten yards from him – on top so I couldn't miss! A beautiful coloured insect he was – red, blue, green and yellow. I let him have 60 rounds [his combat report says 30] at that range, so there wasn't much left of him. I saw him go spinning and slipping down from 14,000 feet. Rough luck, but it's war, and they're Huns.'

Mannock was flying B1552 again on this occasion. Despite these Nieuport Scouts being almost universally known as Nieuport 17s, this machine was in fact a type 23. Aviation buffs have often confused these Nieuport types but they can be forgiven as it is an easy assumption to make that nearly all these early machines were type 17 (XVII). G B Crole also flew this machine in 40, and gained three victories with it. It was later damaged in a crash and once repaired, ended up at 60 TDS (Training Depot Station) at Aboukir, Egypt where it saw out its days.

Two days later Mannock was in an air fight again. He was on an evening patrol and near Douai with five Nieuports led by Bond. Five enemy machines were spotted, then a sixth. Three were fighters, three two-seaters. The time was about 20.15 and the patrol was at around 12,500 feet. Mannock saw the first five north of Douai and he dived towards two of them, firing a whole drum from his Lewis gun. He saw some hits but nothing appeared to have been damaged. He observed the third German going down 'out of control' in a nose-dive following an attack by Billy Bond.

Mannock's diary entry for the 14th gives a misleading picture here. 'Had another scrap the other evening with five Huns N. of Douai. Scalped two of them. Both went down first, although nothing definite as regards their absolute destruction could be vouchsafed. I felt

---

[1] The Battle of Messines, preceded by an enormous mine explosion at 03.10 am, by a charge of 400 tons of ammonal, dug into and beneath the German trench system, after five months of tunnelling. This was immediately followed by an artillery barrage as British troops advanced.

like the victor in a cock-fight! Poor old Shaw went west a few days ago.'

In some lists of Mannock's victories, their authors show these as being two claims, but as the combat report shows, he scored hits but with no apparent effect. The Squadron does not give him any credit for these either. Shaw, who as mentioned earlier, was in correspondence with Norman Franks many years ago, recalled his being brought down, which was on the same day as this action – 7 June:

> 'On 7 June 1917 Mannock was in my Flight at the Battle of Messines when I was shot down. He was close to me at the time and reported me killed but he must have taken me for a Hun DV Albatros which I was following down until he caught fire.'

This was an earlier scrap, shortly after noon, the Nieuports being engaged with the German marine fighters of Marinefeldjasta 1 (MFJ1). They lost one pilot, who came down on the British side, badly wounded, and who died later. Flugmeister Ottomar Haggenmüller bagged Shaw.

These combat successes, real or otherwise, at least showed that Mannock was now on his way. He had overcome his initial hesitancy, and had finally begun to 'see' in the air. All his previous experience was about to bear fruit.

CHAPTER THREE

DEPUTY FLIGHT COMMANDER

June 1917 now entered its second week. Mannock had survived his first weeks in combat and had overcome the feeling from some of his fellow pilots that he was reluctant to engage the enemy. Not only had he survived but he had now been made acting deputy flight leader. Bloody April had passed, the RFC's worst month for casualties, and then May, and while his successes in combat were small, it is necessary to make clear that not every fighter pilot was knocking down opponents at the drop of a hat. While the best way to bring down an opponent was to try and sneak up on them, and open fire before they were aware of any danger, this did not happen that often. Most air fights were the result of two groups of aircraft engaging in an action and the resultant dog-fight, more often than not, ended in stalemate, each side eventually breaking off and going home. A claim or two might be made, more in hope than any real sense of victory, but these so called 'victories' were generally a pilot putting his aircraft into a spin earthwards and hoping the opposing pilot who was starting to get an edge over him, did not follow him down.

In 1917 the RFC fighter pilots were led either by good or indifferent leaders. Most engaged enemy formations, in a fashion a future generation would term 'balls out, hair on fire!' In other words, find your enemy and dive headlong at him. Some of the better flight leaders managed to instil flight discipline into their men and for them only to attack on their signal, having hopefully had some moments to figure out the best way of engaging opponents. Rudimentary tactics were being taught, but these tactics were only as good as any given situation allowed.

The Germans had a better system developed by their Jagdstaffel formations. It did not take long for each Jasta to select a pilot to lead in the air who seemed to have a better feel for the job in hand, and have the necessary skill to hit with his machine-gun fire, the aeroplane he was aiming at. This might seem to the layman a very basic matter, but even good pilots often failed when it came to air-to-air gunnery. Once a German pilot began to down the opposition, he became leader, whatever rank he might hold, and supported by the others, would front an attack and have first crack at a target, before the general mêlée began. More often than not, this would result in at least one kill by this leader, as he was able to concentrate on his attack knowing that his back was protected by the other pilots.

High-scoring pilots such as Baron Manfred von Richthofen, leader of Jasta 11, and soon to become leader of four Jastas (4, 6, 10 and 11) under the heading of Jagdgeschwader Nr.I, used this tactic with much success. Studying Jasta records one can see who these successful leaders in the air were by their scores, being often in double figures, while the rest of the Jasta pilots had scores in ones or twos.

In the RFC and RNAS, pilots with high scores might well be leaders as well but generally they achieved their scores by gaining sufficient experience of air fighting to survive and down opponents, although a number were brought down themselves once a dog-fight began, and everyone tended to look after himself. New pilots in the main had to fend for themselves, and quite often were quickly picked off. An experienced German pilot could spot the novice by the way he handled his aeroplane, or because he opened fire much too soon. The experienced pilot flew with much more confidence, and rarely opened fire until he had got in close, and then only in short bursts. Everything had to be learnt the hard way. However much an experienced pilot tried to instruct a newcomer how to perform and what to do, only by experiencing combat and hopefully surviving his first few encounters could he hope to survive for any period of time.

Mannock slowly learnt how to survive in the air. How to spot enemy aircraft quickly, preferably before their pilots saw him. To manoeuvre his aircraft in combat, while at the same time, judge firing distances and accurate deflection shooting. It was far easier to get oneself shot down than to survive, but Mannock had survived for several weeks, during a period some like to say pilots on the Western Front could only expect to live two or three weeks at most. By this fact alone he must have been above average, and if he could survive a little longer, he might prove to be useful.

* *

Two days after his second victory, Mannock got into a fight with five enemy aircraft in a formation, plus another singleton – three scouts and three two-seaters. He was on an Offensive Patrol at around 8.15 in the evening of the 9th, near Douai. Spotting an enemy formation north of Douai he engaged two of them, loosing off one drum from his Lewis gun. He saw some hits on one but without effect. As he pulled away from this attack, he spotted an Albatros DIII spinning down following an attack by Billy Bond. It was Bond's fifth and final victory.

Mannock soldiered on for another week but on the 17th he had his first period of leave. The preceding days, as he recorded in his diary, had been fairly easy, allowing him some time on the aerial range (gunnery).

He also suffered with a small piece of grit in one eye and it was so painful that he had a job landing. Having been taken into the Mess he promptly fainted. Transferring to hospital the doctor injected some cocaine into him before getting the offending piece of grit out. Then on the 14th he suffered the same fate again. This seems to suggest he was not wearing goggles, but one assumes that after these two alarming events, he did begin to use them.

Mannock also collected yet another machine from St Omer and had a race with one of the new Sopwith Camel fighters beginning to make an appearance in France. He was beaten and was immediately impressed with the Camel's performance. His eye was still giving him a problem though, and on seeing the doctor again, the medic gave him another injection and extracted yet another piece of grit. Then came his leave, and he was quickly off to England.

His leave did not prove a happy time. His mother he found was starting to drink more heavily than she had done before and instead of helping him to relax, he became fed up with her insistence that he send her more money. Brother Paddy, now in the army, could not send her much and his sisters were both having marital problems. He managed a visit to Hanworth aerodrome where he was able to take a look at some new aeroplanes, and was then quite happy to leave London and travel up to Wellingborough and to visit the Eyles. He apparently said to Jim Eyles that knowing his age was rather against him in air fighting, he thought the best course of action was to develop some useful tactics, using brains rather than brawn. He had been thinking a good deal about how to do new things rather than accept the old ways of doing them. 'You watch me bowl them over when I return!' he had said.

Back in London he stayed at the RFC Club, in Bruton Street, a road that ran from Berkeley Square to New Bond Street. A rather boisterous party ended in much broken furniture that he and other incumbents had to pay for.

After a month in England, Mannock returned to the Squadron. In war there are constant changes in operational squadrons and he found several when he got back. Ian Patrick Robert Napier was now a flight commander. 'Old Naps' as he was known, though not because of his age, had arrived at about the same time as Mannock and like Mannock had just two confirmed victories! This Etonian had earlier been with the Argyll and Sutherland Highlanders. His French was excellent and from time to time he was whisked away to be attached to the French 1st Army as a liaison officer, for which he would later receive the *Croix de Guerre* and the *Légion d'Honneur*. He remained with 40 Squadron into the summer of 1918 and won the Military Cross.

Captain Keen and A E 'Steve' Godfrey had by now both been awarded the Military Cross. Keen now had six victories, while Godfrey's score had reached eight. Two of Mannock's pals, Blaxland and Walder had returned to England, and Billy Bond had received a Bar to his MC. The Squadron had even had the pleasure of a visit from the King whilst he was away.

On the downside, G Davis had been lost – on 14 July – ending up as a prisoner, having been brought down by Erwin Böhme. Godfrey Davis had been part of a patrol consisting of Second Lieutenants G L Lloyd, H B Redler, H A Kennedy and W Maclanachan. East of Douai they had run into Jasta 12, six below and four above. In the fight that followed, Davis's Nieuport 17 (A6783) was hit and he was made to make a forced landing in German territory. Böhme reported going after two more Nieuports (Redler and Maclanachan) chasing them back to the lines, Mac's gun having jammed after six rounds. Davis was the German ace's 13th victory. He had only been with 40 Squadron for a month.

Maclanachan had been slightly injured in a near collision just before

Mannock's good friend in 40 Squadron was Mac Maclanachan.

Mannock's return, so it was in hospital that the two men were reunited, but Mac was not seriously hurt. He had been on a late show and landed back after dark. The Squadron's

Maclanachan's Nieuport Scout B3607 which he named 'The Silver Lady'. Mac wrote on this picture: 'A perfect lady, my only love.' Mannock also flew this machine in September 1917 gaining his last victory with 40 Squadron on the 25th.

brigade leader, the youthful 31-year-old, Brigadier-General G S Shepherd DSO MC, who often flew missions despite his rank and position, had been out too, but when he landed a few minutes earlier his engine had packed up and he was left stranded in the middle of a darkened airfield. Maclanachan saw the Nieuport at the last moment, kicked right rudder, dug in a wing and went up on his nose – damaging the propeller – before falling back.

The Squadron lost Captain C L Bath through illness, and Bill Bond took over the Flight, but he was not to last long. Bond was on leave and returned to take over in his new job.

On the 12th, Mannock scored his third and certain victory. He was on a morning OP to Avion, although there is also reference to him being sent off to deal with hostile aircraft at 09.50 whilst engaged in writing letters home. At 10.10 am, south-east of Lens he had spotted two German machines, Mannock flying south-east, gaining height so as to approach from the east. At 11,000 feet over Avion he made his move. Diving down, he opened fire and emptied a drum from some 25 yards range and immediately observed the two-seater start to go down out of control. Mannock, having taken a quick look round, followed to 7,000 feet, seeing the German aircraft make a crash-landing, ending upside-down. He noted the exact spot (Sheet 36c.1 – N 32.d.8.6) which as it happens was inside the British lines.

Having fallen in Allied territory, it was easy to identify the occupants and later, the unit to which they belonged. The pilot, Vizefeldwebel Reubelt, was badly injured and is reported to have died of his injuries, although his name is not listed as such, so he may have become a prisoner. There is a British record, however, of a Willi Reubelt whose date of death is given as 1 January 1918. Was this the same man who survived five months before dying? The problem here is that Mannock noted in his diary of '… the dead and mangled body of the pilot …'

Reubelt's observer, Vizefeldwebel Hermann Johann Böttcher, was wounded and definitely taken into captivity. He eventually ended up in Pattishall prisoner of war camp, near Northampton, and given the PoW number 13038. The machine was a DFW CV, its unit being Schusta (Schutzstaffel) 12 – based at Faumont – a unit that usually flew escort missions for FA211(A), an artillery observation unit. RFC HQ gave 'G' numbers to enemy aircraft that came down in their lines, and this DFW was given G52.

Being within reach, Mannock and others drove to the spot. He managed to collect a few souvenirs although by this time the local soldiers had had first pick of anything worth having. The machine was a complete wreck and in the observer's cockpit he found a dead black and tan terrier, which upset him more than the injuries that he had inflicted on the two crewmen.

Mannock had been flying Nieuport 23 B1682 which he had flown from 1 AD on 12 June. On the squadron it was marked with the number '6'. Lieutenant L G Blaxland had claimed a victory in it on 25 June, then Mannock gained two more. Captain W G Pender was killed flying it on 15 August.

Maclanachan, who had joined 40 Squadron in May, claimed his first victory on 12 July also, another two-seater which he sent spinning down shortly after mid-day. It had taken him two months to score, but there was no suggestion that he was 'slow in coming forward'. Mac had quickly become friends with Mannock. At an early stage Mac had found that a walk with Mannock after dinner made him seem vivid and alive. Mannock was able to speak about other matters than air-fighting and such like. Mac liked his enquiring nature and saw him as one who had the time and equanimity to consider the value of ideals and beliefs in the midst of war. Mac surmised that due to his humble upbringing he appeared to have something of a loneliness about him and therefore welcomed the companionship of a stranger.

On the 13th Mannock scored again. It was another two-seater DFW at 0920 am east of Sallaumines. On a patrol looking for hostile aircraft, they were almost 15,000 feet when they spotted three two-seaters, plus two single-seaters a little further east and higher up. Mannock dived on one of the two-seaters and fired a full drum load of ammunition at it while he closed to 25 yards range. He could see quite clearly his bullets striking the German which began to fall away out of control, but Mannock was unable to watch further as he was then engaged by the other enemy machines. His last view was of it side-slipping and then turning completely upside-down as it fell towards the ground.

He was credited with an 'out of control' victory near Billy-Montigny. Possibly it was an artillery observation machine from Flieger-Abteilung (A) 240, who had a machine shot-up and its observer, Leutnant Heinz Walkermann, wounded. Within an hour Mannock was above another two-seater but held his fire too long and suddenly had to bank away to avoid colliding with it. Although he turned for it again, and fired 40-50 rounds into it, the German kept going towards Douai.

Next morning he tried to repeat these successes and while he did manage to get above yet another two-seater, a tappet rod in his engine broke, which ripped off the engine cowling and forced him to glide down from 15,000 feet. Despite having no engine, his glide brought him to safety although in landing in a field of tall wheat his aircraft turned over, but he scrambled clear unharmed. On the evening of the 19th he almost shot down a British machine south of Lens. It was being fired upon by British AA gunners and this, together with the darkening sky making it difficult to see the machine's markings led him to attack, but luckily he was not on target and no damage was inflicted.

On the morning of the 20th, flying with Keen leading, the patrol began a scrap with three enemy fighters, in which, as Mannock related, were three of the finest Hun pilots he ever wished to meet. The fight lasted ten minutes and despite the odds of two to one, the British flyers were unable to get in a telling hit.

**

Mannock was now awarded the Military Cross. He heard officially on the 19th. When the telephone message arrived he was out on patrol, the call being taken by W R Andrews, one of the administration staff with 40 Squadron. Andrews went off to find him only to discover he was on patrol, so he sent Corporal Godfrey off to the hangars to await his return. Maclanachan was there, read the corporal's message then dashed to Mannock's sleeping quarters to locate his friend's spare uniform jacket. He arranged for the white and mauve MC ribbon to be sewn below the pilots' wings, then left the jacket on the back of the door. Upon his return, Mannock found the tunic which was his first intimation that he had been so honoured.

Bill Bond MC & Bar was killed on 22 July, less than a month after his 28th birthday. He was well liked on the Squadron and had joined the RFC from the King's Own Yorkshire Light Infantry. Leading his flight on the first OP of the day, his Nieuport was blown apart from a direct hit by an anti-aircraft shell over Sallaumines. His wife Aimee wrote a wonderful book about her husband, from recollections and letters. [1]

Mick Mannock's last engagement of July 1917 came on the 28th, east of Lens at 09.30, on another patrol chasing enemy machines. He first observed a two-seater low down, then engaged seven variously coloured Albatros Scouts. He selected one that he described as being purple in colour, with white crosses on its fuselage, swept back wing tips and a fish tail. This would have been an Albatros DV, an improved version of the DIII. Firing approximately 50 rounds from close range, he saw hits but then his Aldis gun-sight fogged up completely and with a broken stay-bolt on the sight's fixing, his aim became inaccurate. The Albatros peeled off east and was attacked by another Nieuport. The fight broke up and the German fighters drew away to the east while losing height.

These machines were from Jasta 12, led by Eduard von Tutschek, and it had been this German ace whom Mannock had fired at. In fact von Tutschek's machine was black, not purple. The black dope on Albatros machines tended to fade slightly and took on a purplish hue, which combined with the green and mauve camouflage on the upper surfaces of the wings, tended to give an overall purplish colouring. The black colouring also tended to accentuate the white edging to the fuselage crosses, and no doubt Mannock's description of 'white' crosses, was really describing this.

The British patrol was by three Nieuports, Tudhope and Kennedy accompanying Mannock this morning. The dog-fight had started soon after the three British machines had crossed the lines, the three pilots fighting a brilliant defensive battle against the seven Germans. Mannock later confessed to Maclanachan that he had never been so frightened in a scrap before. While there were no losses on either side, von Tutschek did claim a victory,

[1] *An Airman's Wife* first appeared in 1918, while a reprint came out in 2006, published by Grub Street.

against Tudhope's machine (B1558). However, he got back, despite his machine being shot to pieces. As so often happened, the desire to bring down an opponent, and then seeing one falling towards the ground, makes the eyes see what the heart wants to see, and von Tutscheck had fallen into this trap. Some of his pilots had obviously seen Tudhope start to go down and as he went down over the lines into the British area, any observers on the ground would also confirm the fall, thus the German ace had his 20th 'victory' confirmed.

John Henry Tudhope had yet to open his account against the Germans but would eventually claim ten victories and win the MC and Bar with the Squadron.

During the afternoon of 5 August Mannock scored again, another 'out of control' type victory. Again the locality was Avion, while out looking for enemy aircraft that had been reported over the lines. The patrol spotted five Albatros Scouts (also referred to by RFC pilots as V-Strutters, due to the machine's V-shaped wing struts) east of Lens. Mannock manoeuvred the patrol into a good position and engaged them over the Drocourt line, south of Hènin Liétard.

Mannock fired almost a complete drum from under 100 yards range and saw hits. The Albatros he had selected for attention turned upside-down and went spinning down but with other enemy aircraft whirling about him he was unable to watch its fall for long. Mannock then picked on another Albatros directly over Lens – and like a week earlier, described it as 'purple' in colour. He scrapped with this one for over ten minutes at 10,000 feet above Avion, emptying the drum at it at close range with no visible effect. Another German slid in behind Mannock's Nieuport forcing him to break off. He also had to change the empty drum for a new one, and by the time he had done this, the German machines were heading off east.

Were these again the black machines of Jasta 12, and was his second opponent von Tutschek again? Might well have been. Back at base, Maclanachan and Tudhope reported seeing the first Albatros going down 'out of control', thereby confirming the victory. The fight had lasted from around 4 pm to 4.10pm, and while Jasta 12 did lose a pilot, the loss occurred much later in the day.

Jasta 12 had become part of Jagdgruppe 4 within the German 6th Army the previous day, a temporary grouping under von Tutschek's command. In addition to his own Jasta, it included Jastas 30 and 37. Von Tutschek now sported the blue and gold *Pour le Mérite* at his throat, having been awarded this highly prized decoration on the 3rd. A week later he was badly wounded by Charles Booker of 8 Naval Squadron, who was flying a Sopwith Triplane, after gaining his 22nd and 23rd victories that same day. He would return in 1918 and run his score to 27 before falling to Herbert Redler on 15 March. Redler, of course, was a pal of Mannock in 40 Squadron, but by March 1918 he had become a flight commander with 24 Squadron flying SE5s.

Mannock was still flying B3554 (type 23) which Redler had collected from 2 AD on 22 July. He was to claim five victories with it before it was damaged on 20 August. Once repaired it too ended its days in Egypt.

The Squadron were involved in another mammoth 'balloon strafe' on 9 August. Maclanachan had just returned to his hut after the evening meal, when Mannock and Bob Hall entered. Mannock, according to Mac, took up a comfortable position against the door post and said:

'You're for the high jump tomorrow.'

'How?' I asked. Mannock and Hall looked at each other devilishly, trying to increase Maclanachan's suspense.

'What the devil do you mean?' demanded Mac again.

'It's quite true, Mac,' said Hall, 'There's a balloon strafe tomorrow.'

'Keep as close to the ground as you jolly well can – five feet if you can manage it. Don't get rattled and fire back if you spot a machine gun emplacement. When you get to the balloon have a good look round to see where the machine guns and 'flaming onion' batteries are, and for God's sake mind the telephone wires both on their side and ours.' Hall then told Mac to keep all this to himself in case it disturb their night's sleep. Then Mannock added:

'It won't worry old Mac,' then turning again to Maclanachan said, 'I promise you I'll count every bullet hole when you get back.'

On the 9th everyone seemed to congregate at Mazingarbe (40 Squadron's advanced landing ground (ALG)) to watch the 'volunteers' – Mac (B1693), Tudhope (B1558), Harrison (A6774), Barlow (B1670) and Herbert (A6771) – go off at 09.30. A loose escort of Mannock (B3554), Captain W G Pender (B1682), Hall (A6733), G B Crole (A6793), Kennedy (B3473) and Godfrey (B1684), also went off at 09.30.

The strafers had the option of heading over in corridors created by a barrage put up by the artillery or to wait until it lifted. Mac decided to wait, but the other four wanted to go with the cover of artillery fire. As he stood by his Nieuport, he chatted with Mannock, Hall and Steve Godfrey. Then he was off, and as he did so saw the balloon assigned to Herbert erupt in flames. In less than a minute he was across the lines and surrounded by machine-gun and rifle fire, zipping across at less than 15 feet.

Mac spotted Harrison, apparently lost, and he pointed a balloon out to him and flew on towards one he had not been aware was there and made for it, right on the deck. The other balloons were being hauled down rapidly, and then he saw soldiers led by some mounted officers directly ahead, coming down a road. Mac zoomed and then dropped over

Pilots of 40 Squadron. Mannock is at rear. In front are Herbert Redler, Lionel Blaxland, John Barlow and Ian Napier. Bruay, June 1917.

them, the horses scattering with fear, with several of their riders falling off. Then he was heading right for the balloon which was almost down.

He watched as his Buckingham incendiary ammunition streaked into the gasbag but no flame resulted. Again surrounded by ground fire, Mac circled quickly and came in again, emptying his drum of bullets. In order to attack again, he had to clench the stick between his knees to change the drum – and all at less than 200 feet. As he approached for a third run, he could see the balloon looking decidedly limp, but again no flames came from it, so not wanting to waste more bullets, he went for the 'extra' balloon, now down to 200 feet. Firing the rest of his second drum, again without flames erupting, he headed for home.

Landing back at Bruay, Maclanachan began to make his way to the Mess for a cooling drink. Along with Hall, Godfrey and Tudhope, the four of them met Mannock.

'What do you think?' he said, pointing an accusing finger at Mac, 'that blighter has only got one bullet hole in his machine – in the tail plane.' Apparently Kennedy and Harrison's Nieuports had both been badly shot about and Herbert too had collected a few holes and tears. Tudhope had had the worst damage, with lots of holes and yards of German telephone wire round his propeller boss,

Captain I P R Napier MC Ld'H CdG, 40 Squadron.

and one of his prop blades had been split. However, four balloons were credited as destroyed, although Sergeant Herbert's was the only one seen burning, the others were left smoking and deflating. Meantime, the escort claimed one Albatros Scout driven down, while Keen had found and drove down a DFW two-seater which he left smoking.

** **

The Squadron, unlike most of the others in France, had started to operate from this ALG, situated on a small field near Mazingarbe, just behind the front lines, situated half way between Béthune and Lens. It is perhaps four to five miles east of Bruay. This forward position had been set up so pilots could wait at 'readiness' and be 'scrambled' and in the air at a moment's notice, and thus be able to intercept hostile aircraft that much sooner. As these reported hostile machines would mostly be flying much lower than German aircraft seen high over their own territory – either heading for the British balloon lines, or about to ground strafe the trenches – there was less need to gain precious height before coming into contact. Maclanachan, in yet another of his many 'McScotch' articles wrote of 'Mazingarbe and Mannock' in *Popular Flying*, March 1936. I have used extracts from the article here:

'To all who served with 40 Squadron in the summer of 1917, "Mazingarbe" must be almost a magic word. It signifies a small clover field amidst the desolate waste of trenches, shell holes, ruined mines and brick works, barbed wire and shell-pocked "holdings", that stretched from La Bassée Canal to the Scarpe. Owing to the absence of landmarks round it, we incorrectly named it Mazingarbe, after a village that had existed two miles to the north. The clover field is officially mentioned as Petit Sains and Mazingarbe.

'Being a mile and a half from the trenches, the field was used as an advance landing ground from which we carried out many of our duties and voluntary patrols. It was the official starting point for our third Balloon Strafe, for the attack by 40 and 43 [Squadrons] during the capture of Hill 70, for the early morning trench-strafing carried out in retaliation for similar work carried out by the Germans on our trenches, and for the quick take-off that was required when chasing the enemy two-seaters away from the lines, or when protecting our balloons. The "ground" was equipped with telephone and wireless, and on receipt of a message that a hostile machine was approaching the lines, one of us would take off to chase or down the venturesome enemy. Our maps were divided into sections, with letters to correspond with those used by the wireless people and observers on the ground, so that, by merely giving us a letter, either by telephone, if we were on the ground, or by laying out the letter in large white canvas strips on the ground, if we happened to be in the air, we could immediately dash off to the correct locality.

'This latter work was purely voluntary, and Mannock, Keen, Zulu Lloyd, Pettigrew, Redler, Lemon, Tudhope, Kennedy and I, usually arranged amongst ourselves that two or three of us would be on the ground or in the air, merely as a protective measure for our artillery observation machines and balloons.

'Mick and I, either with Tudhope or Kennedy of "A" Flight, frequently used the ground in the afternoons, and, apart from the pleasure of carrying out a bit of strafing, we could sneak into Béthune for tea without having to ask for a tender to take us there. Mazingarbe created a feeling of freedom and of being intimately connected with the war. Apart from the usual morning and afternoon bombardments of Bully-Grenay, only half a mile away, the ground itself was occasionally shelled. There was no fuss or bother about reporting flights, and we were able to go off unostentatiously on whatever "business" attracted us, thus making Mazingarbe the ideal "better 'ole" for enthusiasts.

'One afternoon I was inside the small hut telephoning a combat report to the Squadron when there were excited shouts from outside. Mannock's engine revved furiously and I heard him take off in a hurry. Putting down the receiver I darted out. Mick was in the distance over Vimy, chasing an Albatros that had evidently been attempting to bring down one of our balloons. The German, finding Mannock barring his way had turned back, and when I saw them the Albatros was at approximately 500 feet, with Mick close on its tail. It was truly a breathless chase. The German squirmed and twisted in attempts to avoid Mick, or to get his guns on to Mick's Nieuport. Mick had always declared that 'one' on our side of the lines was 'as good as gone' but it appeared as if this fellow might get away, until Mannock, thinking he was going to lose his prey, pulled up in a final zoom to dive on his enemy, and sent him crashing to the ground with bullet wounds in his [right] leg and arm, on our side of the lines. [In the crash the German broke his left arm.] [The action] had taken only four minutes.

'Mick landed immediately and set out to salve what remained of the machine. The German, one von Bartrap [sic], was rescued by the Canadians, but very little remained of the Albatros after the enemy ['s artillery fire] had vented their wrath on it.'

This event took place mid-afternoon on 12 August and the German pilot, whose actual name was Leutnant Joachim Lambert Robert Hermann von Bertrab, had made the foray across into British territory, to attack a balloon of the 2nd Balloon Wing near Neuville St Vaast. This combat has been written about so often that perhaps it is worth recording Mannock's actual combat report narrative here:

'Albatros Scout vee type with all black body and wings and 220(?) h.p. Mercédes engine, armament 2 Spandau guns.

'Hostile machine observed at 3-10 p.m. crossing our lines South of Thelus.

'E.A. attempted to attack our balloon West of that point and descended to low altitude for that purpose. Nieuport engaged E.A. at approximately 1,000 ft. over Neuville St. Vaast and fired 70 rounds during the course of a close combat. The hostile machine was observed to be hit, a glow of fire appearing in the nacelle, and glided down under reasonable capable control South and East of Petit Vimy, landing down wind and turning over on touching the ground.

'Prisoner, Lieut. Von Bertropp [sic], sustained fracture of left arm and flesh wounds in right arm and leg, and was taken to hospital immediately on landing.

'Machine was in very good condition, although upside down, but was unfortunately affected by eventual hostile gunfire.'

Von Bertrab was a pilot with Jasta 30 (within von Tutschek's JGr 4), and had thus far achieved five victories in air combat. Before joining the air service he had been with Niedersächsisches Field Artillery Regiment Nr.46. Once a pilot, he had served with FA71, as well as Fokkerstaffel Metz. Of his five victories, no less than four had been achieved on one day, 6 April 1917. Early that morning he had engaged and downed two Martinsyde G100 'Elephants' from 27 Squadron, which had been part of a bomb raid on Ath, Belgium. Later that morning he claimed credit for two Sopwith 1½ Strutters of 45 Squadron, which he caused to collide over Pecq during a reconnaissance to Lille. His fifth victory had been a FE2d of 20 Squadron, on 13 May.

Von Bertrab, after treatment for his injuries, ended up in a British prison camp near Taunton, South

Von Bertrab with his distinctive black Albatros Scout.

Devon, given PoW number 478. He continued to fly post-WW1 and was killed in a flying accident near Boitzenberg, some 60 miles north of Berlin, Germany, on 28 July 1922.

His Albatros DIII Scout had black fuselage and tail with the fuselage cross in what appears to be pale grey, edged white. On the fuselage, beneath the cockpit was a shooting-star/comet motif, thought to be either yellow or red, edged possibly in white. His awards were the Iron Cross 1st and 2nd Class, and the Brunswick House Order with Swords – the Order of Henry the Lion, plus the Brunswick War Merit Cross.

** **

This had been Mick Mannock's sixth official victory, and number seven and eight came three days later, on the 15th. The first was whilst on a late morning patrol, ordered off from the ALG shortly before noon as enemy aircraft had been spotted from there through a telescope. Near Lens just about noon, an Albatros Scout was seen, Mannock engaging in company with Captain Keen. Mannock fired some 20 rounds from medium range and the German made a hasty retreat into some clouds.

Leutnant Joachim von Bertrab, Jasta 30, brought down by Mannock on 12 August 1917.

After several minutes, Mannock spotted a two-seater together with another Albatros Scout heading his way, north over Lens, at 10,000 feet. He began to follow and close the gap, and when he had done so, opened fire on the scout at 12.50 pm, just south of Lens. He fired 60 rounds at close range without being observed and the Albatros went down nose first through thick clouds and was lost to view.

Although from the combat report it does not seem very likely that either German aircraft was hit, Mannock was mentioned in RFC Communiqué No.101, as having scored an 'out of control' victory.

The day was far from over and at 19.30 over Lens on an Offensive Patrol, Mannock was in another fight. He dived and engaged an Albatros Scout, firing 30 rounds but almost immediately this German was engaged by another Nieuport.

He turned towards a second Albatros – green mottled wings and a black tail – at 11,000 feet south of La Bassée, above the front lines. Pouring 60 rounds into this machine, Mannock saw hits in the fuselage and near the cockpit. The Albatros began to lose height and appeared out of control. Men on the ALG at Mazingarbe watched as the German machine continued down in an uncontrolled manner but at 1,000 feet the pilot appeared to regain some measure of control just east of the lines north of Lens. Mannock had already pulled away, to replenish the Lewis ammunition drum and to watch for other enemy machines.

It had been a busy day for 40 Squadron with six enemy aircraft claimed. Apart from

Mannock's two – rather suspect – claims, Keen had claimed another two 'out of control' during the morning, Bob Hall had sent another Albatros down in flames at 12.50, and G B Crole another 'out of control' at 18.45. This was Hall's fifth and final victory, and he returned to England for a rest. He then flew with 44 Home Defence Squadron (Sopwith Camels) until February 1918. For his work he was awarded the Military Cross and left the RAF in 1920, returning to his native South Africa.

These were also the last victories of Arthur Keen, at least for 1917. His total now had risen to 12. He was later to return to 40 as its commanding officer in June 1918, following the death at that time of Major R S Dallas DSO DSC. Leading 40, Keen claimed two more but was then severely burned in a flying accident on 15 August 1918, and died from his injuries on 12 September.

The day's loss, however, was a new flight commander, 30-year-old Captain W G Pender MC, shot down by Oberleutnant Hans Bethge, Staffelführer of Jasta 30 during the last OP of the day. Jasta 30 had had Leutnant Heinrich Brügmann wounded over Douvrin on this 15th August, and he died of his wounds on his way to hospital, at 2 pm that afternoon [1]. Which of 40 Squadron's claims might have involved Brügmann is uncertain, although quite obviously he was a victim in the mid-day action, so either Hall or Mannock.

Mannock had now become acting flight commander, a position quickly confirmed. His combat reports now showed his new rank of captain (acting) for these August air fights, so he had now jumped up from second lieutenant. In fact, his two combat reports for 15 August noted captain for the mid-day action, but still 2/Lt for the evening fight, so even the recording officer was uncertain or had made an error during the day's activities. Reports from the 17th onwards, however, clearly note captain.

On the 17th Mannock was out over Lens at mid-morning looking for enemy aircraft. At 10.50 he found a DFW two-seater slightly to the south and west of the city and attacked it at 17,000 feet. According to his combat report, the DFW was coloured yellow, red, green and blue, with a light coloured band around the fuselage behind the observer's cockpit.

Getting his sights on he fired off a whole drum of Lewis in bursts of ten rounds each closing to very close range. The German observer fired back and hit the Nieuport twice but then the two-seater heeled over and went down in a slow spin, leaving a trail of black smoke from its tail section.

Mannock followed it down for 3-4,000 feet while it was still seemingly out of control and went into a cloud layer. Maclanachan also followed the German machine down and below the cloud seeing it continue down east of Sallaumines and eventually hit the ground in what he described as a triangular field north-west of the town.

Twenty minutes later, while west of Lens, Mannock spotted another DFW, this one with a coloured mottled effect. It was at 15,000 feet and the time was 11.10. With a new drum in place Mannock opened fire again but this time with no apparent effect and the pilot merely put his nose down eastwards, the observer firing back as they went. With the drum now empty Mannock pulled away to replenish it and was not able to close with the hostile machine which was now heading towards Douai, as his engine began to play up.

The first DFW was Mannock's ninth victory. This may have been a machine from RHBZ 6 (Reihenbildzug), a special photographic section within a normal abteilung. This unit had an observer, Oberleutnant Karl Heine severely injured this date; presumably his pilot survived unharmed.

[1] His date of death is also given as 18 August.

CHAPTER FOUR

FLIGHT COMMANDER

Things had definitely moved forward for Mannock over the summer. Gone now were any thoughts about his ability as a fighting pilot, and if indeed there was anything the matter with his sight, this had either been surmounted by him, was something that has been exaggerated, or it came and went and did not cause him too much trouble.

He was also proving a good and popular flight leader. Perhaps being that much older than most of the squadron pilots gave him that extra maturity which in turn made it more likely that a man with his outlook, and now much combat experience, would make it his business to help, guide and protect his men as much as possible. He was always eager to engage the enemy, but in a calculated way. Maximum damage for minimal risk.

By this time, Mannock had been credited with nine victories, the same total he himself noted in a letter home. Of these, four had been destroyed, including those two brought down on the Allied side, and five 'out of control'.

Maclanachan flew with Mannock mid-afternoon of 18 August, and they chased a DFW two-seater over Lens and then lost it in cloud, but it was now flying east and away from the front. Two days later Mannock made a good job of virtually writing off Nieuport B3554. He took off from Bruay at 14.45 to fly over to Mazingarbe, but as he did so ten minutes later, overshot the field and ran into a haystack. Although he was unhurt, the Nieuport suffered the following damage: top main planes, fuselage and undercarriage strained, wheel axle bent, propeller and gun mounting smashed, engine mount broken and a section of the fuselage badly twisted.

There were several actions on 22 August. Mannock led an OP south of La Bassée between 05.10 and 06.15, with Maclanachan, Harrison, Tudhope and Kennedy behind him. They saw a two-seater east of Lens trying to sneak over to the British side of the lines. Mannock loosed-off 20 rounds at it as it turned rapidly for home, firing off a red and green light, no doubt hoping to confuse the attackers into thinking it was a British machine. They were back on the ground for just 45 minutes before the same five were going out again at 07.00 for a seventy-minute OP between La Bassée and Vitry, these efforts in order to keep German observation machines from taking photographs or directing artillery fire. The third sortie came in the late afternoon.

I make no excuse for again using here words from another Maclanachan article he wrote for *Popular Flying* (July 1935 issue), under the heading of 'Mannock's Way', that concerned this third patrol. With nobody now to interview about events that occurred in WW1 we can only refer to earlier written words by such men as Maclanachan, who was in any event a keen observer of men and events.

'On a beautiful summer evening in August 1917, just before dinner, Mannock and

Padre Keymer were indulging in one of their usual arguments in 40 Squadron's Mess at Bruay.

'The Squadron had steadily been losing young pilots and our brave old Padre was in a despondent mood. His wealth of kindliness and quiet courage rebelled at the deaths of so many young men and filled him with the desire to join the fighting forces himself. Mannock was opposing him.

'"My dear Padre, there are enough of us here to do the fighting. We've got the Huns so well "under" we have to go and dig 'em out. And we can keep them there too. We need the influence of good men like you behind the lines here – particularly over the younger fellows. Yours is really a greater work than fighting and – with all due respect to your courage and your spirit – how old are you? How do you think you would fare as a fighting pilot?"

'I had often heard them arguing in this strain, for every time the Padre heard of the death of one of his protégés his bitterness welled over.

'Knowing that the argument would only finish by Mannock attacking the Padre on religious grounds, and threatening to defrock him, I went over to the piano, just behind Mick, opened the cover quietly and struck a sharp chord. Mannock jumped.

'Although supposed to be the fittest men in the army, it was extraordinary the instantaneous reacting a fighting pilot would show on hearing a sudden and unexpected burst of noise. Mannock himself often "put the wind-up" the mess by hitting the wooden walls of the hut with a stone, or using his powerful lungs to imitate an *Archie* burst, or the *tat-tat-tat* of a machine gun. Besides, there was the uncanny superstition in the Squadron that any pilot who played the piano was doomed.

'"God Almighty," Mannock jumped up, "I'll,__ I'll __" He glared at me and then at the Padre.

'"Excuse me, Padre," he said apologetically, "that wasn't blasphemy, it was a real prayer. There's Mac playing that confounded thing – and Kennedy did it the other night. Why doesn't Tilney give it away or blow it up?" He turned to me. "You needn't laugh. I don't want to lose the lot of you."

'I remembered something Kennedy had told me two or three nights previously. "Did Ken play it?" I asked. Mick nodded.

'"He accompanied Mick until we stopped him. I'm not superstitious," observed the Padre, "but there certainly seems to be something sinister about that piano. You knew it – then why did *you* touch it?"

'"Yes I know but – it's really queer. The other night Ken and I were sleeping at Mazingarbe and he told me he had a hunch that he wouldn't last more than two or three days."

'They were both very serious and as nothing depressed me more than sentiment and superstition, I turned round and struck a few more chords on the piano. Mannock came over threateningly. "If you don't stop that I'll knock ___"

'"Shut up you two," the Padre broke in abruptly, and we noticed that Kennedy, followed by several others, was entering the Mess. As it was such a lovely evening, everyone had changed into slacks.

'"What about a drink, Mac?" someone asked, and as I was in charge of the bar, I, followed by Kennedy, retired to mix our renowned "Lady Killer" cocktails. Silently he watched me measuring the ingredients, then, when I was pouring out the drinks, he said quietly. "Thank God it's all over for today, Mac. I haven't been able to get that feeling out of my mind." I told him I was glad too. He was a close friend, and as the subject was distasteful, I gave him one tray of drinks and followed him into the Mess with another. We were helping ourselves when Major Tilney, the CO, hurried into the Mess.

'"Blast them!" he burst out. "Some fool of an observer has reported that Droignies aerodrome is deserted, and we've got to corroborate the report to-night." As a CO, Major Tilney was considerate. We were tired. Our work that month had included a balloon strafe on the 10th, a hectic day during the attack on Lens on the 15th, and almost incessant flying. He looked round the mess, and continued. "It's a dirty job – as if it matters whether we find out to-night or to-morrow morning. I've tried to put it off, but they say they must know before dark – looks like a job for you Mac. You know those aerodromes around Douai.

'"All right, Sir," I replied. "Let's have our drinks first." Mannock expostulated. "But look here Major, Droignies is just behind Douai; we can't let Mac go over there alone at this time – all low-flying Huns will be after him. What about an escort?" And, without waiting to hear what the CO had to say he turned round to the others: "Who'll come! It'll be a damned fine lark."

'Hall jumped up. "That's the idea. Let's all be in it." Steve Godfrey, Crole and Harrison acquiesced, but Major Tilney remonstrated. "Look here Mick, we'll leave it to Mac. Would you rather go alone or with an escort?" he asked me. "Alone," I replied.

'Both Mannock and Hall insisted that it was unfair to put the question in that way, as I could only give the one answer, and that way, as the pilots from the five aerodromes round Douai would have a chance to take off to intercept a low flying machine, I should have little chance of getting back. I thought it was making a mountain out of a mole-hill, but Mick clinched the argument by saying that as I was going anyway, it would not matter to me whether or not the rest of the Squadron used me as bait.

Lieutenant R N Hall MC, 40 Squadron, from South Africa.

'With his usual enthusiasm for special stunts Mannock wanted to take the whole Squadron to raid the German aerodromes, but Tilney wisely decreed that the Flight that was to take morning patrol should stay behind. He was thinking of the mechanics, many of whom would probably have to be up all night working on our machines in preparation for the next morning.

'We made our plans hurriedly. Mannock was to lead the first flight, while the second was to follow about a thousand feet above him. I was to contour chase right over to Douai and then, when I had got corroboration, to climb up underneath the formation.

'Forgetting that the others intended getting their height before crossing the lines, I took off immediately they had assembled over the aerodrome. Like the others, I had changed into slacks for dinner, and as flying close to the ground always made our engines uncomfortably hot, I wore only a light raincoat and no flying cap. As a precaution, in case of a forced landing on the German side of the lines, my RFC cap and chequebook were in my pocket.

'Flying between ten and twenty feet from the ground I crossed the front line to the east of Vimy, where to my great relief, the machine gun fire that met me was not nearly so bad as it had been on the morning of the balloon strafe. There were only about ten seconds of real firing from the trenches before my machine was skimming over green clover fields. As usually happened, the lull brought a feeling of peace and security – the worst was over, and, except for the immaculate Hindenburg-Drocourt trenches, there was little sign of the war beyond two or three miles from the front line. In passing over a peaceful village I could see women moving about in the road and grey-clad German soldiers standing about in groups.

'As I was flying at less than a hundred feet from the ground the *Archie* gunners could not have hit me, even if they had been aware of my presence. My chief danger lay in meeting low flying scouts or of someone telephoning ahead to the aerodromes, but to my relief I did not see any machines until I was approaching Douai when I spotted five fighters to the north at about five or six thousand feet. Looking round to ascertain Mannock's position I observed a few specks amidst clouds of *Archie* bursts, to the north-west, while to the south-east was another large flight, obviously German, as they were flying towards Douai and were losing height.

'On reaching my objective I flew round the aerodrome at two or three feet, but, except for a few German soldiers, who might have been a guard, there was no sign of occupation by aeroplanes. The hangars were shut up. The Germans were running to the easternmost hangar and, debating as to whether or not I should spend ammunition on them or save it for the inevitable 'scrap' that was about to take place, I decided to keep my drums intact and to climb towards the escort.

'My machine had reached five thousand feet when Mannock attacked the enemy flight that had been approaching from the south-west and was now directly above me. Within a few seconds the air was full of whirling, stunting machines. From the struggling mass, one dropped in the unmistakeable uncontrolled spin. It was a German Albatros.

'Zooming quickly as I let down my double Lewis gun in order to fire up into any of the Germans that got above me, I had almost gained their level when, to my horror, I saw one of our own Nieuports careering downwards in a mad dive, streaks of smoke issuing from behind it, while the sun vividly lit up the aluminium-painted fuselage and red-white-and-blue circles. There was another Albatros above me, circling round feverishly. As I fired a burst from both guns right into the front of the fuselage, the first *Archie* shells exploded in our midst. The German batteries at the front had got our range and bombarded us regardless of whether their shells were hitting friend or foe. Added to the anxiety of being shot at by machine guns were the two more terrifying dangers of meeting an *Archie* shell, or crashing into another machine.

'In the most intense part of the fight, my machine passed right across Mannock's tail, only a few feet above him. I could see that his eye was glued to his Aldis sight, aiming at an Albatros, but that inexplicable something which warned seasoned pilots of the proximity of another machine, made him turn his head abruptly, to realise in a fraction of a second that mine was a friendly machine. I shall never forget the scared expression on his face as he instinctively cowered.

'Turning round into the scrap again, I succeeded in getting on the tail of another German, but by side-slipping and diving he prevented me from getting my guns to bear on him. After following him down to a thousand feet, I gave up the attempt and, on turning westward, discovered that my Nieuport was again alone. In the distance a long trail of *Archie* bursts indicated the course of Mannock's return flight.

'Again I felt lonely. I was hot, tired and disgruntled – I had seen one of our machines going down – was it Kennedy's? Mannock had always declared that there was no merit in bringing down two Germans if we lost one of our own good pilots.

'Dreading the sound of more machine guns, I flew towards the lines, climbing steadily and zig-zagging to mislead the *Archie* gunners. On reaching Oppy another Nieuport joined me, Crole's, and we flew together home to our aerodrome at Bruay. When my machine stopped on the ground Mannock ran out.

'"Thank God you're safe old boy! Where's Ken? I thought you had gone too." I asked him who was missing. "Only Ken," he said mournfully. "I saw him going down."

'Then I knew that, after what I had also seen, we should never see Kennedy again. The remainder of the flights were gathered round the Orderly Room, filling in combat reports and arguing.

'Godfrey and Hall, both valiant scrappers, declared that Mick had given them no chance to close-in before he attacked and that had he manoeuvred properly their Flight could have headed-off the Germans. Mannock rounded on them, saying that the Albatroses were losing height and would have got away, and that, if the upper flight had taken advantage of the extra height, they could have been in the thick of the scrap. "And besides," he added, "it was only a matter of a few seconds before they would have seen Mac. Seven of them. I hold back? Not bloody likely."

'Amid the excitement I filled in my combat report, accurately stating the condition in which I had found the German aerodrome. Everyone else had forgotten the object of the expedition. We were able to claim several victories, but to Mannock and myself these counted as nothing – we had lost our friend.

'Poor old Ken. He had been in all our scraps that month, had gone over with me on the balloon strafe. Mannock, Kennedy and I had discovered a secret rendezvous in Béthune where we frequently had tea together. Kennedy's was the first serious loss the Flight had suffered since Mannock took command and Mannock felt his death keenly.'

Although Mac had seen that Albatros going down seemingly out of control, no confirmation was allowed to Mannock, and there is no indication that a second Albatros was credited to the Squadron either. Mannock had fired into his Albatros from 25 yards range and saw it going down in a spiral, but he was too busy to watch it further. Lieutenant Harry Alexander Taylor Kennedy, aged 22, came from Hamilton, Ontario, Canada. He had previously served with the Canadian Infantry. He lies in Cabaret-Rouge Cemetery, France.

Only one Nieuport Scout was claimed by a German pilot late in the day, and that by Leutnant R Wendelmuth of Jasta 8, east of Ypres at 18.35 pm German time, which was one hour ahead of Allied time, which is way too far north of Douai to be Kennedy. 40 Squadron's ten-man patrol had taken off at 17.40, so the time is wrong too, 40 Squadron only taking off at the time of Jasta 8's action.

One item of interest while reading Maclanachan's account of this episode, is that he carried two Lewis guns on the top wing. While this was not frowned upon, the problem was that the extra weight of the second gun tended to affect the Nieuport's performance. Individual pilots had to weigh (no pun intended) the disadvantage of performance against the extra fire-power two guns gave, provided the pilot was on target.

The last few days of August proved quiet, little action being seen from 27 August to 2 September, and it wasn't until 4 September that 40 Squadron next added to their combat log. In the meantime, some of the latest Nieuport Scouts had started to arrive. It has always been difficult to differentiate between Nieuport 17s and 23s, but the type 27 had a definite change of rudder and fin. As Mannock described it in his diary: 'The tail plane and rudder are shaped very like a Hun Scout, also the body is fish shaped. The similarities are a source of great concern to our other machines in the air, as we are often mistaken for Huns, and consequently get fired at.'

The Nieuport 27 had a 130 h.p. Le Rhône engine (an increase of 10 h.p.) but its speed did not improve overmuch, perhaps 8-19 mph, over the type 17 or 23. In contrast, the main fighter opposition, like the Albatros DVa, had a 180 or even 200 h.p. engine, although its speed did not increase pro-rata over the Nieuport. However, the fire-power and slightly better manoeuvrability gave the edge to the German pilots. The Nieuport had a slight duration time advantage that was often a blessing when battling against head-winds, trying to get back over the front lines.

Another event which Mannock diarised was that the mechanics had set up the two top wings salvaged from von Bertrab's Albatros, in the Flight hangar, with Mannock's name on it plus the date and place where it had come down. Then three American newspaper men had paid a visit to Bruay and Major Tilney made Mannock tell them the story of his victory over von Bertrab, and they also wanted bits off the wings as souvenirs. Mannock also arranged for the carpenter to fashion a model of the Albatros from wood from one of the wings.

* *

Mick Mannock made out three combat reports on 4 September. The first was for an action fought at around 09.45 am south of Béthune. Yet another DFW two-seater was spotted, this one over Noeux-les-Mines at 17,000 feet. Mannock engaged and he fired no fewer than three drums of ammunition at it at close range, the combat continuing well east of Lens. As he was firing he saw the observer slump down and hang over the side of his cockpit. The DFW went into a steep dive but to him the pilot looked in control of his machine, and Mannock was forced to disengage now that his ammunition supply was spent. This fight was in full view of the guys on the ALG, causing great excitement. Vizefeldwebel Eddelbüttel, an observer with FA211(A) was reported wounded this date and may have been Mannock's victim.

Combat number two was timed at 11.30 am, another DFW which he engaged over Liéven at 11,000 feet, after being ordered off to drive it away. This machine had already been in action with Captain Keen but had evaded his fire, then Keen had to turn away to change drums. The German was heading for home. Mannock, flying with Sergeant L A Herbert, closed in to open fire at close range, emptying a full drum into it but the DFW pilot manoeuvred away and headed down steeply east of Lens. Mannock broke away to fit another drum and was unable to engage it further. An AA battery confirmed seeing the two-seater going down steeply but its commander was not able to say if it was 'out of control' or not.

He and Herbert appear to have been credited with an 'out of control' victory between them, although Herbert's combat report was marked 'indecisive'. He had climbed away from Mazingarbe on another mission, to escort Corps machines, and had reached 16,000 feet when he saw and attacked the DFW. Opening fire he found he had a problem with his gun. Something had come loose and he was unable to keep the gun steady as he fired. In trying to solve the problem he somehow caught the Bowden cable in the Foster mounting, so the gun – without any help from Herbert – frustratingly fired off the remainder of the ammunition.

Changing drums he chased after the two-seater as it flew east, managed to cut it off over Lens and began firing at long range. Although he saw some tracer bullets hit the machine, which then stalled and nosed-dived, he lost sight of it while changing to his third drum. This is where Mannock took up the attack. It was not unusual for NCO pilots to be with fighter squadrons in 1917, but they were few and far between. He was later commissioned.

A third DFW drew Mannock's attention between 16.05 and 16.30 that afternoon, Mannock heading off from Mazingarbe following another call from the front. Mannock confided in his diary an interesting tactic, which thankfully worked.

> 'I met this unfortunate DFW at about ten thousand feet over Avion coming south-west, and I was travelling south-east. I couldn't recognise the black crosses readily (he was about three hundred yards away and about five hundred feet above me) so I turned my tail towards him and went in the same direction, thinking that if he were British, he wouldn't take any notice of me, and if a Hun, I felt sure he would put his nose down and have a shot (thinking I hadn't seen him). The ruse worked beautifully. His nose went down (pointing at me) and I immediately whipped round, dived and "zoomed" up behind him, before you could say "knife". He tried to turn, but he was much too slow for the Nieuport. I got in about fifty rounds in short bursts whilst on the turn, and he went down in flames, pieces of wing and tail, etc. dropping away from the wreck. It was a horrible sight and made me feel sick. He fell down in our own lines, and I followed to the ground, although I didn't land. The boys gave me a great ovation.'

In his combat report he was less detailed but says that at 9,000 feet he engaged the two-seater north of Petit Vimy, attacking at first from above. He then manoeuvred behind the German and fired 70 rounds at close range. As he did so smoke began to trail from the machine that eventually turned into flames. The DFW went down and hit the ground near Souchez, the exact position noted by Mannock being T.15 Sheet 56c. This time the anti-aircraft boys were able to confirm the German machine going down in flames, but of course, it fell inside British lines so there was no doubt about this one.

The machine came from FA235(A), its crew of Unteroffizier Georg Frischkorn (aged 21, from Bitsche, south-east of Saarbrücken) and his observer, Leutnant Fritz Frech (23, from Königsberg) were both killed. The machine was a complete wreck but was still given the British code G.68 for captured aircraft.

Mannock had been flying B3607 on this day, as type 24 Nieuport. Maclanachan had flown this in from 2 AD and it had been marked with the letter 'L'. Mannock was to claim five victories in it during September. (In early October it was returned to 2 AD for overhaul, and later went to 1 Squadron, but was lost in a mid-air collision on 9 January 1918.)

The next day, the 5th, Mannock was driven to the spot where his DFW had crashed, in a motor-bike sidecar, hoping to collect some souvenirs from the two-seater but nothing remained of the machine. The two dead airmen had gone by this time but he was told that there had been a small dog in the observer's cockpit, which likewise had not survived.

* *

September 1917 would prove a busy month for Mannock and 40 Squadron. On the 5th he was up again chasing two-seaters in the early evening, finding them east of Lens at 10,000 feet. He attacked one giving it about 15 rounds before his gun jammed, so he had to break off. Being unable to clear it, he flew back to Mazingarbe.

On the 6th he was again sent aloft from Mazingarbe along with Tudhope, at 05.50. German aircraft were spotted north of Lens and the two British pilots drove them east. For reasons that are not explained, Mannock at least reduced height and just north of Vimy, flying at 1,000 feet, he was fired on – presumably from German trench positions. Mannock was off again after a reported German and shortly before 9 am found the almost inevitable DFW two-seater near Lens. Diving from 14,000 feet to the DFW's 6,000 feet, he saw it was already being engaged by another Nieuport – Lieutenant W L Harrison – who had likewise been sent off but who had covered the sky at a lower altitude. Looking down, Mannock could pick out the well-known features of the Metallurgique Works of Lens. He also saw two Albatros Scouts beginning an attack on Harrison, the nearest being close on his companion's tail.

Mannock pulled away from his line towards the DFW, made a rapid sharp turn and placed himself behind the offending Albatros and blazed away with a whole drum from his Lewis gun. Some of the shots must have hit home for the German pilot nosed down very steeply but Mannock was already making sure the other Albatros was not going to cause a problem, so he lost sight of the first one. However, 'C' Battery, anti-aircraft, later reported seeing the Scout force-land, although under control, near Lens.

Bill Harrison lived to fight another day, and indeed, went on to gain 11 victories with 40 Squadron. From Toronto, Canada, William Leeming Harrison was only 19 years old but had already served with the Canterbury Mounted Rifles before transferring to the RFC in May 1917. That summer he joined C Flight, 40 Squadron, and had scored one victory thus far, a balloon on 9 August. By the time Mannock left the Squadron in January, Harrison had yet to gain his second victory, but by the start of April 1918, had bagged 11. His 12th and last was obtained later that month as a flight commander with No.1 Squadron, but he was then wounded. He received the MC and Bar.

According to the Squadron record book, Mannock was in action yet again during a patrol between 11.15 and 12.25, which is assumed to be an indecisive encounter.

The poor weather over the next few days limited much aerial activity with ground mist and low cloud. On the 11th conditions improved and at 11.15 am Mannock, again off alone on an EA Patrol from the ALG, spotted three two-seaters between Thelus and Oppy. There had been two initially but they were joined by a third during his attack. In all he fired off all three drums at varying ranges and saw one of the two-seaters go down out of control from 15,000 feet as the fight drifted right above Oppy Wood. Now out of ammunition, he reluctantly gave up the pursuit of the other two and turned for home. Ground AA observers watched the fight but due to mist and haze at low level were unable to confirm if the German machine had crashed.

As at this date, Mannock noted his score as being 13$^1/_2$. This today would be interpreted as 14. It is uncertain as to how he came to this personal total but it is not far off what appears to be a more official figure of 12.

There were new fighters on the Western Front now. On the British side the SE5 and Sopwith Camel were increasing in numbers since they had first appeared in the late spring and early summer respectively. Both were single-seater types and both would remain as front line aeroplanes till war's end. A two-seat fighter, the Bristol F2b, had also arrived in the late spring and after an initially poor start, became another good machine which would also see out the war.

On the German side, the Albatros DVa was the machine most RFC units encountered during the summer and autumn of 1917, and a new machine, not dissimilar to the Albatros, the Pfalz DIII and DIIIa was about to make its debut. It was not as well liked as the Albatros and in some respects was not as good as the Albatros, but it showed up in several Jastas, even though it might be relegated to the more junior pilots. In September the new, distinctive, Fokker Dr.I Triplane was starting to appear. It was a fast and agile machine and much-liked by many, including the Red Baron – Manfred von Richthofen – the first three being given to his Jagdgeschwader and flown by him, Werner Voss and Kurt Wolff. After a short period it was withdrawn to strengthen its top wing assembly but returned in early 1918 where it continued till the early summer, before the arrival in strength of what has become known as the best German fighter of WW1, the Fokker DVII biplane.

The pilots of 40 Squadron soldiered on with the Nieuport Scouts, which in good and experienced hands could easily hold their own against all-comers. Mannock scored again on 20 September, at 17.35 hours that afternoon. However, his first patrol was timed at between 09.00 and 10.45 from the ALG. He patrolled from Lens to Arras initially at 18,000 feet and observed an artillery-spotting two-seater to the east. By positioning himself expertly he prevented the German crew from getting anywhere near the front, thus stopping them from carrying out their work, although he was unable to get close enough to engage. But he had been spotted by German fighters, five of which attacked him over Méricourt but seeing the Nieuport pilot was aware of their presence by turning towards them, the German fighters turned away and dived eastwards.

Then came the late afternoon action. Mannock led out four pilots: Tudhope in B3617, Harrison in B3605, Maclanachan in A6789 and a new pilot, G E H McElroy, in B3541, at 16.45. Harrison found his engine was not running smoothly so turned back, landed, had it fixed and was off again at 17.10. Meantime, Mannock had started patrolling the line Fresnoy to La Bassée, and in doing so spotted a two-seater, a type he initially could not identify, well east of Lens, heading north-west.

Mannock led his men into the sun, turned, then began to fly a parallel course with the two-seater until it had crossed the lines somewhere above Vermelles. Mannock now attacked, opening fire from close range with some 60 rounds. Tudhope now opened fire (30 rounds) and he observed pieces breaking off after Mannock's attack, and the German went down vertically, leaving a trail of smoke near Hulloch. Although a little further away, Maclanachan also saw the two-seater going down smoking badly. Unfortunately none of the three pilots saw it crash, losing it in the darkening gloom and ground haze.

Mannock was credited with an 'out of control' victory. It is possible this was a DFW from FA240(A). This unit had two crews shot-up this date. Pilot Unteroffizier Kalbreiher was wounded and his observer, Leutnant Artur Beauchamp killed. Unteroffizier Eddelbüttel and his observer, Leutnant Kuhn, were both wounded. (Whether this Eddelbüttel or the one Mannock wounded on 4 September – FA211(A) – are in any way connected, is not clear.)

CHAPTER FIVE

FINAL DAYS WITH FORTY

Forty Squadron lost another pilot on 23 September 1917, Second Lieutenant J L Barlow. John Lancashire Barlow was 19 and came from Wivenhoe, Essex. He had been on a show led by Mannock, taking off at 15.50 pm. There were five Nieuports in this Offensive Patrol: Mannock in B3541, McElroy in B3617, Barlow B1670, Harrison B3605 and Sergeant Herbert in B3512.

At 7,000 feet near Oppy, Herbert saw two enemy machines east of Oppy, waggled his wings then went down to engage one, firing 20 rounds at it as the German pilot pulled round and went east. He then went after another two-seater he spotted crossing the lines near Oppy and gave this 20 rounds too, from 300 yards, but saw no results. Mannock was close by, also firing at the first German at long range, but then the second one not only crossed the lines but must not have seen his Nieuport – probably concentrating on Herbert's machine – and flew right across Mannock's machine at the same height.

Mannock opened fire at this machine, which he described as yellow and green, from 150 yards and it immediately started down

Lieutenant George McElroy flew Nieuports alongside Mannock in 1917 but he did not start scoring victories until the SE5 arrived.

and went into a spin whereupon the wings crumpled up. McElroy and Harrison confirmed seeing this too. Mannock later flew B3607, another type 23 which had a brief life with 60 Squadron in August but had been flown to 1 AD for some work. It was then sent to 40 Squadron – flown in by Mac Maclanachan – for the use of Brigadier General G S Shepherd, the officer commanding 1 Brigade RFC. However, an aircraft is an aircraft so it is not surprising that if short of machines, 40 used it too. After all, they serviced it. It was returned to 2 AD in October and like so many other Nieuports, wound up in Egypt.

A short time before the action on the 23rd, Maclanachan had taken off from Mazingarbe following a report of a German machine up over the lines. He saw the offending Albatros DV heading away east but Mac was then attacked by two more. He turned under these, pulled his gun down and fired up into one of them. As he did so the second German attacked but 'Mac' again dipped under this machine and fired again – the rest of the drum from 20 yards. This Albatros turned over and started down in a slow spin and, with the other two Germans now out of sight, he followed the spinning V-strutter down over Hénin-Liétard and then saw it in a field on the ground, one set of wings pointing skyward. It was the Scotsman's sixth victory.

It is sometimes difficult to reconcile combat claims with losses – at least known losses. One would imagine that Mannock's two-seater crew, having had their machine crumple up and fall to earth, would have had difficulty in surviving such an event. There were a few German two-seater crews killed this day, but not apparently in the area of Oppy. Of course, sometimes the records of where men fell and where they were buried, becomes confused, so that while a crew appear to have been brought down at A, then buried at B, the B becomes the place they fell. There appears to be no German records of lost aircraft that have survived. Even the few experts in German archival material confirm this, so that unless the personnel of these lost machines were either killed or badly injured, one can find very little about an aircraft lost where the pilot and or observer survived.

It does not help in reading British combat reports when a pilot writes that his opponent crashed, or crashed and burned. Any casualty really depends on the degree or severity of the crash. What a pilot sees from height as a crash, may in reality be little more than a rough landing. Even if the machine turns over and a wing is ripped off, this does not mean any of the occupants were more than shaken-up, with perhaps a few cuts and bruises. After all, any self-respecting fighter pilot likes to believe that his victims were smashed to pieces in a 'crash' but it is quite obvious that with some degree of control over a damaged aeroplane, some sort of 'good' landing often resulted in the inmates walking away with little more than a few lacerations. Thus in this case, while it certainly appears that Mannock's two-seater crew would have received some sort of wound or injury, to tie it down to a specific unit or crew isn't possible from the information at hand.

By the same token, the unsatisfactory 'out of control' claims are more often than not moral victories, and the vast majority of pilots on both sides did not spin uncontrolled into the ground. All that can be said is that the two-seater crew that did survive to fight another day, were at least thwarted in their assigned task, and the Jasta pilot similarly was out of the fight for the moment, and not interfering with Allied aircraft doing their work.

It was on this 23 September evening that the great Werner Voss, leader of Jasta 10 within von Richthofen's JGI, was killed in one of the new Fokker Triplanes. His fight with SE5s of 60 Squadron and then the subsequent battle against five SE5s from 56 Squadron has gone down in history. That he put holes into, and damaged, in total, seven British fighters in this action, says much for his prowess and the nimbleness of the Triplane in the hands of a master.

* *

Two days later Mannock was up engaging more two-seaters but they were his last for the momentous year of 1917. Mannock, in B3607, led a patrol shortly after 10 am, in company with McElroy in B3617. A second pair, Harrison in B3606 and Tudhope in B3541, took off five minutes later. Several enemy machines were observed well to the east and low down early in the patrol. Mannock went down on one north of Armentières firing a drum of Lewis at close range and the two-seater dived east apparently damaged. Changing the drum he saw another two-seater over Béthune which he was unable to engage due to its height, but at least he saw it turn east and leave the area.

Lieutenant H S Wolff, 40 Squadron in an SE5A. Note Aldis gunsight.

Spotting yet another recce aircraft at 16,000 feet he attacked and fired a drum at point blank range from behind. The German's propeller stopped and he began to glide east. It was some way over the lines, so Mannock, now low on ammunition, left the German crew and broke off the action. Neither appear to have been claimed by him and certainly no combat reports survive, if they were ever written out, so it shows that even firing at close range did not mean certain success, but at least the observing eyes of the German crews were put off their work.

Landing back at around 11.35 (McElroy had got back at 10.45), lunch was taken and then Mannock led off McElroy (B3561) and Tudhope (B3541) at 15.05 pm. Almost as soon as they were over the front line Mannock observed a two-seater Rumpler coming towards Lens from the north-east. He engaged it immediately and opened fire at 100 yards as the crew, now fully aware of the danger, turned eastwards. Mannock fired off a full drum and the Rumpler began to steepen its dive in the direction of Sallaumines. Pulling up to change drums, he then saw the German still going down, diving steeply. It seemed a certainty that the Rumpler would not pull out, and later its fall appears to have been confirmed by 'C' Artillery Battery near Liévin. Tudhope had also engaged another German machine and it too went down and away eastwards.

Mannock's victims seem to have been a crew from FA224(A)w, Vizefeldwebel Karl Meckes and Leutnant Paul Friedrich Otto. Twenty-seven-year-old Meckes was badly injured and died two days later, being buried in Lambersort cemetery. Otto, from Güstrow, Mecklenburg, died instantly. The Germans reported their fall being at Gondecourt, so the wounded Meckes had struggled a short way north-east before crashing.

Another interesting pilot to join 40 Squadron, was Henry Samson Wolff, aged 18. He arrived on 23 September and would celebrate his 19th birthday in November. He was only around five foot tall so quickly gained a couple of nicknames: The 'Mighty Atom', and 'Little Samson'. On 31 October he was in action, and in a letter to Norman Franks in 1972, recalled:

'Saw two Huns east of Lens as soon as we crossed the lines. We then proceeded north and saw one solitary Hun two-seater and dived to attack, when twelve Albatros scouts came for us. A fight apparently ensued while I was attacking the two-seater. Maclanachan was leading the patrol with another pilot. Before we took-off Mac had called me to one side and said that whatever happens I was to stick close to him. Now, concentrating on the two-seater I was fired on by the Albatri and did not realise I was in a real "party scrap". I saw the Hun two-seater go down out of control then joined up with Mac, who was never far away from me, and then we made for base.

'When I landed I found I had several shots through my top plane but a few inches from my reserve petrol tank and realised my narrow escape. Mac came up to me and asked what I thought of the scrap. I asked, what scrap? Only then did he point to the holes in my wings. Later on in the Mess, Mick Mannock accused Mac of being a "murderer" for leading such a young one on to a decoy, which as such had stood out a mile. This of course was said in a joke as he and Mac were great pals.

'With regard to Maclanachan, he was quite an outstanding pilot and full of "guts". He was a very great friend of Mick Mannock and they often went out on patrols together. Like

Hans Waldhausen's Albatros that Tudhope forced down on 27 September 1917.

Mannock and McElroy, Mac was a born fighter. Another chap I recall was Lieutenant W Harrison, affectionately known as "Harry". A tall angular fellow who had the reputation of not being able to formate and was always seen in the air just that long bit away from the Flight formation, either higher or lower or away at one side.'

**

John Tudhope shared a famous victory on the 27th, thereby gaining his second success. He shared it, not with another 40 Squadron pilot, but with a RNAS one, Flight Commander C D Booker DSC of 8 Naval Squadron, flying a Sopwith Camel. What made it famous was that the pilot was forced down inside British lines, where he was captured, and the man had had some recent and rapid, spectacular success.

Oberleutnant Hans Waldhausen was a 25-year-old former artillery officer, from Mainz/Rhein. An army cadet since 1911 he had served with the 1st and 4th Guards Field Artillery Regiments, and then with the 76th Baden Field Artillery but had been wounded in the early weeks of the war. In 1915 he transferred to aviation, becoming an observer with FA53 and a year later trained to become a pilot. Flying with a Bavarian unit, FA76, he volunteered for single-seaters, and following further instruction, was posted to Jasta 37 on 26 July 1917.

Lieutenant John Tudhope MC, another friend in 40 Squadron in 1917.

He learnt his trade as a fighter pilot slowly, not scoring any successes in aerial combat until he shot down a British Sopwith $1^1/_2$ Strutter on 19 September, and a Martinsyde G100, which was not confirmed. He was more successful over another Martinsyde on the 24th and on the 25th flamed a balloon near Béthune. Thus on the afternoon of 27 September, with just three victories to his name, he attacked and destroyed a balloon south-west of Roulette at 17.05, then an RE8 two-seater five minutes later, while at 18.15 he attacked and shot down another balloon at Neuville St.Vaast.

It was then that his short run of luck spectacularly ran out. Charles Booker was returning from a patrol along with two of his pilots, and observed the German Albatros east of Lens. Before he could close to engage, the German pilot had darted across the trenches and flamed the balloon, but by then Booker had cut him off and attacked. Almost at the same time,

Tudhope, having been sent aloft from Mazingarbe, made his attack too. Badly hit by both attacks, Waldhausen had no choice but to put down his crippled Albatros as quickly as possible, which he did near Souchez, the area covered by the British 5th Army. However, the German had managed a quick burst into Tudhope's approaching Nieuport, forcing him to make a descent too, finishing up in a shell hole and turning over. One could say that this was victory number four for the German, his seventh in total.

It was Booker's first victory in a Camel, and his 23rd overall. Most of his earlier claims had been whilst piloting a Sopwith Triplane. He would go on to achieve 29 victories before his own death in action in August 1918, whilst commanding 201 Squadron RAF.

The downed Albatros DV, serial number 2284/17, was given the British serial G.75. Its varnished ply-wood fuselage gave it – and all other Albatros Scouts – a yellowish colouring and on its fuselage sides, apart from the German cross, it carried a star and crescent motif. Waldhausen had been wounded in the head and one wrist, and had also suffered facial bruising upon crash-landing. History appears to accord him the title of 'The Eagle of Lens' but exactly when is unclear. He was hardly a well-known predator within his area of operations, and all his victories covered a period of just over one week! Nevertheless, he survived to study law and become a judge. He served in this capacity during WW2 with the German Luftwaffe, and died in 1976.

Maclanachan had written up the whole episode, published in 1936 as part of his article on 40's time at Mazingarbe. It makes interesting reading, not just because of Mick Mannock's very different part in the affair, but because, like most stories, there is far more to it than just the plain facts. Mac wrote:

'During tea [one day] [Mick] paused in the middle of an argument on the rival merits of French and British diplomacy. "Look here, young Mac, that one this afternoon pulls you level with me this month. I can't darned well have that – shall have to look to my laurels!"

'In my mind there was no question of any competition with Mick. This propensity of his for establishing friendly rivalries, unspoilt by any tinge of jealousy, always amused me. When he could manage it he would even play Tudhope and myself against each other, purely with the object of livening things up and of getting the best out of both of us. Mick has won the title of *King of Air Fighters* (vide the book of that name by Squadron Leader Ira Jones DSO MC DFC MM) but no one had less desire to be considered as the leader, the commanding officer, or the "King" than Mick. His only objective was victory for the Flight, the Squadron, and the Army. The "A" Flight pilots, NCOs and AMs knew it, and as Gilbert [F T Gilbert – see later] put it: ".. we were a happy lot." His remarks to me that afternoon could have been translated "come on – let's have a friendly game seeing which of us will kill most of our country's enemies."

'Before we left the ground at Mazingarbe, Mick declared that the Flight's total was going to be increased still further, ".. even though it's got to be a balloon." True enough; he succeeded in cutting another notch in our totem pole by sending one of the enemy down to destruction in the lines just east of Oppy [the two-seater on 23 September]. Unless there was something particularly interesting about them, we never discussed our scraps, so I never heard the details of this one.

'The next day we held one of our Flight discussion meetings at which Mick insisted on the necessity of pressing for victories. I remember him saying at the end, "We'll teach them; they can't darned well show their noses near the line."

'Almost as if in defiance of this dictum, one particularly daring German, flying an Albatros, succeeded in carrying out three or four successful raids on our side of the lines. We heard several reports, all of which credited him with having destroyed several of our balloons, and with shooting down three or four RE8s and one AW.

'Mannock was furious, and for two days, he, Tud, or I patrolled frantically over the lines waiting to catch the German on his next venture. There was one feature about war flying on which most pilots agreed; once a pilot has been bitten by the balloon-strafing bug, he cannot resist further temptation. We knew by this fellow's success that he would come over again, and we hoped to be there when he did. On the evening of the 26th September [actually the 25th] he shot down a balloon, and in the early morning [evening] of the 27th another gas-bag was sent to its flaming end, along with another RE8 [an hour before].

'In the afternoon of that day all three of us were at Mazingarbe, two waiting while the other patrolled. There was no sign of the German, and at last Mick had a brain-wave, one of those inspirations that arise after some careful thinking. "That fellow won't come over this afternoon. He's going to come this evening when we should be at dinner – but we aren't going to take dinner until after we've got him. We'll sit here till dark."

'Mick then telephoned to one of the KB [Kite Balloon] sections to ascertain if that supposition were correct. Everyone of the raids was carried out at the orthodox British meal times, during which our activity usually slackened. Lone flyers were not likely to be in the air, and the official patrols took place at too great a height to be a danger to a low flying machine. The German was clever.

'We held a debate on the tactics we should employ were we in the position of the German, and I ended the argument by saying that if we attempted to emulate the raider, and knew of the existence of a hostile landing ground so close to the trenches, I should have one of the forward observation posts keeping a close look-out for machines descending in our vicinity.

'"That clinches it then," Mick said, "we've got to let them see us returning to Bruay, no humbug about it. Then we can come back when it's nearly dark and patrol above the balloons." He telephoned to the KB sections, asking them if they would send the balloons up *without any observers in the baskets*. On the economics of war a balloon without an observer is cheap bait for an enemy of the Albatros pilot's calibre.

'After a refresher in the Mess, we returned to the aerodrome, arranging that Tud was to patrol behind the two balloons nearest the Scarpe [river], Mick was to take those between Souchez and Mazingarbe, and I was to guard the two between the landing ground and the La Bassée Canal.

'While it was still daylight, I flew about half a mile to the west of my two balloons and two or three thousand feet above them. After half an hour of watchful patrolling I felt sick and my head commenced to throb badly. Everything seemed unreal and, thinking the twilight might be playing tricks with my eyesight, I commenced to fly between the two balloons and only a few hundred feet above them.

'Suddenly the second balloon to the south of Mazingarbe went up in flames and, as the fiery fragments slowly wound their way towards the earth, I streaked for the balloon next in line. It was too dark to see far, but I found the balloon and circled over it waiting for the attacker. The section pulled their gas-bag down slowly, and, after ten minutes, my head throbbing worse than ever, I returned to Bruay, without having seen any sign of the Albatros. There I learnt that Tudhope had crashed the German among the crumpled ruins of Souchez.

'Major Tilney, Tud, Wolff and I, drove out to the spot and found Mannock in command of the Albatros. It was a beautiful plywood model bearing both the black German iron cross and the Turkish crescent as national markings. The pilot was wounded and the Canadian Infantry, declaring that he had shot at the observer who jumped with his parachute, wanted to reward him for his chivalry.

'Mannock, I heard, had saved the German, a bristly headed schoolmaster, from the gentle attentions of the indignant infantrymen. It transpired that Mick had had engine trouble, had landed at Mazingarbe, and, while the mechanics were attending to his machine, Tud had landed also, with his engine missing badly. As the latter was taxi-ing towards Mick's machine, the balloon was set alight and Mannock yelled: "Look Tud, there you go, hell for leather, you'll get him." Or words to that effect.

'Amidst spluttering and coughing, Tud's machine struggled into the air, and within a minute he had shot the German down. There was great jubilation that night in the balloon section. Mick's and Tudhope's healths were drunk in the best of all beverages.

'This episode illustrates quite clearly how much Mannock brought his quick Irish intelligence to bear on his methods. Not one of the rest of us would have taken the trouble to enquire as to when the raids took place, and the victory was due as much to Mick's wit as it was to Tud's shooting, courage and determination in taking off with a dud engine. Also, Mannock's confidence in Tudhope's ability to catch the German was such that he himself made no attempt to join in. This was typical of Mick and his enthusiasm over the conquest was even greater than Tud's. It was a positive joy to him when one of us obtained a victory.

'There were two features about this adventure, however, which may require a little explanation. First my headache was caused by a very unusual fault. The propeller was loose and, when my fitter examined it the next morning he found that each of the bolts holding the boss to the plate had almost burnt its way through the wood. Had I been another ten minutes in the air the propeller would have pulled itself from the shaft. [So presumably the almost undetected shuddering had caused the headache.]

'The second was concerning the observer in the balloon. Mannock had asked if the balloons could be left up *without observers*, but the commanders of the sections had evidently decided that there was no need for this precaution.

'Many years after the War I was recounting this yarn to several friends without giving the details, which I thought would be of little interest to them, when one of my listeners offered to complete the story. Chuckling with mirth he told us that he was sitting in the basket of the balloon nearest Mazingarbe when he saw the one to the south of him descending to its flaming end. He immediately climbed on to the edge of his basket preparatory to jumping. Then, hearing the angry noise of an engine above him, he was about to let go when he caught sight of the red, white and blue circles of my Nieuport. He then related how, overcome with relief after these anxious moments, he tumbled headlong into the basket to lie there until the balloon was hauled down.'

One of 40's senior ground crew was Frederick T Gilbert (known as 'Bogey'), who wrote an article in the April 1935 edition of *Popular Flying*. He mentions this action involving Tudhope:

'Mannock was out to win, but not to grab all the Huns for himself. On September 27th, 1917, a Sunday evening, Mannock and Tudhope had landed at Mazingarbe, Tudhope with a cylinder missing. Before it could be attended to, the telephone orderly ran out and shouted: "H.A. approaching!" Sure enough, there he was, after the kite balloon at Aix Noulette. Mannock said, "I'll go to the line and cut him off. You try to get him, Tud."

'Well Tudhope with his dud engine went after the Hun. The Hun dived on the balloon, sent it down in flames. Not content, he zoomed up, and dived a second time, and machine-gunned the crew on the ground. This gave Tudhope time to get his height, and he got on the Hun's tail, shot his switch away and wounded him. He landed at Souchez.

'A Canadian, thinking that he had fired at the observer on the second dive, blacked the Hun's eyes for him. He was a proper square-headed Prussian, a major just come back from the Turkish front. He had only been on the Western Front fourteen days, and he had got down seven of our machines and five balloons. The Hun's machine was made of plywood and had the Turk's crescent and star, and the German cross on the side. I heard that he was sent to G.H.Q. at St. Omer, but escaped and was recaptured at Aire.

'I mention this to show that Mannock did not "hog" all the Huns. He encouraged his pilots, and trained them, and helped them to get victories.'

Fred Gilbert had a wealth of stories about 40 and Mannock. He recalled for Vernon Smyth in the 1950s the following incident:

'Mannock was seated in the Mess one afternoon playing cards with another officer, when a stranger looked in at the door, clad in flying kit. "Come in, old man, and have a drink." "I want your C.O.," said the stranger in a cold and distant manner. "Never mind," said Mick, "don't be a bloody fool, come and have a drink."

'The stranger partially undid his flying regalia. It was General Longcroft. Mannock, quite unabashed, smashed his fist into his other palm – "Bang goes my squadron!" said Mick.' [1]

As the April 1935 edition of *Popular Flying* came out, the same H S Wolff who had served in 40 Squadron, read the article and wrote to Mr Gilbert via the magazine. His letter dated 25 March 1935 reads:

[1] Brigadier-General C A H Longcroft was OC 5 Brigade, RFC, and later the first Commandant of the RAF College, Cranwell, in 1920. He retired in 1925, Air Vice-Marshal Sir Charles Longcroft KCB DSO AFC Ld'H. He had learnt to fly in early 1912, during service with the Welsh Regiment (Aero Certificate Number 192). On the occasion of this incident, Longcroft was 34 years old, so just four years older than Mick. Longcroft died in February 1958.

Dear Mr. Gilbert,

I was extremely interested to read your article in the April issue about 40 Squadron. I went overseas with them in September 1917, returning to England in May 1918. Major Tilney was my first CO and Captain Keen my first Flight Commander. As you know, we had Nieuports in those days. Afterwards dear old Tud was my Flight Commander, then Major Dallas took command of the Squadron after poor old Tilney came down when his wings collapsed in the air.

Micky Mannock was there the whole time with me and left just before me to get his Squadron. He certainly was one of the finest airmen produced, and one of the stoutest fellows one could ever wish to meet. I recollect sitting in my Armstrong hut with him one night when we were both due to go on leave on the morrow together – he was in A Flight and I in C Flight, (I had a dawn patrol just before catching the tender for Boulogne and he [his Flight] did not have a patrol until the afternoon, and was, therefore, quite free to enjoy his leave).

He came to my hut and chatted to me about the shows we could see together in London, and remarked that it was a bit unpleasant having to patrol just before "blighty". I naturally agreed with him and said, "Well, you're lucky Mick, you miss yours." "Oh," he said, "I think I'll try and snatch another Hun before I go." The next morning he was up at dawn with us and practically followed me the whole way through the patrol almost like a guardian angel from beginning to end, sitting high up well in the rear. We missed him towards the end of the patrol, and when he landed, sure enough, to use his own words, he had found a nice fat one.

H S Wolff.

There had been another witness to the action against Waldhausen. Harry Marchant was one of the Canadian soldiers on the ground and saw the fight. He later wrote of the event, from an address at Guestling, near Hastings, Sussex:

'I happened to be one of the Canadians at Souchez when the German was brought down, and what excitement it caused. That he deliberately shot at the observer [in the balloon] was correct enough, because we saw the tracers, and that caused the hostility. I don't think any of us knew that it was Mannock that helped him away out of trouble. [The story] was so real and well written that I lived it all over again the evening I read it, and was there in the ruins of Souchez where he crashed.'

It is appropriate to mention here another soldier who wrote to Vernon Smyth during his research in the 1950s about Mannock. Myles Waller, then living in Boston, Lincolnshire, and in 1917 serving with the 28th London Regiment, The Artist's Rifles, often saw Mick Mannock above them in the sky, and on several occasions actually came up to the front line on visits. He remembered him as: '… rather tall, somewhat untidy and most unassuming in his ways [and] had a quiet but genuine sense of humour.'

Mannock has never been described as a poet, but during research, the following poem was found. Due to the date Mannock signed it, the ditty must have followed the downing of Waldhausen.

There was a little Hun
Who ventured o'er the lines,
(a risky thing to do
In these riskiest of times).
Said the airman on his tail,
In a voice so sweet and calm,
'Another thousand revs. wouldn't
do you any harm.'

E Mannock
R.F.C.
Octr. 1917.

* *

Early in October 1917 Mick took some well-earned leave, only his second since arriving in France in April. This month, on the 18th, also saw the announcement of a Bar to Mannock's Military Cross. The famous Battle of Cambrai commenced on 20 November while he was still back in England, and then the Squadron finally changed its equipment from the Nieuport Scout to the SE5a fighters in December. The SE5 was not new to France. Indeed, 56 Squadron had brought out the first of this type way back in April, at the time of Mannock's debut to the front. He would fly and fight with the SE5a for the rest of his combat career. He did not get off to a good start, for Mannock damaged SE5 B4884 on 23 November in a forced landing at Dainville following engine trouble.

Mannock kept up a regular correspondence with his family, and one letter that has survived is dated 21 November, to his sister Jess:

40 Sq.
R.F.C.
B.E.F.
21/11/17

Dear Jess,

Greetings. Hope all is well at Birmingham. Am still safe, but cannot tell how long I shall remain lucky. Plenty of work for the airmen and plenty of casualties.

Am doing special air work by myself now. A big feather in my cap. Am expecting the D.S.O. soon, but may get a white cross instead. Who cares anyway.

It's great fun out here chasing the Huns on the ground. The squadron has done some wonderful work, and has been specially congratulated by the G.O.C.

How's Ted? Ask him to write me when he can.

I suppose you are still munitioning, or have you got 'fed up'? We want shells.

Hope Mum and Norah and the kiddies are going strong.

Cheerio,
Ed.

(PS) Have got 16 Huns down up to date.

Obviously Jess was, like many women at the time, making munitions in the factories producing guns, shells and bullets. Times were certainly changing in wartime Britain, women becoming more independent and taking on men's work with so few males being available at home.

Of interest is him telling Jess about his lone sorties. These of course were flown from Mazingarbe, taking off rapidly whenever German machines were either seen, or reported by front line observers. On what he based his assumption of a DSO is unclear. Perhaps he was being humorous, especially when saying then that he might get instead, a 'white cross': i.e. a wooden cross on his grave.

His score is more or less that agreed by official figures as at this date. Arguably 15, but obviously his 'own' tally included one that is perhaps questioned today.

**

In the April 1935 edition of *Popular Flying* mentioned earlier about '40', Mr F T Gilbert refers to several of the Squadron's pilots, including one story about Mannock and McElroy:

> 'Mannock came to Forty at Treizennes, about early April. I saw the right-hand bottom plane of his Nieuport break in two at 2,000 feet. Fortunately he did not attempt to turn, but glided over the hangars, fired his gun, and finished up in a ploughed field, unhurt. He gave his rigger some work, eighteen tail skids in succession, in bad landings.
>
> 'Mannock was very highly strung. I saw him at our advance landing ground at Mazingarbe one day when a Hun had got on his tail, and McElroy, too. The Hun had shot part of the king-post away, which has the rudder and elevator connected. McElroy had some bullets smash one of the tubes in the fuselage at his side, and then go into the oil tank at the bottom. Poor Mac was soaked to the waist in caster oil. Mannock said, "Who the hell does he think he's shooting at? Does he know I hold a first-class pilot's ticket? I'll give him shoot, trying to shoot my tail off!"'

There was a new pilot on the Squadron in December, Captain G H Lewis. Gwilym Lewis was a new flight commander, having already been in France with 32 Squadron in 1916. He would become an ace with 40 and win the DFC in 1918. Very much the gentlemen, one can imagine him being less boisterous than some of the other pilots. This is supported by a comment by C W Usher, who was in 'Zulu' Lloyd's B Flight, who many years later said that Lewis was known as 'Noisy' Lewis: '… a charming but particularly silent individual.' In 1976 Lewis wrote a book about his WW1 experiences (*Wings over the Somme* published by William Kimber & Co) that he formulated from his letters home. He mentions Mannock several times and knew him fairly well.

> 'I think I told you that we have got an expert Hun-strafer here. Captain Mannock MC and bar; someone said he has got 17 Huns. Anyway he strafes about on his own, and seems to enjoy himself fairly well. I believe he will be going home soon. He is an excellent fellow.'

Despite the conversion to the new SE5 machines with all the potential it offered, Mannock did not get off to a great start. On 9 December he had written: 'We chase the Huns out of the sky with our new bus. They won't stand up to it at all. Rather rotten luck.' However, he was less enthused a week later, writing: 'Had a few (very few) scraps since last leave, but my guns have let me down badly. Had one a few days ago, and drove an Albatros down from 11,000 feet to 3,000 feet, then my guns jammed and he got away. Very annoying!'

The SE5 carried two guns. Like the Nieuport it had one drum-fed .303 Lewis gun on the top wing, set to fire over the whirling blades of the propeller, that just like the Nieuport, could be pulled down to both reload with a fresh drum, or to fire upwards into the undersides of an enemy. The other was a belt-fed .303 Vickers machine gun in front of the pilot, slightly offset to the left, firing through the blades of the propeller using a synchronising gear.

The SE5 was powered by a 200 h.p. Hispano-Suiza engine, which gave it a speed of around 118 mph at 10,000 feet – more in a dive. The type had been slow to arrive in numbers due to the fact that a newer hoped-for engine had proved unreliable, which kept some 400 airframes languishing in various stores and depots until early 1918. 56, 60 and 84 were the only three operational squadrons in France, but as the year of 1917 drew to a close, 40 and 41 re-equipped, followed by 68 and 24 by Christmas.

Regarding Christmas, there is another surviving letter from Mannock to his niece Marjorie. Although it is undated, it was obviously written on the run-up to the festive period:

Dear little Marjorie,

I have very great pleasure in acknowledging your kind letter dated the 25th of last month, and thank you very much for the thought which bid you to write.

I am afraid I have no news for you, which the censor would allow me to give, but I hope if I am still spared, to see you some time just after Xmas. I tried very hard to remain out here until the war ends, but the Authorities would not allow me to stay, as they said they thought I was in need of a rest in England.

I'm sorry you don't take kindly to your school duties, but I feel sure that when you get older, you will be sorry, like I have been, that you did not take fuller advantages of learning. It is very nice to know more about a subject, than the person to whom you are talking. And again, those persons who cannot work with their brains, have to work much harder with their hands, and it is always nicer and cleaner, if not easier, to work with one's brain.

I'm afraid I shall not be able to send you any Xmas presents from France as the only presents we ever get out here are bullets, shells, rain, and early morning jobs. Some of us are lucky enough to get a present in the shape of a wound when we are sent home to England to get better, the sooner to get sent out here again for further altercation.

Well, I must close now as it's about 1-30 in the morning and there are lots of jobs to do tomorrow.

Love to all,

Yours,
Uncle Eddie

* *

Mannock's winter gun problems were experienced by many other pilots also. Despite improvements with anti-freezing lubricants, there was always a problem in cold winter weather that caused gun mechanisms to clog and freeze up, especially at height. Thus a frustrating time for him and others, and it was not until New Year's Day that he was again successful. It was also the day he was finally due to leave 40 Squadron. His papers and travel documents were all dated 2 January 1918.

It was another special mission, flown alone, having been sent up after a reported two-seater over the front. He left the ground at 11.10 and made height to 15,000 feet over Fampoux, east of Arras. Arriving here, he saw a German two-seater being engaged by two Sopwith Camels (8 Naval Squadron based at St Eloi, where the nearby ruined monastery was a wonderful landmark for its pilots). As he watched the German pilot seemed to elude his antagonists and dive towards the north-east.

Mannock went down after the German – which he identified as a DFW, coloured with purple chequered markings. At 12,000 feet both Mannock and the German observer began to exchange fire, but then his Lewis gun jammed. However, he closed right in, following the diving machine to around 3,000 feet, and fired 20 rounds from the Vickers. Damage from his gun and the speed of the dive caused the two-seater's right wings to crumple up and the machine crashed near Fampoux, inside Allied lines. Another SE5 flying nearby, piloted by Lieutenant [A.B.] Shilstone, observed the combat and confirmed Mannock's claim. [1]

Despite Mannock claiming in his combat report that his opponents had been flying a DFW, the actual machine was a Hannover CLIII, with a 200 h.p. Opel engine, from FA288(A). Mannock gives the time of the actual combat as 11.35. The wreckage was given the British serial G.121. The German crew were Vizefeldwebel Fritz Korbacher, a Bavarian aged 25 from Arnstein, south-west of Schweinfurt, but living in Munich, and Leutnant Wilhelm Klein, a month short of his 25th birthday, coming from Kaiserslautern, in the Rhineland, and listed as a Bavarian. Klein's remains are within a *Kameradengräb* (mass grave) at the German cemetery of St Laurent Blangy, east of Arras.

The following day Mannock left for England. There is no doubt that his going was felt deeply by 40 Squadron pilots and ground personnel alike. His character and personality had certainly been imprinted on everyone and his slow start had been totally forgotten. He left as a valued flight commander with a reasonable score of victories achieved mostly over the summer. A Canadian with the Squadron, W G Soltau [2], related to Ira Jones for his book on Mannock, the following about the day he left for 'Blighty':

'I also recollect some small incidents of his great popularity among men, both mechanics and other ranks, as well as junior officers. How he made them sing sometimes during the concerts and sing-songs, and how they always responded to his leadership in all things!

'In January 1918, I was ordered to the south of France for a rest, and at the same time Mannock was ordered back to England. Four of us decided to make the trip to Boulogne in one car, Mannock, McCudden, McElroy and myself. As we left No.40 Squadron, the car was loudly cheered by the officers outside the Mess, and we found the road lined with cheering mechanics. I then realised Mannock's influence over the men ... Mannock was

[1] The authors tried to discover who Lt Shilstone was and with which squadron he was flying, as Mannock mentions him by name in his combat report. The only Shilstone we could find was Arthur Bernard, born in Simla, India, where his father was assistant secretary to the R.W. Dept at Ranchi. After Cambridge, Shilstone joined the Artist's Rifles and in early 1917 learnt to fly with the RFC. He went to France on 12 July 1917 but by the end of the month had been posted back to England due to ill-health, and in fact struck off charge and sent to the 2nd Battalion of the Northamptonshire Regiment. When the RFC accountants chased him for being overpaid with flight pay, Shilstone told them that he had no idea he had been posted to this regiment, but meantime had returned to the RFC in September 1917. He was again deleted from RFC records in March 1918, and again sent to the Northamptonshires.
[2] Wilfred Gustave Soltau was with the Intelligence Corps and not with the RFC but the Imperial Army. He had been a private (476033) with the PPCLI and had qualified for the 1915 Star in late 1915. He was commissioned in October 1916 and it is assumed he had some dealings with 40 Squadron due to his intelligence duties. Perhaps being with the Canadian forces that were on 40 Squadron's front.

one of the most loveable men I have ever known, always cheery, witty, courteous, daring, brave, and resourceful. He personified the best type of Irishman. On the way to Boulogne we stopped at a hospital, as there was an Irish sister, named Murphy, who wanted to say au revoir to Mick. His popularity in this sister's mess staggered us as much as it embarrassed him.'

One cannot say at this distance just why McCudden was in the car, for he certainly was not going on leave. He was flying and in action on both 1 and 3 January. 56 Squadron were based at Laviéville, down by Albert, so it seems strange he should motor to Bruay, then on to Boulogne, before returning to Albert.

McElroy, a particular friend now of Mannock's, had just achieved his first victory (28 December) following the arrival of the new SE5s. He was not going on leave either, so perhaps these friends were merely escorting Mannock to the leave ship at Boulogne.

Reading Maclanachan's book puts a slightly different light on these events. He starts by referring to McElroy's first victory:

'On landing, my first question to the others was to find out which of them had attacked the twelve Albatros. McIrish was the culprit, and after hearing my opinion of his courage, his success and his *lack* of discipline, he was attempting to defend his action by saying: "I thought you meant to attack the lot the way you swung round," when Mick climbed out of his machine. "Which of you was it?" "Mac," I said, and McElroy waited, expecting some praise from his fellow-countryman. There was a lively twinkle in Mick's eyes as he said: "What do you think our Pygmalion duty is, to risk our lives protecting you, you hot-headed Irish spleen? You might have lost Mac the whole blinking flight. Couldn't you see what Mac was going to do?"

'Poor McElroy, he did not know now whether we were serious or not, and only after having filled in our reports did I congratulate him on his first "blood". There was no doubt that the Albatros had gone down to its destruction. Mick then gave him a severe lecture on tactics and flight policy – telling him that against fourteen of the enemy we should really have had little chance in a dog-fight. "Remember, McIrish, none of us want to see you "go" as you certainly will if you behave in that high-blooded Irish way of yours. You leave it to your leader. The Flight might have had half a dozen of them if you hadn't split them up."

'The mess was lively that day, for two other pilots were able to claim victories, and everyone in the Squadron had been engaged in a fight of some sort. Mick openly showed his pride in A Flight.

'Two days later, however, Mick came to the door of my hut, his old time grin covering his rugged countenance. Holding out a yellow ticket he said: "Got my ticket, old boy. Home to good old Blighty and then back for the big fight!" I was momentarily relieved, and laughed at him for having suggested that I was going home too. "Don't you worry, Mac, you're coming with me. Your ticket is round there as well. They wouldn't give it to me. We've only got 48-hours to get out of France, and we'll be together still."'

Then, on their last day, Maclanachan recorded the events of 1 January:

'This morning the temptation to have a last destructive raid against the enemy was strong. My luck was in, for after contour-chasing to Douai I dropped my bombs from 200 feet, getting direct hits on the tracks, after which I returned to empty my ammunition into the German trenches.

'Mick's trip was even more fortunate. Taking his usual beat between Lens and Hénin-Liétard, he met a two-seater and shot it down into our trenches. It was the first day of the year, Mick had begun well.

'That evening there was a quiet farewell dinner:

> Huites Natives, Potage de Fampaux,
> Carrelets Fritz, Boeuf Roti au Ration,
> Asperges en branches, Fruits de Bruay,
> Bambouches des Heraldes, Dessert.
> Café.

'Combined with Lady Killers and champagne it was a merry meal, at the end of which Major Tilney made a blushing speech. He spoke in most glowing terms of Mick's courage and of his ability as a flight commander.

'The next morning, when the 48-hours had elapsed, I was helping Finlay to pack my belongings when the feeling of having been thwarted again returned. I went to Mick's hut where he too was in the midst of packing. "What about a last go at them?" I asked. "That's an idea, I wonder if we can risk it. What time is the tender coming for us?" "Two o'clock."

'It was then almost eleven, and we hurried to the aerodrome. Mick's machine was nearest the entrance to the hangar, and by the time Davidge and Biggs were getting mine out Mick had revved his engine and was taking off. The sound of a machine leaving the ground drew Major Tilney's attention from squadron affairs, and as I was about to climb into my SE he came over from the orderly room. "Look here, Mac, you can't go up, you're already struck off the strength." "Hang it all, Major. Mick's just gone up. I'm to meet him over the lines," I said. "But neither of you has any right to have a machine."

Mannock standing outside his hut, 40 Squadron 1917.

'We argued about it for two or three minutes, finally agreeing that as mine was the most valuable machine in the Squadron, because of my extra "gadgets", official anger might be mollified if I took the worst machine – Harrison's – the machine on which we had all learnt to fly SE5s.'

Maclanachan flew out and actually encountered a DFW but just as he was starting to engage it, he lost oil pressure and had to return to the aerodrome. After a hurried lunch Mick asked Mac to do him a favour. He was meeting a Canadian pal and also wanted to see some people on the way to Boulogne, so wanted Mac to go in the car while he went in the tender.

This he did, and Mac also recorded the send off they had from everyone on the Squadron, so perhaps rather than remembering McCudden on the journey, Soltau had meant to say Maclanachan. They all met up in Boulogne, dined in a small select restaurant and then shared a room at the Hotel de Louvre, ready to sail at 09.30 the next morning. To his surprise, Mick confided to Mac that he was not looking forward to the trip as he was not a good sailor. Considering all the twists, turns and other manoeuvres Mick performed in the air, Mac could hardly believe it.

Gwilym Lewis wrote in a letter home that Mannock was leaving 40:

'Our expert, Captain Edward Mannock, has recently been sent home, very much against his will. He has been out here about eight or ten months, and has 18 Huns to his credit. He got his last this side of the lines the day before he left. He even went up on the morning he was due to leave. I told him to be sure to call on you if he had a chance. He is one of the finest personalities I have ever met. Very popular by all he met, and a regular hero in this squadron. He loved fighting but hated killing – I believe it used to upset him for days after sometimes. He was originally in the ranks and I know you would like him if for no other reason than he is the most arrogant socialist!

'He told me he would be staying at the RFC Club, so if he doesn't call on you, you may think it worthwhile to rout him out. He was jolly good to me when I arrived first. A new flight commander to an old squadron is always looked on with suspicion, and by his being nice to me everyone was.'

Captain Gwylim Lewis of 40 Squadron pictured in 1918.

**

At this juncture it seems pertinent to look at Mannock's victory score. In all, his biographer, Ira Jones, gave him a score of 21 while flying with 40 Squadron. Mannock had submitted, as far as is known, 23 combat reports, although not all would have concerned a positive victory. It is difficult to reconcile any figure and substantiate it with information known today. In mid-August 1917 Mannock had noted his score as nine, and then after 11 September, he gave it as $13^{1}/_{2}$. The half would have been a share, although RFC pilots hardly ever counted shares in fractions. 13^1/$_2$ would mean 14, even if some of the 13 had also been shared. A victory, whether claimed singly or by two or three pilots, gave each participant 'one' victory. This system should not be confused with scoring in WW2 where halves or quarters, etc, were noted as just that. Where that system fell down for the historian is that a score of say, 8^1/$_2$ could not only mean eight singly plus one shared with another pilot, but could also mean seven destroyed and three half shares, which, when added together, made 8^1/$_2$!

There are undoubtedly anomalies in looking at Mannock's combat record, for there are enemy aircraft driven down, and at least one other 'forced to land'. In the early days of air fighting, a victory was almost anything. The mere driving away of a hostile machine was, in its day, a sort of victory. A victory need not, and indeed did not, mean a hostile machine 'destroyed'. Again, in the early days of men such as Albert Ball VC, German pilots were far more inclined to go down and land, with reasons for doing so varying from what was politely called 'wind up' – wonderful WW1 expression for frightened or scared – to a mortal wound. In those early air battles where aircraft numbers were far fewer than the summer of 1917 onwards, it was far less likely that a German airman who decided to land – for whatever reason – would be shot-up on the ground. Chivalry was still respected. For that reason, where the result was in doubt, a 'victory' might be awarded for forcing an opponent to land. After all, quite apart from the possibility that the enemy pilot might be seriously or even mortally wounded, he had been stopped from carrying out his assigned mission. If that had been directing artillery fire on to British troops, then it was indeed some sort of 'victory'. There could also be confusion in surviving records about those 'driven down' claims. Driven down meant just that, driven away from the front, interrupting the opponent's task, and with the time it took to fly away and regain the necessary height to start that task again, might well exceed the fuel limit of the aeroplane. The confusion also continued when the 'out of control' claims might also be termed as 'driven down out of control'. Driven down meant driven off, 'driven down out of control' should mean a possible kill, although more likely just a hostile pilot spinning down out of the combat zone which had become too dangerous.

Looking at Mannock's record rationally one could come to a total of 16 victories, made up of three definitely destroyed, including one balloon, four forced down inside Allied lines in various states of disrepair and captured, and ten 'out of control'. So, without the 'probables' he had achieved seven definite kills, but the total of 16 must still be considered his score at this time. It must be remembered that all WW1 British fighter aces worked with this system. Only with the resurgence of interest in WW1 aviation in the late 1950s did some comparisons start to be made using yardsticks from the recent conflict of WW2.

In the Second World War, a pilot was only credited with victories which were deemed as definitely destroyed. Probables and damaged were noted but not included as part of an overall score. Thus a pilot who had achieved ten destroyed, four probables and two damaged (10-4-2), had a score of 10, whereas in WW1, that figure would most likely be recorded somewhere as a possible 16. The early pulp-fiction writers of the 1930s, the time WW1 aviation first had its enthusiasts and followers, often knew little of the niceties of the scoring system, and more often than not a pilot's score was referred to as, say, 20 'destroyed' rather than 14 destroyed and six out of control. When I [Norman Franks] started out on the road of WW1 aviation history more than forty years ago, one thought in my head was that if a man like McCudden had 'destroyed' 57 German aircraft, how many others had he damaged or had probably destroyed? It took a while before I realised I was confusing WW2 to WW1 scoring and their different crediting systems, and that amongst those 57, the probables – the out of control claims – helped to make up that total.

CHAPTER SIX

74 SQUADRON

No sooner had his boat docked than Mannock was quickly on his way to London, followed by trips to Birmingham and Northampton for a good rest. He had spent some time visiting friends and meeting up with flying colleagues in London at the various haunts frequented by RFC officers. On 11 January he dropped a line to his sister Jess, on RFC headed note-paper, while staying at the RFC officer's main watering hole in London, situated between New Bond Street and Berkeley Square:

> Royal Flying Corps Club
> 13, Bruton Street,
> Berkeley Square, W.
> 11/1/1918

Dear Jess,

Home again for a month or two, and am staying at the above address for a while. I hope you are all quite well and keeping cheerful in these fierce times.

I am trying to arrange to see Paddy in town here during the next week, and am hanging on until then, when I shall take a run along to Birmingham to see you all. Hope Mother is quite fit.

Haven't heard from Ted at all! I hope he is O.K.

Well, no more now, and excuse brevity.

Yours,
Eddie

Towards the end of January, Mannock was posted on attachment to the Wireless Experimental Establishment (WEE) at Biggin Hill.

It was not the Biggin Hill of later fame, but it had been established in 1916 to house the wireless testing park, that had earlier been at Mannock's old stamping ground at Joyce Green. Biggin Hill is on high ground, south of Croydon/Bromley and north-east of Sevenoaks. Such elevation was especially useful for wireless experiments. The unit grew quickly, to become the WEE, under Major H T B Childs.

The base had no aircraft, except one unarmed Sopwith Pup, but with the increase in Zeppelin and then Gotha bomber raids, newly formed 141 Squadron took up residence as part of London's air defence. 141 had a variety of aircraft until it took on two-seater Bristol F2b fighters in March. The Squadron arrived on 8 February 1918, virtually coinciding with

Mannock's posting. Not that there was any other connection, because by mid-February he was posted to 74 Squadron at London Colney. This Squadron had been formed at Northolt in July 1917 as a Training Depot Squadron (TDS), then a Training Squadron (TS), which meant that in due course it would cease to be a training unit and become a fully fledged RFC squadron, fit for operations, with, hopefully, a trained-up bunch of pilots ready for action.

Mannock had been agitating to get back into action ever since his rest leave was over and at the time he was told to go to 74, he wrote to Jim Eyles:

> 'Just got my instructions. As you know, I have been trying very hard to get out to France again. Well, I have been posted to No.74 Training Squadron at London Colney [to the south-east of St Albans, Hertfordshire] and we are proceeding overseas next month. Hooray! I feel horribly glad about it. We shall be flying the same machines as I flew in No.40 Squadron – SE5s.'

Exactly when 74 was designated as (a) a fighter squadron, and (b) with what equipment is uncertain. This was a time when the three main RFC single-seat fighters were the Sopwith Camel, Sopwith Dolphin and the SE5a. In France the big German March offensive (Operation Michael) would start on 21 March, an event that would put several plans for new squadrons awry. At least one new squadron was due to equip with Dolphins, while two more had almost completed their 'working up' on this type, but casualties during the March battles stripped these two squadrons of their equipment, and the new one had its equipment changed from Dolphins to SE5s. Even some of the SE5 squadron working up in England, had to lose some of their machines to supplement losses in France. 85 Squadron, later to be associated with Mick Mannock, had been designated a Dolphin squadron, but due to the lack of new machines, its equipment was changed to SE5s.

Although most SE5 pilots liked the machine, there had always been a question as to why it did not carry twin Vickers guns, rather than just one, plus the top-wing Lewis. One assumes that because the latter had been reasonably effective on the Nieuports, and also because Albert Ball had had some input into the final design, the armament was retained. Even Mannock and Caldwell questioned the armament and it seems that initially they both liked the Dolphin a little more than the SE5!

One change that was made in 74, said to be Mannock's idea, was to remove the Aldis

Mannock (right) with Henry Dolan MC, 74 Squadron. Dolan was killed in action on 12 May 1918 after downing seven German aircraft.

telescopic gun-sight and put a Vickers ring-sight on the centre line, just to the right of the muzzle of the Vickers gun, and this was lined up with a bead sight just in front of the cockpit windshield. Although the Aldis had been used with the Nieuport, it was less than useful in close-up fighting and it had the habit of collecting oil on the forward lens that made it impossible to use.

* *

Being in England with his new squadron enabled Mick to make a flying visit to his adoptive town of Wellingborough. He flew there on 27 February, landing at a place called Long Marsh. No doubt he had alerted Jim Eyles of his visit and quite a crowd had assembled, which must have included Jim and his wife, plus small son Ernest, now aged five. In WW2, Ernest would serve with the RAF and one has to wonder if this visit and the display Mick put on for the crowd, influenced his choice of service in that conflict.

Just over two weeks later, on 17 March, Mick repeated this visit, taking with him once again Henry Dolan. Both trips were reported by the local newspaper, and this second trip had Wellingborough School's cricket ground as the destination. Jim and May would have been among the welcoming assembly and when the two pilots took off for home, they put on another dazzling display to enthral them all. Both these flying visits were duly recorded in the *Wellingborough News*, the first in a March 1918 edition:

Captain Mannock's Wonderful Display at Wellingborough

'When two aeroplanes appeared over Wellingborough on Sunday afternoon and began scouting about above the town, the inhabitants realised that a treat was in store, and flocked into the streets and open spaces in readiness for the performance. When it was observed that the red streamers of a patrol leader were attached to one of the machines it was easily guessed that Flight Commander Edward Mannock MC, the well-known Wellingborough airman, was one of the visitors. It was a correct guess, the daring flier having come, accompanied by Lieut. Dolan (in the second machine). The planes were single-seaters of the latest and best type, with 180 h.p. engines, built especially for scouting and fighting, and were the finest machines that have ever been flown over Wellingborough.

'Scarcely had the airmen reached the town when they commenced a sensational exhibition of trick flying, which thrilled the thousands of spectators. It seemed to the watchers that the airmen could do anything they liked with their machines, for they looped the loop, made sudden descents and ascents, made short circles, and banked in all methods and directions. A sudden swoop from the clouds, and as sudden a return to the heights, particularly impressed the crowds.

'The first performance did not last long, and the machines descended for a time in Long Marsh. Special constables guarded them for a time, whilst "Paddy" and the Lieutenant had tea with a Wellingborough friend, and then, at 5.30, a re-ascent was made. A great crowd of people in the field had an exciting time as the two roaring 'planes literally jumped into the air and shot up overhead. The performance which followed was even better than the first, for in addition to looping, the Flight Commander carried out an amazing vertical bank, and the Lieutenant who, although he had not yet been out to France, is a clever pilot, was responsible for an exhibition of "rolling" – a new trick often used at the front but seldom seen in England. After a short but astonishing display the generous entertainers made off for home.

'We understand that Flight Commander Mannock will within a short time be leaving for the front as a member of a famous fighting squadron. He has already 17 enemy machines to his credit, and is known as one of the foremost airmen. Everyone in Wellingborough and district will wish him the best of luck, fresh laurels, and a safe return.'

Mention of the second flight into Wellingborough was reported in a May edition of the *Wellingborough News*, which is recorded in the next chapter.

**

At the start of its life, 74 had Avro trainers and was commanded by Major A H O'Hara-Wood, an Australian from Melbourne. He would later take charge of 4 AFC Squadron and fall whilst commanding 46 Squadron a month before the Armistice. In November 1917 Major the Honourable L J E Twisleton-Wykeham-Fiennes took over from O'Hara Wood, and was CO as Mannock arrived, but on 1 March 1918, Major A S W Dore succeeded him, seeing the unit move from a training to an operational squadron. However, three weeks into his leadership came the man who would head 74 during all its time in France, New Zealander, Major Keith Logan Caldwell MC, from Wellington.

Despite his tender years, he was only 22, he had learnt to fly in New Zealand in 1915 before travelling to England to try for the RFC. Successful, he first flew with 8 Squadron, which used BE2d two-seater reconnaissance aircraft, from July to November 1916, and then moved to fighters, going to 60 Squadron, that had, like 40 Squadron, Nieuport Scouts. Apart from some sick leave in March and April 1917, Caldwell survived to the early autumn, gaining a Military Cross and claiming nine victories, which included an earlier one while with 8 Squadron. As was mentioned in Chapter Three, he was known to everyone as 'Grid' because he always referred to aeroplanes as grids. In 60 he had W A Bishop as a fellow pilot.

After 60 Squadron he had been at the Special School of Flying (SSF) at Gosport, run by Major Robert Smith-Barry. This was

Mannock's CO in 74 Squadron was Major K L Caldwell MC, who had earlier flown with 60 Squadron.

a specialised unit, whose pilots were virtually hand-picked by Smith-Barry in order to train them to train others, especially would-be instructors, in an attempt to have as many pupils as possible to be good instructors. In this way he hoped that, in turn, their trainees would not only become worthwhile pilots at the front, but also survive their training! All of those picked had good front line experience, with a number coming from 60 Squadron, which had been Smith-Barry's unit in France.

** **

The Squadron's new CO found that Mannock was his A Flight commander. Caldwell was later to recall that Mannock was about six feet tall, quite thin and with a ruddy complexion. He had reddish-brown hair and invariably carried a cane. In his speech there was no sign of an Irish accent. I can quote here from a 1964 tape recording made by Keith Caldwell, referring to when the two men met again. He hadn't thought much more about their first meeting on the occasion of going to 40 Squadron with Zulu Lloyd, but:

> '…. in early 1918, I met Mannock at London Colney where a new training squadron was being formed and I was fortunate in being the new CO, and delighted to find that Mannock was the senior flight commander in charge of A Flight. With Captain Mannock to give a lead, I felt we might spin when we went overseas and got up against the enemy, and so it was to be. We had five down on the first day [of combat], of which Mannock got one and his Flight two others, tho' they say Mannock was really the cause of these two others going down.'

Mannock, as senior flight commander, immediately began to imbue his pilots with that press-on spirit he had helped formulate in 40 Squadron. His presence was well-felt, for the pilots in the other two Flights equally knew they could learn what they needed to pick-up

Pilots of 74 Squadron, April 1918. Rear (left to right): A G Lewis, B Roxburgh-Smith, H Hamer, P J Stuart-Smith, H E Dolan, H G Clements, R E Bright, C E L Skedden, H Coverdale and J I T Jones. Seated on chairs: W J Cairnes, W E Young, K L Caldwell, J J E M Everard, E Mannock. In front: P F C Howe, J R Piggott, G M Atkinson and W B Giles.

quickly from this tall, dark, ruggedly handsome man, who was not boastful despite his MC ribbon and Bar rosette beneath his wings, and would tell them honestly exactly how things were. There would be no 'mollycoddling'. Air fighting was a serious business and death, in several gruesome forms, awaited the unwary. Some experienced pilots tended to say little to newcomers, working on the basis that 'you'll learn in due course', but more often than not, death interrupted the youngsters' learning curves. One chap Mannock did pick out and often flew with in the early days with 74, was Henry Dolan, the pilot he had flown up to Wellingborough with in February and March. Mick had obviously seen something in him that he thought worth taking time to foster.

Mannock was a different man now. Much of his air fighting in 40 Squadron had been 'lone wolf' stuff, often operating alone from Mazingarbe. Experienced pilots were still just about able to survive doing this, but Mannock knew that by 1918 it had become far too dangerous to go out over the lines by himself. War in the air was now a patrol war, patrols which were led by experienced and caring flight commanders. For Mannock, the pilots became his main concern after destroying the enemy. Even though he had ended his time with 40 Squadron as a flight leader, he was now fully aware of his responsibilities to his men, particularly his Flight comrades. It was his job to look after them.

Commanders of B and C Flights were Captain W E Young and Captain W J Cairnes respectively. Wilfred Ernest Young was 26 and came from Bournemouth. After serving with the Dorset Regiment he transferred to the RFC and had seen action flying French Spads with 19 Squadron during the first half of 1917, gaining three victories. He would survive the war, commanding 1 Squadron from August 1918 and be awarded the Distinguished Flying Cross (DFC).

William Jamieson Cairnes [1] came from Drogheda, Ireland and was 21, and had been educated at both Rugby and Cambridge. Following service with the 5th Battalion of the Leinster Regiment, he had also moved to aviation whilst in Egypt but seems to have suffered slight injuries during training. Returning to the UK in November 1916, he, like Young, had flown with 19 Squadron, and had similarly claimed three victories. Therefore both these men had known each other for some time and shared adventures and dangers together. Unhappily Cairnes would not survive his time with 74, being killed in action on 1 June 1918.

Most of the pilots had seen no active duty in France and were keen to absorb every bit of help and advice that they could. Death was no respecter of inexperience, and the 'devil always took the hindmost'. Caldwell was equally keen to make his squadron a good one and he too had the intelligence to impart as much information as he could to his chicks. Mannock's lectures on air fighting techniques were always well attended, and the one thing he managed to thrust home, and which became a well known phrase with them, was: "*Gentlemen, always above; seldom on the same level; never underneath.*" Like most RFC squadrons, the pilots came from a variety of places and backgrounds.

Of Mannock's A Flight, Lieutenant Benjamin Roxburgh-Smith came from Bromley, SE London (now Kent). Born in April 1884 he was just on 34, so little wonder he was known as 'Dad'; or sometimes 'Rox'. A married man with a family, he had worked in the Glyn, Mills & Currie Bank in London since 1908 and had joined the RFC direct, in August 1916. His first squadron was 65 but he was injured in a crash and following this became an instructor until finally posted to 74. He would become one of the Squadron's top scorers and in later life lived in Rhodesia.

[1] Sometimes incorrectly spelt and recorded as Cairns.

Lieutenant Henry Hamer was 20 and was living in Worcestershire when he joined the RFC from Denstone College, Staffordshire in April 1916. He had, however, already learnt to fly at his own expense at the Hall's Flying School, Hendon in 1915. He spent two months with 60 Squadron in France in early 1917, then flew with 44 Home Defence (HD) Squadron in England before being sent to 74. He would survive the war and live till 1956.

Lieutenant Henry Eric 'Bolo' Dolan, from Ealing, was 22. He enlisted while in Canada and became part of the 1st Canadian contingent and had won the MC in France as an artillery officer. He became a particular pal of Mannock and in his short spell of operational flying with 74 would down seven enemy machines before he himself fell in combat.

Lieutenant Percy Frank Charles Howe was a South African, from Bremersdorf, Swaziland, who had been educated in the Cape Colony. He was 20 and had joined the RFC in April 1917 and been sent to 74 while it was a training unit, in November. Due to his background he was known as 'Swazi' Howe.

Another flight commander with 74 Squadron was W J Cairnes, but he was killed in action on 1 June 1918.

Lieutenant Harris George Clements – or 'Clem' – was 25 and although born at Chilham, Kent, had emigrated to Canada with his elder brother, worked on the land, and was a student in Calgary when the war started. He had joined and then been commissioned into the 9th Reserve Battalion of the Alberta Regiment, later requesting a move to flying in August 1917. His posting to 74 TS came in October as soon as he got his 'wings', and apparently Mannock selected him for A Flight after watching him come in and make a good landing! A minor ace with the Squadron he survived his time in France, and of later being an instructor. Post-war he lived in Leicester till his death, having lost both of his sons in Bomber Command in WW2. Clem died in May 1983.

The last pilot was Lieutenant Geoffrey Murland Atkinson. He has been described as a Scot, but his address when he joined the RFC was Defanwy, South Wales, and his pre-war occupation between 1912-14, was a school-master, in Constantinople. Born in October 1891, he was commissioned into the General List and joined the RFC in July 1917. Once he had gained his 'wings', he was sent to 74 Squadron in October – around the time of his 26th birthday – and went with it to France in March 1918.

B Flight's pilots consisted of: Clive Beverley Glynn, from Liverpool, aged 25, who had been a Captain with the Liverpool Regiment and retained this rank in the RFC. His first squadron had been 56, which he joined in June 1917, but he was not with them long before being sent back to England. He joined 74 prior to its move to France and survived 1918 with the unit, winning the DFC and becoming a flight commander. He was known as 'Glynski'.

Henry Hamer, Taffy Jones and Charles Skedden. Skedden was killed in a crash on 8 May 1918.

Lieutenant Andrew Cameron 'Dixie' Kiddie, was another South African, hailing from Kimberley. He was 28 and like many of his countrymen, had served in West Africa early in the war. Coming to England to join the RFC his first squadron had been 32, flying DH5 fighters, and with them he scored one victory. He then became an instructor, and by all accounts a very good one, before being posted to 74. Short, fat and with a podgy face he became known as 'the Old Man'. He flew with them until the Armistice, becoming a flight commander and winning the DFC and Bar, and the Belgian *Croix de Guerre*. His final victory score stood at 15.

Lieutenant Gerald Radford Savage was 26, and another from South Africa (Pretoria). A law student with the Transvaal University College in 1911, he had already worked as a solicitor and notary public between 1906-1910. So, if his birth date is correct (20 January 1892), he was a very young lad of 14 when he started, so perhaps he was little more than an office boy with ambition. Joining the RFC in June 1917, he trained at the Central Flying School when it was at Hendon, in the summer of that year, before being posted to 74 in February 1918. 'Zulu' Savage he was called – or was it Savage Zulu?

Lieutenant John Robert Piggott, was from Worcester, but was living in Stoke on Trent when the war started. Just 19 when he joined 74, so little wonder he was called 'Boy'. However, he had already been in uniform, with 'E' Company, 13th Training Reserve Battalion while working in an architect and surveyors office. He had enlisted into the RFC in August 1917 and flew with 74 till early July 1918.

Lieutenant Ronald Ernest Bright was even younger than Piggott, being just short of his 18th birthday when 74 went to France. 'Buddy' Bright hailed from Oxford and had joined the RFC in May 1917. He joined 74 on 12 March 1918 but was killed in early May.

Lieutenant Philip James Stuart-Smith, aged 22, came from London, Ontario, and was married. He had been with Lord Strathcona's Horse, part of the Canadian Corps of Cavalry, prior to joining the RFC in May 1917. After training with 56 TS he had moved to 74 in March 1918. For reasons which may have been obvious to his comrades, he was known as 'Poet'. He would be killed in May.

C Flight's pilots was headed by Lieutenant Wilfred Bertie Giles, from Westbury Park, Bristol. Known as 'Twist' he was approaching his 22nd birthday and had been an insurance official with the Alliance Assurance Company between 1911-1915, so he was another junior starter. He had served with the Somerset Light Infantry prior to joining the RFC, having been wounded on the Somme front in 1916. Initially flying as an observer with 43 Squadron in their Sopwith $1^1/_2$ Strutters, he gained one (shared) victory using his rear gun. Accepted for pilot training, he was posted to 74 Squadron where he gained a further four victories to become an ace. Injured in a crash in early August 1918, he survived the war and returned to the world of insurance. A good and long lasting friend of Taffy Jones who was also in C Flight, he later married Jones's widow.

Lieutenant Reginald Allan 'Queenie' Birch, from Southport, Lancashire, was another youngster, aged 19. After attending Southport's University School between 1913 and August 1916, he had joined the RFC in April 1917. Trained with 81 and 56 Training Squadrons he had also had a spell at the prestigious School of Special Flying, Gosport, in November 1917. He came to 74 in March 1918 and would survive to return home in September.

Lieutenant Charles Edward Lloyd Skedden was an American, from Minneapolis, Minnesota. He had joined the RFC in Canada, after enlisting into the 6th Reserve Battalion, CEF, part of the 1st Central Ontario Regiment. He had transferred to the RFC in September 1917 and been posted to 74 TS at Christmas. He would be lost in May 1918.

Lieutenant Sydney Claude Hamilton Begbie came from north-west London's Regent's Park area, although born in Fareham, Hants, and had first seen service as an officer with the 3rd East Surrey Regiment. Being with the Royal Flying Corps from April 1916, he had some of his training at the Central Flying School but in early 1917 had a period in hospital. Finally he was sent to 74 TS in February 1918. He was one of the first squadron pilots to be lost aged just 21.

Lieutenant Leonard Atwoode Richardson was another American, and known as 'Spearmint'. He too had come via Canada, where he had lived in New Brunswick, arriving on 74 in March aged 23. An engineering student at the prestigious Massachusetts Institute of Technology (MIT), he had worked for the Morgan Auto Company in Worcester, USA, pre-war. He had arrived on 74 on 23 March but would be wounded in combat on 19 July 1918. He was famous for inventing a cocktail, which became known as the '74 Viper'! Little wonder he was called 'The Cocktail King'.

Lieutenant James Ira Thomas Jones was probably the most famous name to come from 74 Squadron after Mick Mannock. Born in St Clears, Carmarthen, Wales, in April 1896, he was just on 22 years old. A clerk in civilian life he joined the Territorials in 1913 to add some excitement to his life and while awaiting call-up when war came, trained as a civilian wireless operator. Joining the RFC as a 1st class air mechanic he served in France with 10 Squadron in 1915 and the following year volunteered to fly as an observer. While acting with a ground wireless station at the front, he rescued two wounded artillery men, for which he received the

Military Medal and the Russian Medal of St George. Later accepted for pilot training, he ended up with 74 Squadron at London Colney and although not in his Flight, soon became a firm friend of his mentor, Edward Mannock MC. Taffy Jones continued to be a friend after his hero's death writing not only Mannock's biography (*King of Air Fighters*), but also a history of 74 Squadron in which Mannock had a prominent position, in the book *Tiger Squadron*. Jones gained the DSO DFC and Bar to add to his decorations and achieved 37 victories in air combat – one more than Mannock scored while with the Squadron, and thereby becoming 74's top ace.

The three main ground officers in 74, were Lieutenants Coverdale, Mansfield and Lewis – gunnery/armament officer, equipment officer and recording officer (adjutant) respectively.

Harry Coverdale was a married man of 29, who had resided in Thames Ditton, although during the war his wife was in Sutton, Surrey. He had been an English Rugby international. A ship-broker by profession he had joined the 17th London Regiment and with the RFC was appointed assistant instructor in gunnery in December 1917. He was assigned to 74 in February 1918.

Clifford Mansfield was 26 and from Crewe, Cheshire. Between 1909-1915 he had been a technical clerk with the L & NW Railway, at Crewe. Joining the colours he had been a shorthand writer to the chief electrical engineer, Lieutenant-Colonel F H C Leigh and commissioned in November 1917, then posted to 74 Squadron.

Although Lieutenant Arthur Gordon 'Lew' Lewis was the recording officer, he was only with 74 a short while, having to leave following a knee injury. He was 22 and came from Exmouth, Devon, although he was later living in London. A civil servant working at the War Office between December 1914 and January 1917, he managed to join the 23rd London Regiment, then transferred to the RFC that May. He was posted to 74 on 8 March 1918, and left in April.

74's noted adjutant after Lewis was an Irishman, 37-year-old Captain William Joseph Julius Everard Mount Everard, of the Irish Guards, whose wife was the Honourable Victoria Everard of north-west London. He had addresses in County Down and Tipperary, Ireland, and Barnes, London SW13. Among several attributes was that he was fluent in French, Spanish and Arabic. He was sent to 74 in October 1917.

**

While waiting for the order to fly out, Mick decided to fly up and visit the Eyles family and took Clements with him. They went north in a two-seater, and landed in a field at Wellingborough, being met by a car that Mick had organised. Driven to the Eyles's home they then had dinner at the Hind Hotel before returning south.

**

With the big German offensive raging in France, 74 Squadron were keen and eager to get out and join the fray. Then on 27 March came the order to fly from London Colney to Goldhanger, Essex, right on the east coast close to the inlet of the River Blackwater. This was a Home Defence airfield where, until recently, 37 HD Squadron had awaited German raiders. For a couple of days 74 sat there expectantly. On the one hand they might be sent up against German Gotha bombers, or, as was hoped, receive the call for France. Everyone knew it was imminent as a ground party had already left a few days earlier, under 'Splitpins' Mansfield. They had arrived as the battle started and had their own brand of excitement for a few days.

Jones recalls an incident while at Goldhanger concerning a local policeman from the village who objected to the squadron singing some renowned RFC songs of a dubious

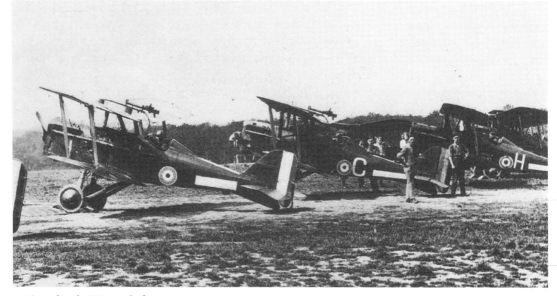

74 Squadron's SE5s ready for France.

nature, in one of the hotel bars. Mannock resented the intrusion, offering the man a drink, or the street! Fortunately the policeman saw the funny side of the offer and chose the drink.

At last, on the 30th came the order to go. Taking to the air, the pilots' first stop was St Omer aerodrome, for a long while the time-honoured place for incoming ferry pilots and squadrons. It was the main depot for the RFC in northern France, and they all landed safely on the 31st – except for Taffy Jones and Bertie Giles, who had mishaps. Never a good pilot when it came to landing, Jones turned his SE5 over upon his arrival, but so too had Giles. Jones was carrying the squadron mascot, a black puppy named 'Contact' and the dog promptly threw up. The very next day the RFC ceased to exist, it becoming amalgamated with the Royal Naval Air Service to form the new Royal Air Force (1 April 1918).

On this auspicious date the squadron took off for Teteghem aerodrome, near Dunkirk. It was not a large airfield, often referred to as the 'tennis court' in consequence. A week later they moved to La Lovie, to the west of Ypres near Poperinghe, until finally, on the 11th they flew into Clairmarais, just east of St Omer, where 74 would remain until early August. To be exact, there were two airfields at Clairmarais, one known as Clairmarais North, the other as Clairmarais South. 74 used the northern one. To say the Squadron moved again in August is correct but perhaps misleading, for it only transferred from the northern airfield to the southern one! They were a mile apart. The new airfield was L-shaped and on a slope, measuring 300 by 150 yards with a ten-foot hedge on one side and tall trees along another. Bets were made on who would be the first to crash! The Squadron became part of 11 Wing and shared the base with the Camels of 54 Squadron.

By the time 74 had begun to settle into its now more permanent base, the main thrusts of Germany's Operation Michael were at an end. Like the majority of offensives on either side, they were never maintained to any great degree, mainly because the support in logistics generally failed. The armies of both sides were often so surprised that, on those rare occasions when a break-through had been achieved, they did not have the necessary strength nor support to hammer home and sustain any advantage.

Consequently the Germans having made successful in-roads into the British positions towards Amiens, pushing back the British 5th Army some 50 miles by 4 April, which was an almost unprecedented amount of territory, it then failed as the British finally rallied and the German support structure failed. The Germans then began a second assault on 9 April, (Operation Georgette) with a desperate effort to break through a little further north, through to the River Lys and the La Bassée area, in the hope of moving to the North Sea/Channel coast. If they could achieve this it would finally roll-up the remaining Belgian territory on the coast, cut off a large part of the British forces east of Calais, and help to dominate the Straits of Dover. The pilots of 74 Squadron, along with others, were now faced with this new offensive and for 74 its baptism of fire was about to start.

The British High Command had envisaged this move and had decided to relieve two Portuguese divisions in the area under threat, which had to be replaced by some very tired British divisions. The dangers were known, and on the 11th, Field Marshal Douglas Haig made his famous 'backs to the wall' Order of the Day, forbidding any retirements, and holding out to the last man.

By the 12th the German advance had reached Merville and beyond Armentières to the south of the attack line, and despite the retreat by the Portuguese, the line began to hold. However, the Germans had not made too much of a dent further north, to the east of Ypres. By the 25th, the German centre had passed Bailleuil but now began to falter.

The critical day of the battle was the 12th and the RAF was up in force trying to stem the progress of German troops on the ground and their supporting aircraft in the sky above.

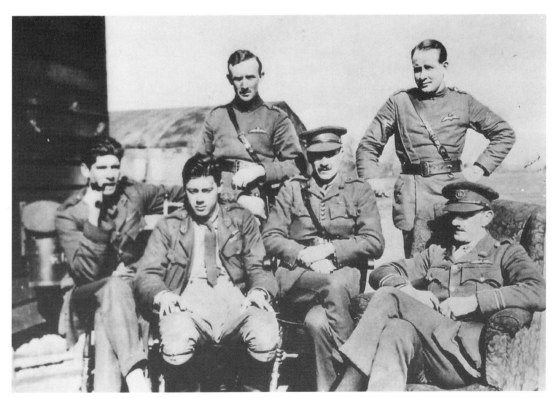

Senior officers in 74 Squadron: Ben Roxburgh-Smith and Andrew Kiddie at the back. Seated are: Mannock, Keith Caldwell, Everard (adj), and Wilfred Young.

At 08.25 that morning it fell to 74's A Flight commander to open the scoring for the unit. Mannock led an OP to the east of Merville where the advancing Germans were now digging in. German fighters were in evidence, providing cover for their two-seater artillery machines and the trench-strafing schlachtflieger units.

He observed an enemy patrol of multi-coloured Albatros Scouts between 12-13,000 feet and went straight into the attack, having manoeuvred to the east, so that the morning sun was behind him. He opened fire with both guns at one V-strutter from 30 yards and head-on while just above the German. As they passed each other, Mannock turned swiftly, opening fire again from behind. The Albatros staggered and began to go down out of control. Quickly realising that a general engagement had developed between the enemy machines and his embryo pilots he plunged into the fight and later was able to observe two enemy aircraft crash to the ground below the scene of action, one appearing to fall to the guns of Bolo Dolan.

Cairnes's C Flight had flown the first patrol of the day, Mannock being out on the airfield to see them depart, and asking them not to disturb the Huns too much before he led his patrol out. In the event they did get into a scrap but neither side scored any hits.

When Mannock led his Flight out shortly after C Flight returned, Jones recalled that Mannock's last instruction to his pilots had been, succinctly: 'Remember, to fight is not enough. You must kill.'

There was much air fighting this day, on both sides so it is difficult to deduce who 74 were fighting with on this early patrol. Jasta 29 lost a pilot near Armentières on the 12th and operating from their base at Phalempin, south of Lille, were certainly flying in the area. As mentioned previously, the Germans seem only to record for posterity, losses in personnel and not aircraft, so if indeed Mannock saw two enemy fighters crash, it really depends on the 'degree of crash' that occurred. The lost pilot was Vizfeldwebel Gilbert Wagner, aged 24 from Mittersheim. He had achieved four victories.

Mick was wreathed in smiles when he and his patrol landed. The honour of the Squadron's first kill went to him although it could equally have been Dolan, as both men reported their victories at 08.25. Dolan later told the others than Mannock swooped down on the enemy like a hawk on its prey.

Mick and A Flight were out again after lunch and in the vicinity of the Bois de Phalempin, south of Lille, he spotted an air fight in progress north of the La Bassée Canal but continued to circle above the mêlée, awaiting an opportunity to select victims and pounce. As he circled he saw two enemy scouts appear just a few hundred feet right below his formation and made ready to attack.

For some reason that isn't explained, his pilots began to dive down on the two Germans. Perhaps he signalled them to do so, or perhaps they were just too eager to await his signal. In any event it was he who followed the other SE5s down, as each pilot in turn fired off a burst into one of the black and yellow coloured Albatros Scouts. After Mannock took his turn, he followed one German fighter down for a few thousand feet while the others covered him. It certainly appeared out of control but then the pilot seemed to regain some measure of control at 5,000 feet, but eventually they saw it crash north-east of the wood, just east of Carvin. In his combat report Mannock stated that credit should go to the Flight as a whole, obviously wanting to give encouragement to his fledglings. No doubt it did, but everyone thought it was the flight commander's fire that had done the damage.

Later that evening B Flight, including the CO, got into another fight with German fighters and Caldwell and Young both claimed victories. Thus on 74's first real day of action they had claimed five of the enemy, while the RAF claimed numerous others. 43 Squadron with its Camels alone claimed a total of 13 (one pilot put in for six!), and 24 Squadron claimed seven. German pilot casualties amounted to about six with another captured and two more wounded, so the battle front must have been 'littered' with crashed German aircraft where pilots had walked, or perhaps limped, away!

After this day of high activity, poor weather curtailed operations over the next few days and in any event, the German ground attacks had started to tail off. On 21 April the news came through that the German ace, Baron Manfred von Richthofen, who had achieved 80 victories, had fallen in action. When Mannock heard about it he is reputed to have said that he hoped the Baron had burned all the way down!

On this same day, 74 were back in action once more. Dolan claimed a two-seater while Cairnes and Skedden each sent Albatros Scouts down out of control. Skedden was lucky not to have been killed, a bullet actually passing through his flying helmet, slightly creasing his skull. Luck in air fighting is everything.

However, the Squadron suffered its first combat loss, Begbie failing to return from an evening action which began over Armentières. What happened to him? Not clear except that he had left St Omer on patrol at 17.20 – Armentières to Laventie – and failed to return. He was witnessed in action at 13,000 feet and then seen to go down on fire into the German lines where he died of wounds the next day, and was buried at Lille. Leutnant Kurt Legal of Jasta 52, based at Provin, may have been involved, claiming an SE5 down near Bailleul at 19.25 German time (18.25 British time), right up in the front line battle area. It was Legal's second victory but six days later he was killed in a flying accident.

That evening in the Mess, a toast was made to Begbie's memory, and glasses were also raised for the death of von Richthofen, although Mannock did not share the others' views.

**

Mannock scored again on the 23rd, a Pfalz DIII which he described as having a black body, white tipped tail (rudder?) and silver and black chequered top wings. He had led out an OP in the late afternoon and shortly after 6 pm east of Merville, flying at 14,000 feet, he spotted a German formation and quickly manoeuvred to engage. Diving on the rear of the formation, he selected a target and fired 120 rounds in three bursts at very close range. As his bullets splattered around the pilot area, he saw an explosion in the cockpit. Whether a signal flare had been hit is unclear but volumes of smoke poured out and the Pfalz turned upside down and fell vertically, striking the ground near Meurillon. Bolo Dolan confirmed its demise and after some ineffective shots at a couple of other German machines, Mannock led the patrol towards home.

Jasta 7 had their aircraft painted black with white tails, and in April the unit was based at Ste. Marguerite, just north of Lille. On this day they had Leutnant Paul Lotz wounded in combat. By this time Lotz had secured four victories and upon his return to the front in June, he took command of Jasta 44, ending the war with at least nine victories. He died in a flying accident on 23 October 1918, aged 23. Another Jasta 7 pilot, Gefreiter Jupp Böhne, was also shot-up in combat and forced to make a landing east of Merville, so it is possible that either of these men, or both, were hit by Mannock.

There were plenty of patrols over the next few days, especially on the 25th due to the Battle of Kemmel Ridge. Like all high ground in northern France, Mount Kemmel dominated the area and all strategic spots like this were fought over regularly during WW1. However, no successful combats were had until the 29th, Mannock scoring yet again, his 20th victory.

The mission on this late morning sortie was a Line Patrol – patrolling the front lines in order to protect British two-seaters working above the front on artillery duties or photo reconnaissance. South of Dickebusch Lake – a prominent feature in this shell-pocked and desolate region south of Ypres – Mannock spied a formation of around ten enemy fighters. The one he selected was different from the others, noting in his combat report that it was a 'strange type … very long fuselage, swept back wing tip [and] very pronounced mackerel shaped tail.'

Ben Roxburgh-Smith in his SE5A marked with a I on the cowling.

The formation was that of Jasta 2, or Jasta Boelcke as it had been named, the Staffel formally led by the German ace Oswald Boelcke in the autumn of 1916. When he died in combat on 28 October of that year, it was decreed that his unit be named after him. Today it was being led by Leutnant Karl Bolle and nearby were the Fokker Triplanes of Jasta 36. Mannock's good eyes did not deceive him for it was indeed an unusual machine within Jasta B's group. It was a Fokker DV.

The Jasta was about to change its equipment from Albatros DV and Pfalz DIII machines to Fokker Dr.I Triplanes and needed to gain experience on rotary-engined aircraft, rather than in-line engined fighters. So the Fokker DV, although a biplane, and a type not really up to front line operations, was being flown this day mainly to 'make the numbers up' as well as for experience. It was being piloted by Leutnant Ludwig Vortmann, a 22-year-old from Reckling, north of Essen.

As the fight began, Mannock picked on this unusual-looking machine, firing some 40 rounds into it during a frontal attack. The Fokker biplane immediately burst into flames and fell to earth, breaking up as it went. Meantime, Dolan fired at an Albatros and claimed that this too began to fall apart as it went down, while Captain Glynn went after a Triplane. He had been flying to the left of Mannock and had spotted the Triplane coming on from his left so pulled round towards it. As the two fighters closed with each other, Glynn began firing from both guns.

For a moment, as the two aircraft flashed past each other, Glynn lost sight of the Fokker but Mannock and Dolan saw it diving vertically and crash to the ground. This was Glynn's first victory and he had scored well. The Triplane was being flown by the Staffelführer of Jasta 36, Leutnant Heinrich Bongartz, in Triplane 575/17, who was hit in the arm but more seriously by a bullet to the head. This bullet smashed into his left temple, eye and nose, but he managed to crash land near Mount Kemmel. Bongartz was an ace with 33 victories and holder of the *Pour le Mérite*, and this wounding put him out of the war. He was 26. He retained interest in flying post WW1 and died in January 1946.

Shortly after this action, Ben Roxburgh-Smith shot down an LVG C-type two-seater, although it has also been recorded as a Halberstadt in the 2nd Brigade work summaries. As the fight with Jasta B and Jasta 36 began to dissolve, Mannock had headed back towards the lines and spotted another German near Dickebusch Lake and dived to attack. As he began to fire, his gun jammed, so he pulled away to let 'Rox' and Dolan have a crack. Rox was just about to let fly when Dolan's SE5 cut right across in front of him, which apart from putting him off his aim, frightened him to death. However, Dolan, over-eager as ever, overshot the target after firing 70 rounds, which let Rox have another chance to open fire.

Swooping up below the German, his fire appeared to knock out the observer and then the pilot began a downward spiral with its engine off, the SE5 following, still firing, until the two-seater crunched into the ground near to the lines at Onderdom. Now low-down, Roxburgh-Smith came under intense ground fire but he swiftly headed west, safety being helped by a red signal flare fired by his flight commander. On landing, rather than massive congratulations, Rox got a dressing down by Mannock for following the German down for far too long and endangering himself to enemy gunfire, a serious 'black' in Mannock's view.

The LVG was probably from Schutzstaffel 13 based at Ingelmünster. They lost Flieger Hans Vollmeyer and gunner Unteroffizier Paul Weyher, the latter having been with the unit since the previous September. It is reported

Lieutenant P F C 'Swazi' Howe, who, as the nick-name suggests, came from Swaziland, Cape Colony, South Africa. After gaining five victories he was wounded on 15 July 1918.

they fell near Bailleul. The next afternoon Dolan and Mannock were out after two-seaters, this time finding a Halberstadt CLII from Schutzstaffel 28b, based at Bisseghem.

The location was again near Dickesbusch Lake and although both men attacked, Mannock seems to have given most of the credit to his young friend. The two-seater came down inside British lines and was given a G number – 'G/2nd Bgde 6'. Things had changed recently. No longer was there a sequential 'G' number given to each captured machine, now each RAF brigade gave any captured aircraft (or wreck) in their area of influence a brigade number. Thus this downed Halberstadt fell in 2nd Brigade's area, the sixth such aircraft to be 'captured' since the new numbering system came into being in early April. It seems that the pilot was 'borrowed' from Schutzstaffel 10 (they shared the airfield at Bisseghem), Vizefeldwebel Speer, who was taken prisoner, but the observer, a Schusta 28b man, Flieger Anton Zimmermann, was seriously wounded and died on 1 May.

According to Jones in his book on Mannock (*King of Air Fighters*) Mannock showed how much he hated the Germans, for Keith Caldwell is quoted as saying:

'Mannock and Dolan were up together, and on seeing British 'archie' bursting on our side of the lines, they chased along to see what could be done. They spotted a Hun two-seater beetling back towards the lines, and got down just in time to prevent this.

'The Hun crashed, but not badly, and most people would have been content with this, but not Mannock, who dived half a dozen times at the machine, spraying bullets at the pilot and the observer, who were still showing signs of life. I witnessed this business, and flew alongside of Mick, yelling at the top of my voice (which was rather useless), and warning him to stop.

'On being questioned as to his wild behaviour after we had landed, he heatedly replied, "The swines are better dead – no prisoners for me!"'

Thus ended April and 74 Squadron's first month in France. The pilots had claimed more than a dozen German aircraft shot down for the loss of just one pilot in action. May would see more than a trebling of victories, but losses too increased. Grid Caldwell's tape records:

'Mannock, of course, was in his element being back in France again, and was a good influence in the Squadron. He enhanced his reputation still more by being a magnificent patrol leader, with a capacity for bringing his Flight into an attacking position with reduced risk to his followers. That's where he was so very good, getting up high and the sun being behind him, stalking his enemy, then going down very, very quickly, slowing down a little before he got there, giving his chaps time to get into a firing position. The record shows that there was a list of about 70 enemy aircraft accounted for by his Flight with very few losses. This was during a period of just three months.

'Mannock's own score of course, mounted rapidly during this time, four on one day, three on two other occasions. Nearly all his successes were won in front of his followers, so they could see how it was done, and his tuition and example was of great value to his Flight and to the Squadron generally.'

CHAPTER SEVEN

ZENITH OF A FIGHTER PILOT

May opened for 74 and for Mannock with a two-seater shot down on the 3rd. He was leading an evening patrol with Dolan, Kiddie and Clements, prowling the front in order to ward off any German fighters that might think of interfering with British corps aircraft, but instead, found a two-seater LVG (2nd Brigade noted it as an Albatros C). It was at low altitude, 3,000 feet, and the four SE5s went down on it and each got in bursts as the enemy pilot twisted and dived to escape the onslaught.

Finally it plunged to the ground in a spin east of Merville, and once again Mick wanted it known that his men should share the kill. 'As several members of the patrol', he wrote in his report, 'took a close part in the destruction of this machine, the credit for such, in my opinion, cannot easily be given to any individual member of the patrol.' This was fine and it therefore gave each participant a share, but under the system of scoring, it still meant that <u>each</u> pilot was awarded <u>one victory</u>. It is in this way that the story had to have emerged that he gave away victories to others, when in fact he did not have to do so in order to boost his youngster's scores. Everyone got a piece!

The two-seater is thought to have been a machine of FA32, and its crew, Unteroffizier Fritz Schöning, 24, from Sibbersdorf, and Leutnant Fritz Beuttler, from Stuttgart, and nine days away from his 23rd birthday. Both were killed and are buried at Seclin.

Although Mannock had warned his men to take care when engaging Fokker Dr.I Triplanes, knowing that these nimble fighters could turn on the proverbial sixpence and get behind you before you had time to see what was happening, he had personally had few encounters with this machine, which in any event was now becoming less and less prevalent over the front. Its time had passed, and the last great exponent of the Triplane – Baron von Richthofen – was now dead. Only Jacob Jacobs, leader of Jasta 7 still flew one regularly. In fact he had two and always tried to lead his Staffel in one. Despite the lack of rotary engines for his two machines he had a standing order for any front line army unit which could salvage any rotary-engined British machine's power plant, mostly the Camel, and get it to him. A crate of champagne would be their reward.

On 6 May however, Mannock ran into four, plus one Albatros Scout, at 09.20, for there were still a number of Dr.Is distributed along the front line jagdstaffeln. It was common for many fighter units to have a variety of aircraft on strength at various times, Albatros and Pfalz Scouts, the odd Triplane and so on. On this May morning he was in a fight with these five fighters which began over Dickesbusch Lake. Mannock dived on one 'three-decker', firing short bursts. It turned on its back, and went down to crash near Gheluvelt, map ref given as 28.0.4. That afternoon Dolan and Roxburgh-Smith shot down two more Triplane north-east of Ypres, at around 15.30, so all-in-all it was a bit of a 'Tripehound' day. Major Caldwell had supported Rox in his action but made no individual claim.

Taffy Jones seated in his SE5A. Note the huge fur flying gauntlet.

Mannock's victim is thought to have been Leutnant Günther Derlin of Jasta 20, shot down and killed near Ploegsteert Wood, although this seems, if the locality is correct, to be a bit too far south, as the Jasta was operating from Rumbeke, which is much further to the north, past Ypres. Derlin was 27 and came from Berlin. Gheluvelt is much nearer Zillebeke so he may have fallen to either Rox or Dolan. There is no time given for Derlin's fall which makes things difficult to reconcile.

Ira 'Taffy' Jones made his first claim on the 8th, a two-seater in flames between Bailleul and Nieppe, but it was not a good day for the Squadron. For a while now some of the SE5s had carried 20 lb Cooper bombs to drop on enemy troops or transports – or just to cause a nuisance to the harassed German soldiery below. On this morning B and C Flight had taken off early, within a few minutes of each other, intent on dropping their bombs on Menin. Jones later recorded in his diary:

'It was my intention to climb steadily as far as Ypres, which I had hoped to pass at an altitude of 15,000 feet, and then fly east, using the Menin road as my guide and dropping my eggs [bombs] over the objective.

'When I got to Ypres, I was still only a few feet above 11,000 feet, so I decided to climb to the requisite 15,000 before crossing. I continued climbing in the direction of Houthulst Forest, all the time searching the sky eastwards for machines.

'Suddenly I spotted two formations, one of six and the other of ten. The six I recognised as B Flight, and the ten as enemy Triplanes. B Flight was at about 16,000 feet, halfway between Ypres and Menin. The Huns were a couple of thousand feet higher, over Menin, making for Ypres.

'"Young is for it," I said to myself. I wondered if he had seen the enemy. I felt he must have. Then my confidence wavered. A terrible feeling of helplessness came over me. How could I warn him? I was three miles away. Instinctively, I thought of shouting, then I realised the childishness of the thought. I felt I must do something quickly. I fired as many red lights as I had. Giles, Skedden and Birch did the same, but Young did not alter course. He was making straight for the enemy. It was a terrible sight. There was I, a helpless spectator of a cruel play which was about to be enacted, the killing of friends.

'The Hun leader was very clever. He led his flight southwards, going away at right angles from Young. I think he was afraid Young had seen him and that he would rightly turn round, make for our lines, and get away. So he encouraged him to continue his eastern flight. I could almost sense the devil's thoughts. I ordered my Flight to drop their bombs, and pointed the nose of my machine in the direction of Menin, climbing as steeply as I could.

'When Young got over Menin, he dropped his eggs, then turned round and made for Ypres. As soon as he did this, the Hun leader also turned round. His flight came hell for leather towards Ypres to cut Young off. Young was now at 18,000 feet, the Huns at 19,000 feet, and my Flight 3,000 feet lower. I decided to take my Flight below the impending fight in order to help push off any stray Huns who might drop out of the battle above. It was a silly thing to do, really, but I thought there was every chance that a B Flight machine might come down below the fight with a Hun on its tail. We could have knocked him off.

'The Triplanes cut off the SEs over Gheluvelt, and the unequal contest started immediately, the Hun leader firing on Kiddie. Kiddie turned under him and avoided his bullets. The fight soon developed into the usual dog-fight. It was a grim business we witnessed. There we were below the battle, just circling round and round, looking upwards at our pals fighting for their lives. We could do nothing to help. Nothing! Nothing but look on in a state of anger and helplessness. It was a terrible feeling. May I never have to endure it again. I would prefer a dozen Huns on my tail, any time of the day.

'Within a minute of the start of the fight we saw an SE come hurtling down, smoking badly, before bursting into flames. It passed quite near me, but owing to the smoke I could not recognise the number on the nose. I know now it was poor old Stuart-Smith. A little later on, another SE passed down, burning fiercely. It was Bright. By God, it was a grim sight! Then an SE came spinning through, with a Tripe following. "This is my chance," I said as I saw the enemy pass below us.

'I made a dive after him and so did the others. I had not dived for more than a few seconds when I felt my machine vibrating badly and the engine over-revving. I tried to pull my throttle back. It was jammed full bore. I had to pull out gently, and as I did so, I saw Skedden and Giles whiz past after the Hun, firing for all they were worth.

'The Hun, hearing the machine guns behind him, left the SE5 and dived away east.

The SE came out of the spin at about 2,000 feet, then glided towards our lines. We saw him crash in the trenches. It was dear old Piggott. Whether his machine crashed on the enemy's lines or on ours we are not sure. But it was a real smasher. We have little hope of his being alive. As we have no news of him, he is no doubt a goner.'

This was not the end of the matter. Jones managed to get his machine back to Clairmarais but before landing, saw Skedden fly in and cheerfully chuck his usual half-roll on top of a loop, but in doing so both his wings collapsed. The wreck fell right in the middle of the aerodrome and burned. Jones could not bear to land so near his burning pal – with whom he shared a hut – so landed at nearby Clairmarais South.

That evening Jones took some revenge by flaming a C-type and as he flew back across the trenches had the satisfaction of seeing many waving soldiers who had seen the action.

What Jones had witnessed earlier was the demise of Stuart-Smith (C1078), and Bright (B8374), plus the senseless death of Skedden (C6445). Fortunately, Piggott (B8502) survived his shoot down, although his machine was destroyed. Young, in a badly shot-up SE had to land at Marie Capelle airfield, so it was only Kiddie who landed at base, and even his SE was severely shot about. Their victors had been the experienced pilots of Jasta 26, who put in claims for four SE5s – Leutnants Fritz Loerzer, Helmut Lange, Vizefeldwebels Erich Buder and Fritz Classen. All were, or would become aces, Loerzer being the brother of Bruno, until recently leader of Jasta 26 but now commander of Jagdgeschwader Nr.III.

The sudden loss of three pilots was a sobering event for the new Squadron. The great adventure had become more serious and certainly more chastening. The empty tables at dinner that evening only slowed the boys down for a moment and soon the drink was flowing and songs were being sung. It was their way of dealing with death. Most squadrons were the same.

On May 8th, Mick wrote a brief letter to his cousin Patrick, and while much of it is of a personal nature, he does mention his score:

Dear Patrick,

I owe you several letters of thanks for your copies of "Whitecraft", duly received. I think your editorial efforts are to be commended. I should like to contribute some 'real live stuff' if you are agreeable, and we can 'come together' about the matter of the price (ahem!).

You may be interested to know that my bag now amounts to 23 or 24 (I'm not sure of the exact figure). Not bad for an old man, eh?

The Hun Triplanes are getting it in the neck.

How are they all at home? I hope mother is keeping well and Kathleen. Of course Dora is going strong as I gather from your current number.

Paddy is out here with a Tank Battalion, still a L/Corporal. I haven't succeeded in getting into personal touch with him yet, but hope to do so soon.

Regards to Miss Adele and love to Kath, mother and Dora.

Yours,
Edward

The previous year, Mick had met Patrick [1] at Hanworth, while Jim Eyles was visiting London towards the end of Mick's leave. Ira Jones quotes Patrick in *King of Air Fighters*:

'On June 26th, 1917, I was at Hanworth Aerodrome, where I had a job with Whitehead Aircraft. There had been a crash when a Sopwith was being tested by the firm's pilot, named Sykes, who was injured. On the scene I suddenly saw Edward with his friend Eyles – a surprise visit. Edward, who asked me when Whitehead was going to make some really up-to-date machines, laughed a lot at the crash. Somehow it was obviously amusement at the mishap, not callousness; for he made it his business to ask after Sykes. He stayed with me some days at Barnes. On the 29th, with my father, dining out, we met a certain sporting baronet, and I recall Edward expressing contempt for him, saying what a pity it was that such people mattered because they had a handle to their names. The next day he went back to France.'

**

Mick was out with Dolan in the early evening of 11 May on a special mission and just to the north-east of Armentières, flying at 14,000 feet, they spotted a German formation of eight fighters, Mannock picking out a silver and black Pfalz Scout, sporting a red nose. They were east of the Germans with a few hundred feet of height in their favour, so hoping the enemy pilots would be concentrating more to the west, the two men dived into the attack from behind. However, the last machine which he was after suddenly turned as the pilot spotted the danger. Mannock followed his manoeuvres, firing as his guns came to bear until they were down to 6,000 feet. Here the Pfalz suddenly burst into flames and fell and as it did so, Mannock saw another German machine fall by him, out of control.

Looking up he saw Dolan was still engaging the other Germans and climbed to help but then the opposition swiftly made off east before he could get within range. From his combat report, Mannock implies that his burning victim was followed by another Pfalz spinning down, presumably shot down by Dolan, although elsewhere there is a suggestion that both men scored victories. In the event, it seems only one Pfalz was destroyed but whether officially shared or the second one did not crash, is unclear. The loss was Leutnant Otto Aeckerle of Jasta 47w, flying Pfalz DIIIa 5916/17, whose death was reported at 18.35 German time (17.35 British time) over Deulemont à Lys. Aeckerle, from Biberach, in the Black Forest area, would have celebrated his 24th birthday the next day. He is buried at Menin.

The next evening Mannock was in amongst them again, a formation of eight German fighters, some brown and black Albatros scouts and dark-coloured Pfalz DIIIs. Orders required a patrol in squadron strength, and as Caldwell was away from Clairmarais, Mannock led it. At around 18.20 hours, in the vicinity of Wulverghem, north-east of Menin, they came across the German formation as it passed north from Armentières. Mannock led his men south and east whilst gaining height, then, having put them into a position he favoured, attacked from the south-east with an advantage of 1,000 feet over the enemy.

He closed in on the rearmost machine and opened fire at right angles to it. The German pilot tried to side-slip out of the way and crashed into another Albatros that had just started

---

[1] Patrick had a well-known father, John Patrick Mannock, being a professional billiard player. J P Mannock, known as Jack, lived in London, and had been born in 1859, a brother of Mick's father Edward. His son Patrick had been born in Parkhurst Road, Upper Holloway, London, on Christmas Eve, 1887, so was just seven months younger than Mick. Jack Mannock had begun his professional career in London in 1878, aged 19. In January 1891 he patented a design for a billiard cue that incorporated several innovations. Later many other designers modelled their cues on his ground-breaking work. J P Mannock cues can still be bought and are sought after on the internet today.

to bank away. Both machines fell to pieces and went down.

Mannock was immediately behind a Pfalz, firing almost a whole drum of Lewis gun ammunition and a similar amount from the Vickers. The fighter went down in a vertical dive and smashed into the ground. As he pulled up and round, he looked down to see several enemy fighters going down, apparently out of control from the general engagement. Upon counting up the score after they had landed, 74 made it six, three to Mannock, and one each to Young, Bertie Giles and Roxburgh-Smith. Sadly one SE5 failed to make it back. Dolan was missing.

This was some blow for Mannock. He had been flying with Dolan almost constantly for the last month and had found him an aggressive pilot, never hesitating to dive headlong into the enemy whenever and wherever he found them. On the German side it was one of those odd days when there appears to be no official claims and equally no losses. However, at 19.10 German time Leutnant Raven Freiherr von Barnekow, of Jasta 20, claimed an SE5a south of Dickesbusch, so on the German side of the lines, and this has to be Bolo Dolan. He is buried at La Laiterie Cemetery, near Kemmel, Belgium.

There are certainly no reported German fatalities among fighter units this date, so that if 74 Squadron really did achieve six victories, and two Albatros Scouts colliding and starting to fall to pieces from several thousand feet up should have caused some discomfort to someone, then we face again this 'degree of crash' as seen by excited pilots full of adrenalin pumping through their veins, and perhaps seeing what they wanted, or at least felt, they should see. Parachutes were beginning to be used by German pilots but there were none seen nor reported by either side on this day.

News of Henry Dolan's loss soon found its way to Wellingborough, no doubt by one of Mannock's letters to Jim Eyles. In the 24 May edition of the *Wellingborough News*, the following was recorded along with the better news of Mick's latest decoration:

Henry Dolan's grave, La Laiterie cemetery.

THE D.S.O.
Capt. Mannock, of Wellingborough, Gets Further Honours

'A fresh and well-deserved honour has, we are informed, been awarded to Captain and Flight Commander Edward Mannock, the brilliant young Wellingborough airman.

'It is commonly known information that "Paddy" has already, by exceptional bravery and ability in bringing down enemy planes, won the Military Cross and bar. Now he is able to inform a Wellingborough friend that last Sunday he was given a higher honour – the D.S.O. He now has to his credit the magnificent total of 41 Boche machines "downed", this first-rate number having been approached by rapid strides during the past few weeks. The Captain is still flying the little fighting machines with which he gave exhibitions over Wellingborough in March, and the flight under his command is doing big things.

'In the letter in which Captain Mannock sends the news of his own success there is also mentioned a matter which will be regretted by Wellingborough people. It is the fact that Lieut. Dolan, a member of the same squadron, is missing. This officer was the one who twice accompanied Capt. Mannock in his flights over the town. His first visit was on Wednesday Feb. 27th, when both officers came over in the same machines, alighting for a time in Long Marsh; and his second and last on Sunday, March 17th, when the officers came in single-seaters, giving a thrilling show of aviation during the afternoon and evening. Describing the action in which Lieut. Dolan was shot down, Capt. Mannock says that six British machines attacked eight German scouting planes, six of which they sent to the earth, three falling to the Captain himself. In the fight, Lieut. Dolan was apparently hit, for his machine was last seen descending to the ground in a spin behind the enemy lines.'

* *

The Squadron suffered another casualty the same day, the 12th, Lieutenant Geoff Atkinson. While there is no actual report, nor is he listed in casualty lists, on his record card (microfilm copies of which are under the National Archive's code Air 76) it is noted that he was wounded on this day and thus disappears from the squadron from this date.

According to Taffy Jones, Mannock was devastated by the loss of Dolan, and he says Mick actually took himself off to his hut and cried. However, later in the Mess he displayed nothing of his obvious sorrow and joined in the merriment that always accompanied losses. Yet it also added to Mannock's ferocious hatred for the enemy. Many of his victims fell in flames and Mannock very often displayed great glee when either he or another 74 pilot sent down an opponent burning. 'Sizzle, sizzle, sizzle, wonk, woof!' or similar expressions generally came from his lips on such occasions. He was a formidable air fighter already, but these recent losses and that of his friend Dolan, made him a veritable terror to be up against. It was personal – up close and personal. He made certain the squadron pilots practised their gunnery. Good flying, he would comment, never killed an enemy. Accurate firing did.

Grid Caldwell and Lieutenant J I T 'Taffy' Jones, 74 Squadron.

He got another 'flamer' on the 16th, Leutnant Hans Nissen from Jasta 54s. This 24-year old from Munkbarup had been with his unit since January and fell near Passchendaele. Leading a patrol Mannock picked out the German formation from 13,000 feet, south of Houthulst Forest. There were about six of them well east of the old Ypres salient. Again he manoeuvred his flock into a favourable position, then attacked from the east. It was 11 am in the morning. Closing right in on one silver and black Pfalz he fired 40 rounds from head-on, then watched as it went down vertically and broke up in the air.

Mannock scored twice on the 17th. In the late morning he was on a special mission, and between Bailleul and le Doulieu found four or five Albatros Scouts circling over this area, while five or six Sopwith Camels were some thousand feet above them. Without waiting to see what the Camel pilots would do, Mannock gave the signal and led his men down, swooping in behind the rearmost German, firing from close range. With a full drum of Lewis and a similar amount from the Vickers, the Albatros staggered under the impact and began to spin down. Before Mannock could see anymore, another Albatros attacked him from above and behind, and now he was forced to spin away. Starting then to come out of his spin and edge west, the German pilot followed and chased him well to the west, right over the Nieppe Forest before finally breaking away east. As far as he could see, the Camels, which in fact came from 210 Squadron, took no part in the engagement, but they were kind enough to confirm that his spinning Albatros erupted in flames and crashed. This fight may well have been with Jasta 52, based at Gondecourt, near Lille.

Earlier than morning, at around 09.30, Taffy Jones had despatched a Hannover two-seater over Merville, and then shortly afterwards, an Albatros C-type 'out of control' over Nieppe, for his 3rd and 4th victories.

After lunch Mannock led out a mission that is noted as a balloon drive, presumably to either attack or force down any balloons up behind the front. North of Ypres, rather than balloons, he saw an Albatros two-seater crossing the lines near the town at 12,000 feet, at 14.30 pm. He climbed north and then east, before making an interception. Diving on the reconnaissance machine, he fired 200 rounds at close range during the fight that he estimated lasted around a minute. The two-seater pilot alternately spun and dived in his endeavours to escape but when down to 4,000 feet flames began to sweep back from the Albatros and going down it eventually struck the ground two miles north-east of Ypres were it continued to burn itself out. This had been a machine from FA288(A), flown by Unteroffizier Andreas Ertl, aged 26, from Kraham, with Oberleutnant Viktor Hepe, aged 34, from Bemke. Both men are buried at Menin. This was also the 30th victory for Mannock.

The Squadron lost two more pilots on this day, one being among the new replacements for Skedden, Bright and Piggott. The three newcomers were Lieutenants Battel, Sifton and Nixon, who had arrived on the 13th. Leigh Morphew Nixon, aged 18 from south London, lasted four days, being shot down by Unteroffizier Marat Schumm of Jasta 52, and falling in flames. Ira Jones had seen Nixon going after a Hun that he had just fired at. Turning round to watch Nixon complete the action (he was interested too because Nixon was flying SE5 C6404, the machine that he usually flew) he was horrified to see the youngster, not on the German's tail, but the German on his. Within seconds Nixon's SE5 was going down on fire. With a German on his tail Nixon had forgotten the golden rule of never diving away from an enemy but to keep turning.

The other loss was Lambert Francis Barton, from Gloucestershire, aged 19. He too fell in flames after apparently being hit by anti-aircraft fire at 7,000 feet. A good many pilots tended to ignore AA fire, or certainly dismiss it as not being a major danger. This is why it was called 'archie' taken from a famous music hall song of the day, where the line "Archibald – certainly not!" was the basis of the name and the contempt. However, enough aircraft were brought down on both sides by AA fire so it was always on the mind of a pilot, that those gunners on the ground might get lucky once in a while. They had had a lot of practice!

Victory No.31 for Mannock came on the 18th, another Albatros C-type, at 08.25 in the morning. Leading an A Flight OP, the pilots watched as a yellow and black Halberstadt two-seater crossed the lines right in front of them, going south from Mont des Cats. Mannock, leading, then flew level with the German and in the same direction until he was well in front if it. It must have been un-nerving for the two-seater crew but they appear to have done little to avoid the inevitable engagement.

Now Mannock winged up and over towards the Hun and fired a burst of about 40 rounds from the front and above as the Halberstadt passed at right angles to him. Then it began to nose down, over the vertical, and remained in this position until it struck the ground near Steenwercke, and burst into flames. They had been at 14,000 feet and the German machine had plunged down from that

Mannock seated in his SE5A D278, spring 1918.

height. Captain Cairnes confirmed seeing it fall but lost sight of it in some ground mist.

The crew were probably 20-year-old Leutnant Karl Fischer, from Malchin, Mecklenburg, and Leutnant Georg Emil Pitz from Sulzbach, near Saarbrücken, aged 33, of FA19. Both were killed and today lie buried in Lambersart cemetery, Lille.

Next day, the 19th, came the news that Captain Mannock had been awarded the Distinguished Service Order. The citation mentions 30 victories. According to Ira Jones, the announcement caused quite a celebration with champagne and the 74 Viper cocktail. A number of guests were invited from nearby squadrons, which included Arthur Cobby, the Australian ace from 4 Squadron AFC, along with E R 'Bow' King and Herbert Watson. P J 'Pip' Clayson and Ernest Owen came from 1 Squadron, C J 'Boetie' Ventor, C G Ross and Tom Harrison from 29 Squadron and three chaps from 85 Squadron, S B 'Nigger' Horn, Malcolm 'Mac' McGregor and W H 'Scruffy' Longton. One has to wonder whether Jones, writing his book on Mannock some years after the war, just picked some or most of these names out of the air! Almost without exception, all had only just started scoring against the Germans, although each one would become top aces before the Armistice. At least one of those names was not even in France with his squadron in May 1918.

No.1 Squadron was at Clairmarais South at this time so obviously some may have been invited over. The Australians were also at Clairmarais while 29 were at St Omer and 85 had only just arrived in France and were up on the coast at Petite Synthe. One imagines Jones 'included' the 85 boys in his list of guests because Mannock would soon be flying with them as 85's commanding officer. One might have thought someone from his old 40 Squadron would have come along, they were still at Bruay so surely one of them could have flown up. True, several of his old cronies were no longer with this unit, but it was still not far to fly, and Napier was still there, so was Gwilym Lewis. According to Lewis, Mick visited 40 just a few days before his DSO was reported. In fact, when the announcement came, Lewis telephoned Mick to congratulate him. Mick apparently told him he now had 41 Huns, but that his fighting partner [Dolan] had been shot down after bringing down nine Huns.

According to a letter to one of Mannock's earlier biographers, James Dudgeon, Andrew Kiddie remembered that it was a great 'do', and that 85 were represented by 'Nigger' Horn, Elliott White Springs, John Grider and Arthur Daniels. There was loads of speeches, and of course, Richardson, 74's 'cocktail king', was up to his usual tricks with the drinks. Several people got pretty well drunk – more than was usually the case.

* *

Mannock hardly lost step and continued his May rampage with two combats on the 21st. For the first time the I/O records the DSO after his name on his combat report forms for this date.

The first action was in the morning above La Couroune, south of Vieux Berquin, at 4,000 feet. A mottled green Hannover two-seater caught his attention, and he dived after it from Mont des Cats to Merville. He had observed the two-seater flying west and had cut off its line of retreat towards the lines. Firing some 40 rounds while closing from the left front position, the German dived vertically and crashed, first striking a tree. He had achieved this victory despite much British AA fire exploding nearby, and the crash was confirmed by his Flight members.

Two more German airmen had been sent to their deaths. Gefreiter Walter Menzel, 21, from Lemmatzsch, and Leutnant Hermann Friedrich August Steinmeyer, 25, from Lieme, of FA9w, lie with the previous crew Mannock had shot down, in Lambersart cemetery, Lille.

That evening, around 7 pm, in the area around and to the south of Hollebeke, 74 claimed six Pfalz Scouts, three falling to Mannock. This must have been a Squadron OP for the other scorers were Major Caldwell and Captain Young. Six silver Pfalz Scouts were observed flying east from the direction of Kemmel at 12,000 feet and the SE5s attacked from the south-west. Mannock selected a target and fired off a long burst at a dark coloured machine that immediately went to pieces.

He then engaged another of similar colouring, fired off the rest of his Lewis ammunition, and also bursts from the Vickers. The machine went into a spin and crashed. Turning in behind a third fighter, this one silver-coloured, which was diving away north as he closed in on it. The German pilot went into a loop, Mannock following, firing his Vickers gun whenever the opportunity presented itself. Heading down to 4,000 feet he kept up the pursuit, the Pfalz side-slipping occasionally, and at about 100 feet up, it suddenly spun away and crashed.

Ira Jones gave a wonderful description of Mannock's fight in his diary:

'In his first [sic] fight, which commenced at 12,000 feet, there were six Pfalz scouts flying east from the direction of Kemmel Hill. He shot one to pieces after firing a long burst from directly behind and above; another, he crashed. It spun into the ground after a deflection shot. Then Mick had a fine set-to with a silver bird while his patrol looked on. It was a wonderful sight. First they waltzed round, with Mick tight on the bright lad's tail. Then the Pfalz half-rolled, falling a few hundred feet below him.

'Mick did the same, firing as soon as he got his enemy in line. The Hun looped. Mick looped too, coming out behind and above the other, firing short bursts. The Pfalz spun. Mick spun also, firing as he did so. This shooting seemed to me a waste of ammunition. The Hun finally pulled out. Mick, who was now down to 4,000 feet, did the same. The Hun started twisting and turning, a sure sign of "wind-up" and Mick administered the coup de grâce with a burst from directly behind at about 25 yards range. The Hun went down, obviously out of control, and crashed.

'This really was a remarkable exhibition of cruel, calculated Hun-strafing. I felt sorry for the Hun. He put up as fine a show of defensive fighting as I've ever seen.'

Once the patrol had landed, Jones had asked Mannock why he had opened fire while both he and the German were spinning, to which Mannock replied: 'To intensify his wind-up!'

Yet again, despite clear identification of four enemy machines crashing and another breaking up in the air, losses in personnel are not recorded. Jasta 16b based at Ste. Marguerite lost Vizfeldeldwebel Hans Schorn near Wytschaete, which is south of Hollebeke, but if this unit or any others lost aircraft but not pilots, there is no record of it. Whatever the truth may be, Mannock's score had now reached 35, and number 36 came the next day, another Pfalz DIII at Fromelles. This was claimed only as out of control and the combat report seems to be missing today, and only a questionable time of 18.15 hours can be found.

However, from Ira Jones's diary it seems that Mannock and Howe met and engaged German fighters during the morning and each scored. It was Swazi's first claim. Shortly before 1 pm Jones bagged a Pfalz, and that evening another, at 18.15 over Fromelles. It certainly looks as if this time and place has been also given as Mannock's claim, rather than in the morning with Howe.

Some poor weather cut flying a bit over the next couple of days, and the Squadron received a surprise visit from General Sir Herbert Plumer, commander of the British 2nd Army. He praised the Squadron for their recent hard work, and then he congratulated Mannock on his DSO. Unlike some officers of field rank, Plumer was well liked, respected and trusted among the ordinary soldiers. He was often to be seen in the front line trenches talking to the men and generally encouraging everyone to do their best. In his book *Tiger Squadron*, Ira Jones recorded (in his diary) a wonderful picture of Plumer meeting Mick Mannock:

'Though he flattered us on our fighting efforts, I have a suspicion that he did not approve of either the cleanliness or mode of our dress. Mick, in particular, "shone" in this direction. With no hat or collar, no Sam Browne [cross belt], long hair, and muffled, he looked a typical bushranger.

'When we had all rolled up (there is no other word), Plumer said to Grid: "Which is

Mannock?" Our D'Artagnon was duly pointed out to him. I really thought Plumer was going to pass right out. However, with a masterly effort he pulled himself together and staggered up to Mick with arm outstretched. Mick's dirty paw clutched his gloved hand and squeezed it in his usual hearty manner. Plumer's face twitched; for a second, I thought he was going to give a yell.

'"Mannock," he said, "let me congratulate you on your DSO and on your first day's work." Mick replied: "We expected that, Sir." Plumer's face wore a puzzled look; then he smiled faintly. I have an idea he went away wondering what sort of fellow this Mannock could be. I don't blame him.

'When Plumer had gone, Grid phoned Van Ryneveld [the wing commander] and told him what the "old man" had said about a DSO. Yes; it was quite true. Van Ryneveld had been asked to keep it quiet until the General had done his stuff.'

Despite what he wrote, Jones had probably got the date wrong about the visit, for as mentioned above, Mannock's combat report for the 21st clearly shows that he had already been told of the DSO. So while the diary entry is recorded as the 24th, it must have been nearer the 19th, a date on which Mannock is thought to have been first notified of it.

* *

Another new pilot in the Squadron was killed on the 25th. Lieutenant Henry O'Hara from Greenock, Scotland (aged 25) crashed on the aerodrome and burnt to death. Another couple of newcomers were Frederick John 'Mike' Hunt, from Hampshire, and a real old war veteran, Sidney Carlin, already the holder of the MC and DCM, awards he received in the front line while with the Royal Engineers. Aged 27, from Hull, Carlin had lost a leg when he won his MC, but now, fitted with a wooden one, he had learnt to fly. He was known as 'Timbertoes' and despite his disability he was to do well with 74, and win the DFC. He would die in the Second World War, serving again with the RAF, at the age of 50! Hunt too would win the DFC and record his wonderful introduction to air fighting from Mick Mannock during his first few days on the Squadron. Hunt was put into Mannock's Flight, and was not allowed to cross the lines for at least a week, yet every day Mannock found time to take him up on practise flights and fights.

Mannock and Roxburgh-Smith were the scorers on the 26th, claiming an Albatros DVa and a Pfalz DIII respectively. Four Albatros Scouts were found south of Bailleul that evening at 7,000 feet, flying west from that town. Mannock circled to the east and in his

Sydney 'Timbertoes' Carlin had won the MC and DCM with the Royal Engineers, but had lost a leg. He won the DFC with 74 Squadron but was taken prisoner on 21 September 1918.

usual way, put himself between them and their own territory, so making sure they had to go through him and not merely fly away east.

He attacked one at the rear and a dog-fight began. His target twisted below him but after two turns, Mannock got in a good burst at right angles and at close range. The DV went into a slow spin and was still spinning at 1,000 feet. Ira Jones got himself into a spot of bother and Mannock went to assist him so did not see the German's final plunge, but Swazi Howe and Twist Giles saw it burning on the ground.

The pace continued on the 29th, Mannock leading a special mission that evening, taking Jones and Clements out with him. Enemy machines were encountered north-east of Armentières and actions were fought between 19.25 and 20.05 pm. Initially, Mannock saw two Albatros C-types flying east from Bailleul around 16,000 feet. Gaining his usual tactical position before engaging he attacked one from the south and at close range blazed away with 80 rounds. Hit, the Albatros staggered and began to go down out of control but flattened out at about 4,000 feet. However, Ira Jones later saw this Albatros crash and burn north-east of Armentières. According to Jones:

'We re-formed at 10,000 feet and proceeded to climb again – looking for trouble. We soon found it: After a while we came across a formation of six SEs; Mick flew close to them, and we recognised by their markings that they were No.85 Squadron – newly arrived from England. The leader turned out to be "Nigger" Horn. Mick waggled his wings, as an invitation to "Nigger" and his flight to follow him. This they did like lambs being led to the slaughter. And here begins my big fight story.

'Just after 8 pm Mick spotted about a dozen Huns coming from the direction of Roubaix; we were then over Lille. As we had not too much time for a fight, having already been up for over an hour, he decided to go straight at them, as we had the advantage of height. The Huns, who were Albatros Scouts, were of the stout variety, and they accepted our head-on challenge. Both Mick and the Hun leader opened fire at one another as they approached from about 300 yards' range, but nothing happened. This burst of fire was the signal for a glorious dog-fight – as fine and as frightening a dog-fight as I've ever been in. Friend and foe fired at and whistled past one another at a tornado pace – it was a real stunner. I have never been so frightened in my life.

'Mick sent a slate-blue Albatros down out of control and Clements crashed his first Hun. He is very bucked about it. …. No.85 Squadron claim an out of control, too. The main thing, however, about this fight is that we did not suffer a casualty. Nigger telephoned Mick during dinner to say that his patrol were drinking double brandies, and could they please follow him again tomorrow!'

According to Mick's combat report, he made out the formation of German fighters at 14,000 feet in this same Armentières locality. Mannock and the others attacked from the south, and he fired 150 rounds at point blank range at one that he described as being slate-blue in colour, which went down completely out of control. He was immediately in behind another Albatros that was turning to attack an SE5. He fired half a drum of Lewis at this machine – his Vickers having jammed – and the German went into a spin. He saw the Albatros continue to spin down to 2,000 feet but was forced to break off the combat as he was unable to clear the Vickers and needed to replace the Lewis drum. He claimed one crashed, one out of control and one driven down. These first two claims would seem to be his 39th and 40th victories.

I [NF] don't want to seem picky, but while Clements did in fact claim an Albatros DV destroyed in this action, it was however his third confirmed victory, and as far as I can see, 85 did not make any claims against scouts, but Mac McGregor did claim a two-seater out of control at 20.30, some short while after this dog-fight. They were still based up in the Dunkirk area but were operating near Armentières this evening.

Air fighting on the 29th was fairly minimal, in fact nothing even got reported in the RAF communiqués this day. The Germans shot down a lot, but mostly down on the French front, hardly anything along the British sectors. One Jasta 7 pilot was wounded in combat but that was all.

Following this event, came the news that Mannock had been awarded a Bar to his DSO. Gwilym Lewis wrote in a letter home as paraphrased in his book:

> 'Mannock came here a few days ago. He has now got a Bar to his DSO and by bringing down three the night [day?] before has now 51 Huns to his credit. James McCudden was the leader on the British side before with 52, so you see you know someone pretty important!'

This score business gets very complicated, especially at this distance, and even more especially as it is difficult to reconcile known facts today, with assumed facts 90 years ago. On 25 May Mannock had written to Jim Eyles that his score now was 41 'victories'. This is the same number as he mentioned to Lewis on the telephone following his DSO awarded a few days earlier. Thus both times it exceeds by some ten the number that seem official as opposed to a personal tally.

On 2 June Mick had written to a friend who was a balloon officer, Captain C M Down. Again he mentions his score, and also mentions the marking on his personal SE5a:

> 'You will be pleased to hear that the official total is now 47 … By the way, they gave me a Bar to my DSO a week ago. I feel absolutely ashamed of myself on this account, as the credit should be given to the other boys, who back me up wonderfully. They think I can do no wrong, with the result that I always have a strong following in a scrap … The boy who took you up is gone – poor devil. He got nine Huns in eight days. A star turn.'

After saying goodbye and to give regards to a couple of Down's friends, Mick concluded by saying: 'Look out for "A". No streamers. Yours, Mick'

The 'A' was his personal aircraft identification letter, while the white horizontal rectangle, or bar, identified 74 Squadron's marking. The reference to streamers was to tell Down his machine carried none. Generally, a single coloured streamer attached to the fin depicted a flight leader, while two streamers from the elevators identified the deputy leader. This was not universal for some squadrons used streamers attached to the wing struts.

Dolan was the boy who 'took you up', having obviously taken Down for a flight in a two-seater for the experience. Down had been on the Souchez front in April 1917, at the time Mannock and 40 Squadron were involved in their balloon strafes.

It is a fact that fighter pilots with a modest score of victories are quite content to say little of their achievements, most being happy to have survived so long to accumulate anything. In contrast, the higher a pilot's score becomes, most appear to be more than a little conscious of other big scores, and begin to include everything they can to their tally, even some dubious claims. It's all sporting, of course, like scoring goals or achieving large run totals in cricket.

More 'deadly' serious of course. McCudden, in fact, had left 56 Squadron at the end of February with a score of 57, so Mannock was still below that. Bob Little DSO & Bar, DSC & Bar, a Naval pilot who had fallen in combat on 27 May, had achieved 47 victories, again more than Mannock at this point. W A Bishop VC DSO MC, the larger than life CO of 85 Squadron, had a tally of 50, and would go on to 'claim' 72 by mid-June, so was also above Mannock in the scoring game at the end of May 1918. Many of Bishop's claims have come under stern criticism in recent years however, including his lone VC action.

Mannock's score increased by one more on the last day of May. Over the north of Wytschaete, at 19.40 in the evening, he shot down a Pfalz DIII out of control, officially victory No.41. He had achieved an amazing twenty victories during the month. He was at the peak of his game; he had reached the zenith of his career.

**

We shall end this chapter with some of the antics that 74 Squadron and Mannock got up to in their off-duty moments. All squadrons did the same. It was a way of letting off steam, of forgetting their trials and tribulations and relaxing after a particular stressful day, or, because most of these fighter pilots were little more than boys, just youthful enthusiasm for life, a life that might well end the next day or the next week.

Most squadrons had record players, the best and easiest way of listening to something other than engine noise or the rattle of machine guns, or the distant and seemingly constant booming of guns from the front. On leave pilots often took in the London shows, and were encouraged to return with the latest records for the Mess. Stage singers such as George Roby, Violet Loraine, Elsie Janis and José Collins were always popular. According to Ira Jones, Mick would often annoy everyone by constantly playing 'The Londonderry Air' ["Oh, Danny boy... "], especially before going out on patrol.

One of his favourite pranks that he enjoyed in company with the CO, was to creep into someone's hut in the early hours of the morning after returning from a 'night out'. Caldwell would carry a pitcher of water and once inside, Mick would give a good impression of someone who had over-indulged on food and drink, and make sounds that appeared to herald the re-appearance of all he had imbibed! As each of these 'retching' sounds came forth, Caldwell would splash an amount of water on the floor. As the victim became aware of what he thought was happening, and about to happen with more severity, he would leap from his cot whereupon Grid would throw the rest of the water on the chap's legs. Peels of laughter would accompany the lad's assumed discomfort. All new comers had to live through this experience to become accepted into the Squadron.

Apparently Mick, on one occasion, did the same to the CO of an adjoining squadron, noted for his poor sense of humour. Whatever his degree of humour was, it was certainly not improved by the incident, although his pilots learnt of it with great delight.

On days with poor weather, both Grid and Mick would organise 'bomb raids' on neighbouring squadrons, using oranges as weapons. Jones recalled they once dropped some 200 oranges on the buildings of 1 Squadron, who retaliated with a 'banana' raid.

CHAPTER EIGHT

FINAL WEEKS WITH 74

The Squadron was beginning to make a name for itself, having achieved quite a number of victories since its arrival in France. This together with its senior flight commander having been awarded the DSO and Bar within a few weeks was news too. Other pilots were also beginning to get recognition.

The CO, Grid Caldwell, had achieved four victories by the end of May, which brought his overall score to 13. Andrew Kiddie had added four to his one claim with 32 Squadron, so had become an ace. 'Dad' Roxburgh-Smith had five victory claims thus far and Bill Cairnes had made it five too on 30 May, possibly six. Ira Jones had been no slouch either. He had scored an amazing 15 victories in May, only five less than his mentor Mannock. Others had all gained one or two kills – Giles, Clements, Birch and Howe. Young had added three to his 19 Squadron score so had six in all. On the last day of May, Ira Jones had received the Military Cross, so another excuse for a party. The euphoria, however, was short lived.

Things looked rosy for the first day of June, as on a dawn patrol, Captain Young bagged a brace of Hannover two-seaters – Hannoverianers they were usually called by the RAF. The first he shot down over Estaires at 04.30 and half an hour later the second one went down over Robecq. At least one of these came from FA32.

Around 2 pm Mannock and Cairnes led patrols out towards Estaires and came into contact with a number of enemy machines, some of them from their old sparing partners, Jacobs's Jasta 7, with others from Jasta 52. The encounter began after Mannock saw the machines east of Merville and immediately attacked from the front and from above, going for a group of Pfalz Scouts. The fight had already begun as he selected the highest enemy machine that had positioned itself behind an SE5, and Mannock began firing away, as he closed right in, with both guns from point blank range. Both bottom wings of the Pfalz ripped away and what was left crashed, witnessed by both Birch and Giles.

Swinging in behind another Pfalz it zoomed upwards and pulling back on the stick, Mannock fired vertically into the machine that burst into flames and went down, confirmed by others in the patrol. Already Mannock was engaging another which he saw making a turn towards him on the same level. He fired several short bursts into this fighter whilst they circled and the German went into a spin, and disappeared from the fight.

When the patrols landed, Captain Cairnes was missing. This was a bitter blow and there was no welcome news later of him having landed elsewhere, or force-landed near the front. He had been shot down by Leutnant Paul Billik, leader of Jasta 52, becoming the German's 19th of an eventual 31 victories. Billik in fact accounted for several British aces during his fighting career: Lieutenant J J Malone DSC, a RNAS pilot who had achieved ten victories, Major A D Carter DSO & Bar of 19 Squadron with 29 victories, and later Captain A Clayden DFC of 32 Squadron, seven victories. He had also shot down and killed Mannock's old squadron commander, Major L A Tilney MC, on 9 March 1918. Billik was finally brought down himself during a huge land battle on 10 August 1918, the opening of the Allied offensive that finally spelt the end of the war. He was probably downed by Lieutenant M C Kinney, of 3 Squadron, flying a Camel. As luck would have it Kinney's claim this day was his first, a Fokker DVII going down to crash land behind the British front line troops, where its pilot was taken prisoner. A novice had overcome a top ace. Four days later Kinney claimed another victory but it was his last.

Jones noted in his book on Mannock that:

'1.6.18. – Poor old Cairnes was shot down this afternoon, and is no doubt dead, as one of his wings came off. It has been a hell of a day for fighting.

'I led a dawn patrol, leaving the ground at 4.30 am. It was a dawn which attracted the eye; there was no cloud, and gently the eastern sky lit up, gradually waking the warriors of the war area to activity. I got up at 3.45 am, had my cold sponge bath to help me to wake up, and then went into the Mess to have the usual cup of tea and biscuit. Giles, Battel [1] and Richardson were the others. As we were a little early, Birch and Richardson continued to slumber, as they were both suffering from a slight headache. I thought this continued sleep was bad for them, so I put on the record of Violet Loraine, singing "College Days". This song woke them up immediately, and simultaneously books and magazines were flying at my head and at the gramophone.

'When we got to the aerodrome, our machines, as well as B Flight's, were ticking over all ready for being flown. The mechanics looked very tired and almost fed up. They had been up since 2.30 am. We took off punctually to time and climbed towards Ypres at about 65 mph – which is the best climbing speed for the SE – turned east just north of Ypres and crossed the lines at 15,000 feet.

'At 5.15 am, I spotted three Albatros Scouts over Armentières, so I led my Flight to the east and above them à la Mick, before attacking. They were completely surprised, but due to bad shooting we failed to bag one. Personally, I forgot to load my guns during my initial dive, and so lost my opportunity.

'After leaving this fight we re-formed quickly, and I made for Dickebusch Lake (which is a favourite landmark of mine), where I could see some of our "white" [archie [2]] bursts trailing a black speck, which was a dark camouflaged Pfalz scout returning from an expedition of balloon-strafing at 3,000 feet. I had to take a right-angle shot at it, and this time, having made sure that my guns were loaded, I was more successful. I did Mick's trick of traversing, and almost immediately we had the joy of seeing the Hun go spinning down and crash a mile and a half east of the lake.

'We foolishly followed him down to the ground, and Battel and I gave him a parting shot into the wreckage. We had to pay the penalty for being so reckless, as on our way back to our lines many bullets perforated our machines, and Battel's SE having been hit

[1] Lt Andew J Battel, a Canadian from Saskatchewan, was shot down and killed on 9 July 1918, aged 18. He has no known grave.
[2] In WW1 German anti-aircraft fire produced black smoke bursts, while Allied bursts were white.

in the engine, had to land in a field behind the trenches. As Mick has always told us, to follow a machine down to the ground is to ask for trouble, but I find the urge irresistible.'

The machines of B Flight landed shortly after Mannock's Flight, and once on the ground his pilots began to rush up to Young's machine, and having climbed out, he was slapped on the back with some enthusiasm as he had downed two Hannovers. Jones continued:

'He [Young] had shot down two two-seaters in flames, one of which fell into our lines. Great show – three Huns before breakfast is not bad and everyone is very bucked.

'As I am going home on leave tomorrow, Grid suggested that I did not do another patrol, but when Mick started teasing me that I would get shot down if I went up with him in the afternoon, I decided to go, as we had a bet of 100 francs on my safe return. As he was leading, I knew this bet was an easy one for me, for his leadership is fool-proof.

'This patrol with Mick in the afternoon led to a dog-fight which was the hottest that I've been in for a few days. Mick led A and C Flights on to seven Pfalz, camouflaged dark blue with white tails, over Estaires at 13,000 feet. For five minutes the ten SEs fought the seven Pfalz almost down to the ground, and when the battle was over one enemy had been shot down in flames, one crashed and one sent down out of control, all by Mick. We lost poor old Cairnes, who was seen to leave the fight with the right wing of his machine breaking away from the fuselage. It spun towards the ground at a terrific rate, and as I watched him disappear into the depths below, a feeling of sickness overcame me. It is a terrible sight to see a pal going to his death.'

Clem Clements was in this fight too, and once told James Dudgeon, another biographer of Mannock, his version of the fight, also mentioning about why 74 had changed from the Aldis to the fore-and-aft gun-sight (see *Cross & Cockade Journal*, Vol 18, No.3, 1987):

'It was the biggest fight, scout to scout, that most of us had ever taken part in. We met up with a large group of Albatros and Pfalz and all hell was let loose. Every second one was avoiding other machines, friend and foe. Machines were swirling about at a tremendous rate, passing only a few feet away – sometimes closer. One was buffeted by their slipstreams and had only fractions of a second to avoid collision. It was terrifying when thought back on. At the time one was far too busy to think of what might happen.

'Only rarely did one get the chance to fire, and this is where the point about the telescopic sight comes in. One's eyes had to be everywhere. EA were passing much too quickly for a pilot to get his eye down to the Aldis and adjust his eye accordingly. Apart from taking too much time it kept the eyes away from their very important job of looking about. To sight on an EA in that way would have been much the same as flying through a mass of stunting machines with one's eyes shut.

'I saw an Albatros out of the corner of my eye, coming from my right and heading straight in front of my bow – from three to nine o'clock. I fired both guns as he crossed in front and was somewhat surprised to see his struts breaking as my rounds went in between his wings. His upper plane snapped away and then his lower wings. He kept going straight down and I lost sight of him for an instant as I passed his stern. But as I turned, not to get him again as he was obviously done for, I caught a glimpse of his going straight down through some lower SEs.

'After landing back at Clairmarais I was advised by Mick Mannock not to claim this Albatros as another officer from the lower SE formation had already claimed it and had been credited with its destruction. He was one of the very few who "poached" claims to increase his score. He did well in the service after the war.'

On the 2nd Mick claimed another Pfalz, this one out of control two miles south of Mount Kemmel, at 15.40. It was a day of indifferent visibility and enemy aircraft activity was slight – as that day's communiqué recorded. However, the number of Allied aircraft claimed by the Germans makes nonsense of this comment, and they too suffered losses. With Mannock's penchant for scoring hits on whatever he attacked, one has to wonder if the pilot Jasta 58 lost east of Bailleul might have been in this Pfalz DIII. Kemmel is only just to the east of this town, and Leutnant Johan Dunkelberg who was shot down and killed this day, was operating from Koekhoek, near Menin, on the German 4th Army front. He came from Barsinghausen, south-west of Hannover and was just a few weeks short of his 22nd birthday.

The weather, at least on the British front, remained cloudy and overcast for the next couple of days or so, and it was not until the 6th that 74 scored again. On this late afternoon patrol they met for the first time the new Fokker DVII fighters, and Mannock sent one down to crash east of Ypres. Mannock, Young, Kiddie and Clements were then out on an evening patrol and at 19.25 east of Ypres they mixed it with some German scouts, and between them they shared the destruction of a Pfalz DIII which crashed west of Roulers. Sadly there are no obvious candidates for these German losses, so again we must contend with 'crashed' aircraft with no apparent fatalities.

Mick Mannock relaxing with a cigarette.

Mannock wrote on 7 June that he now had a total of 51 victories. Of these, 47 appear official. The relevant letter was addressed to Major S E Parker, one of Lieutenant-Colonel Robert Smith-Barry's flight commanders at No.1 School of Special Flying at Gosport. Sidney Parker had taken his 'ticket' in 1 August 1915 and had seen action flying with 60 Squadron in 1916. He later received the AFC and was made an MBE for his services.

74 Squadron RAF
B.E.F.
7/6/18

Dear Major,
Greetings!

Bewilderingly pleased to receive your letter of the 30th, and thanks muchly for all those kind words about the gong. Incidentally they staggered me by the presentation of a bar to same, a few days later.

I think my guns must have gone wrong (not properly aligned) as I couldn't miss the damned Huns. Official score now 47. Office (Squadron) records 51. Not so bad for an old chattering wreck like me, what!

Grid's going strong at times, and feeling fragile at others. "No Greens" is the standing complaint of the Squadron, and the situation from that point of view is a serious one. I don't know what's going to happen when I go away on leave (if I ever do). I'll have three days (and nights) in bed right away.

Old Bishop is out here again and seemingly intends going all out. He has rather a decent crowd – some good Americans – and he ought to do well.

So you're at Gosport now! That means a colonelcy very soon if not already materialised. Well old bean, I shall drop down to see you at the first possible moment, so reserve the nicest 'fairy' in the whole outfit, for the well known hatchet-faced birdman.

Cheerio and much success in your new job. Do drop us a line when you can. Grid sends his good wishes, as does Young and others you know. (I presume you heard that poor Henderson was killed a few days ago.)

Yours sincerely.
Mick

The gong, of course referred to his DSO, and the greens, one assumes, was referring to green (new and untried) pilots. The reference to Henderson most likely referred to Captain K S Henderson of 1 Squadron, who was killed in action on 2 June. 1 and 74 Squadrons were both at Clairmarais.

This was obviously a day for writing letters, for another the same date relates:

They have given me a bar to the DSO, I enclose correspondence in connection therewith. DSO and bar inside 11 days is not so bad for an old man. Total down 51. Officially only 47. No news of poor old Dolan. I have no hope personally. We have lost several people lately, but up to the present I have only been shot about the machine a bit. I have only to beat Mac and old Richthofen now. I hope I shall do it. The other day the CO and I engaged 9 Huns. We chased them miles over their own side. They would not wait. I got one.

Another occasion 5 of us engaged 12. I got 3. One in flames, one in pieces, and one nose-dived to the ground. Great times. Derek's mascot has lost an ear. In combat, I think! I am having a white one put on in its place.

German DFW CV two-seater.

Once again it is totally apparent that he was well aware of his score, and understood that only McCudden and Manfred von Richthofen had scored more victories. Mention of Derek's mascot is interesting. Some small furry toy animal one suspects, dangling somewhere in his cockpit.

On the morning of the 9th, two Flights were out again, Mick's and Young's. They came upon two Albatros two-seaters a couple of miles south of Kemmel shortly after 8 am, with their green and brown camouflage, which aided the crews not at all.

Mannock first spotted them flying below their own balloon line, and he climbed to 10,000 feet and flew south from Mont des Cats, then dived on them from the south, firing both guns into the leading German. It was also attacked almost simultaneously by Messrs Kiddie and Clements and it fell away apparently out of control, and disappeared from view.

Mick immediately engaged the other Albatros from the rear, again firing both guns at intervals as his sights came to bear. Wilf Young then attacked it from behind and as he swung off to one side, Mannock watched as the C-type struck the ground in a glide and turned over, again, just below the enemy balloon line. These claims of one destroyed and one out of control, although both shared, edged the official total a tad nearer the 50 mark, although Mannock himself would no doubt have said 53 in all.

The Squadron lost another pilot on 12 June, an American, Second Lieutenant G F Thompson, from Craig, Missouri. During an OP the SE5s were engaged by the Bavarian Jasta 16 over Armentières that evening. He was last seen spinning down from 15,000 feet, but survived as a prisoner. He was claimed by Leutnant Johan Schäfer, his first of three victories he would score before his own death on 10 October 1918.

Mannock wrote a letter to his sister Jess on 16 June, which referred to Jess's husband Ted, who appears to have suffered an injury in the war, and then he mentions brother Patrick:

Poor old Pat is going through the mill now. The Tank Corps is having a rough time of it. I hope he gets through all right. I suppose you are all still on the munitions job. It must be pretty hard work, but not quite so hard as the war out here. Things are getting a bit intense just lately and I don't quite know how long my nerves will last out. I am rather old now, as airmen go, for fighting. Still, one hopes for the best. I hope mother and Nora are getting along OK. These times are so horrible that occasionally I feel that life is not worth hanging on to myself, but "hope springs eternal in the human breast". I had thoughts of getting married, but …?

I am supposed to be going on leave on the 19th of this month (if I live long enough), and I shall call at Birmingham to see you all.

Cheerio, Yours,
Edward

It is obvious from the tone of this letter that the strain was beginning to tell. He often showed bravado but here the bravado appears to be hiding his innermost thoughts that perhaps he was living on borrowed time. His thoughts on marriage were obviously on hold. It is known that he was interested in a VAD sister, and the name of Sister Flanagan crops up from time to time. Like so many men in war, he no doubt felt that he should not contemplate matrimony until the war had ended.

**

Ira Jones returned from leave on 16 June. Over the four previous days 74 had gained several victories. Clements and Swazi Howe had both shot down Pfalz Scouts on the 12th, 'Timber-toes' Carlin crashed a DFW two-seater on the 13th, and then Howe had bagged two more Pfalz DIIIs on the 15th, which brought his score to five. In his diary for the 16th Jones wrote:

'Back from leave. Giles and I went to a church service and communion in No.1 Hangar this morning. Padre Bankes of No.1 Squadron took it. He shot a good line, as I expected him to. He is one of the better types of padres. No humbug about him.

German LVG CV two-seater.

Two other stalwarts in 74 Squadron were Andrew Kiddie and Sydney Carlin, both of whom became aces.

'While I was in church, Mick was killing Huns over Zillebeke Lake – a couple of black Pfalz. There were eighteen of them against six of ours. Mick tells me he took them completely by surprise, attacking them from above and from the direction of the morning sun. His Flight adopted the dive-and-zoom tactics, while the Huns tried to counter by pulling up the noses of their machines and firing almost in the stall. These tactics of the Hun are quite wrong in my opinion. When the machine is almost in the stall, it is practically stationary, and therefore an easy target. It is strange, though, how only Mick managed to get any Huns. Good shooting I suppose. There is no doubt that once a pilot gets into the knack of deflection shooting, the rest is easy.'

Mannock was leading an early Offensive Patrol and found the enemy at around 07.45, three miles south of Zillebeke Lake. Going into the attack he fired about 50 rounds from head-on, then lost sight of his target as it went beneath him. As he looked back he spotted the Pfalz going down in wide circles and then pile up on the ground at a position he noted as Sheet 28 J 30 C 3 5.

He was immediately after another Pfalz hammering 25 rounds into it and it stalled and spun. Mannock watched it falling for several thousand feet, until he was engaged by another German pilot, and it had not flattened out by then.

Were these the black-painted machines of Jasta 7? They were operating south of Ypres this day, time unfortunately not known, and even claimed a couple of SE5s but they were not credited. They suffered no pilot casualties but aircraft, who knows?

Roxburgh-Smith also claimed a victory this day, a Fokker DVII an hour earlier whilst on an Offensive Patrol south-east of Dickebusch. It was his first this month and his sixth overall. This was the second time 74 Squadron had encountered this formidable new German fighter. The enemy machine was first seen at 19,000 feet. Mannock and Roxburgh-Smith began flying below it to lure the German pilot down under the other SE5s of the patrol, but the enemy pilot was not tempted and refused the bait. Mannock then flew in front of the Fokker and slightly below it, again tempting the enemy pilot to come down to his level. According to the writings of Ira Jones:

> 'It was laughable to watch Mick's machine swinging from side to side (he was kicking his rudder) as he pulled the Hun's leg. Occasionally he would pump handle his controls and the machine would bounce about like a bucking bronco. Very funny it was. I could imagine Mick roaring with laughter.'

While this was going on, Rox had slowly closed in on the Fokker and finally began to fire into it, whereupon it turned onto its back and then flicked into a near vertical dive, straightened out for a few moments, then went into a zoom which ended again with the DVII on its back, so the pilot seemed to be either dead or unconscious. It finally crashed south-east of Dickebusch Lake at 08.45.

* *

The Fokker DVII that RAF squadrons were now meeting in increasing numbers came from a long line of excellent fighter aircraft. The Dutch designer, Anthony Fokker, had his first success with his Fokker monoplane. As a fighting machine at first it was nothing special, but it became so once Fokker and his engineers managed to mount a machine gun in front of the pilot, which had an interrupter gear, allowing bullets to pass between the turning blades of the propeller. This combination of a reasonably manoeuvrable aeroplane and the gun mounting made it a useful single-seat fighter and for a while in 1915-16 it dominated the air fighting above the Western Front. In the hands of some early aggressive fighter pilots, such as Oswald Boelcke, Max Immelmann, Kurt Wintgens, Max von Mulzer, Otto Parschau, Gustav Leffers, *et al*, both the British and French airmen were on the defensive and a comparatively small number of Fokker Eindeckers wrested air superiority over France.

Once these Eindeckers became out-dated by new Allied designs, Fokker introduced Fokker D-type fighters, but then the Albatros Scouts took over the major fighting role in the German Air Service in 1917. Late that year he introduced his Fokker Dr.I Triplane, which for a while became a powerful addition to the Germans' air arsenal, especially as the design found favour with Rittmeister Baron Manfred von Richthofen, by then leader of the first Jagdesgeschwader (JG.I) that comprised four Jagdstaffeln. By that autumn, the Triplane was starting to have problems with the top wing, which occasionally, and unnervingly, tended to break up, but some Albatros Scouts too were having wing troubles, which was why, for a period, the Pfalz DIIIa Scouts started to be met in increasing numbers. As we have seen, Mannock and 74 Squadron had been in battles with this type frequently in recent weeks. The Triplane could still be found but von Richthofen in particular had been eager to have the new Fokker DVII biplane at the front. He had seen the machine back in Germany, and liked it. Fokker's chief designer, Reinhold Platz, had produced a winner. The Baron's death in April 1918 came before the DVII arrived, but it was now coming on line and entering service. It would be a formidable adversary for the British and French airmen – perhaps the best fighter the Germans ever had in World War One.

Like the Triplane, the DVII was constructed using the same formula of wooden cantilever wings and welded steel-tube fuselage. It had a one-piece lower wing and the upper wing was constructed into two separate box-spars. A braced box-girder welded from steel tube gave strength to the fuselage and metal panels covered each side of the engine compartment. Fitted with a 160 hp Mercedes DIII engine, later a 185 hp BMW engine, the machine was easy to fly, responsive to the controls, and helped the average pilot become a good one. When the BMW-engined type came to the front, it gave Allied fighter pilots a bit of a shock, for it had a much better performance while still looking like a Mercedes-powered machine.

However, Mick Mannock was not to meet the DVII much prior to him leaving 74 Squadron, and his final victory with them came an hour or so after Rox had despatched his first Fokker biplane. He would claim a dozen more before the war's end.

Mannock led off his Flight on an Offensive Patrol to Armentières on the 17th, and at 09.45, flying at 15,000 feet he spotted a German two-seater surrounded by bursting anti-aircraft fire over Berques. He immediately gained height to 18,000 and dived on it when directly over Mont des Cats. As he led the Flight down, Clements broke away with engine trouble, but Mannock closed, chasing the German – which he identified as a Halberstadt painted with silver dope. By the time they had descended to about 8,000 feet the German machine had been hit severely, Mannock then watching as it went down in a spinning nose-dive and crashed at position Sheet 36 B.29d. Ira Jones wrote about this action in his book *Tiger Squadron*:

'After breakfast, I went up with Mick's patrol. I felt I could do with a little inspiration from him. I was quite frank with him about why I was going up. He laughed and said: "Taffy, old lad, I've often felt like you. Come up with me, and I'll send one down, sizzle, sizzle, wonk. It will put you right. You can fly on my left. You'll get a better view from there."

'At 9.30 I spotted our "Archie" bursting over Berques. I went up to Mick's level, waggling my wings to attract his attention. I was only ten yards away. When he saw me he just laughed and pointed to the Archie. Marvellous what eyesight he's got, despite his dud eye.

'We commenced to climb eastwards at once, as the Hun was at 18,000 feet, and we were only at 15,000 feet. The first thing Mick always does, if he can, on spotting a Hun is to get on the east of him. He does this for two reasons. One: the Hun must pass him to get home. Two: there is a better chance of surprise attack.

'I should hate to be a Hun. He never knows from what angle he is going to be attacked over his own territory. For our part when we are on our side of the line, we just dream of home and think of some sweet fairy. We never think of a Hun. To us, the war does not commence until we are a few miles over the enemy's lines.

'Well, to continue our patrol. At 9.45 we are getting close to the Hun. Mick decided on a head-on attack. About half a mile away, Clem, who was on Mick's right, was suddenly seen to drop out and dive for home. Mick and I saw him simultaneously. We stared at each other and looked behind. We both thought there might have been Huns diving at us and that Clem was giving us the tip. Later we found that his engine had conked.

'This little episode put Mick off his target slightly, but he continued on his deadly track. When the Hun, a lovely silver Halberstadt, was 200 yards away, he opened fire with a short burst. Almost simultaneously, he dived steeply below the Hun, turned and came up under his tail. The formation did likewise. Our friend was not hit, but was diving steeply away – a foolish thing to do. Mick had now only to dive at the same angle directly behind him and he was sure to be hit. He was in direct line with the flight of the bullets.

'It was a grand sight to watch. There was Mick, just in front of me, doing 180 miles an hour, with the bullets pouring out to the accompaniment of the vicious barking of the two machine guns. At 8,000 feet it was plain that the enemy had bought it. He was going down at a steeper and steeper angle. I pulled out to watch the end. It came in a cloud of dust.

'My blood lust had been re-awakened. My confidence was returning. Good old Mick!'

In this same book, Jones recorded that the Halberstadt he destroyed that day was his fiftieth victory, adding: 'He is a wonderful chap, and so modest.' This it seems, actually brought Mannock's combat score to 52. In any event, he was now sent off on leave the next day, Jones noting that:

'Mick went off on a spot of well-deserved leave this afternoon. It is very noticeable to me, after an absence of ten days from his company, that his nerves are very much on edge. It is easy to spot when a pilot is getting nervy. He becomes very talkative and restless. When I arrived in the Mess this morning, Mick's greeting was: "Are you ready to die for your country, Taffy? Will you have it in flames or in pieces?"'

**

Several years after the end of World War Two, a plaque was placed on the wall of a new block of maisonettes in Canterbury, named Mannock House, not far from where Mick had lived as a boy. It was unveiled by Air Commodore F M F 'Freddy' West VC MC, along with the city mayor, Alderman W S Bean. Among the guests invited to attend was Edward Davis, of Gillingham, who had been Mannock's sergeant-rigger in 74 Squadron. In his pocket he carried a cigarette case that Mannock had given him. Apparently, as Mr Davis said, Mannock had borrowed a cigarette from him, and in typical fashion had returned it by throwing to him a full cigarette case.

**

The day following Mannock's departure, the wing commander, Colonel Pierre Van Ryneveld, a South African, arrived on a visit and spoke to Major Caldwell, telling him that he would be losing Mannock, for after his leave he was going to take command of 85 Squadron. Its CO, Major W A Bishop, was about to end his period as its commander. It came as a bit of a blow to 74, but while unhappy that they were no longer going to be able to have him in the squadron, they were pleased about his promotion. As Jones noted in his diary, it should have happened months ago.

Grid Caldwell immediately sent a wire to the RFC Club in Bruton Street where he suspected Mick would stay. When he later received the message after his journey to London, no doubt Mick had mixed feelings too, but probably 'pushed the boat out' with whomsoever he found staying there too.

Mannock had found the message in an envelope pinned to the club's notice board. It was good news but there were no doubt some misgivings. To lead a flight was one thing, but a whole squadron? He probably knew it was likely. You don't get several decorations and a high score of victories and expect to remain in the background when leadership and experience is required to win a war. Almost immediately he went down with a bout of influenza, but it passed quickly. It is difficult to say whether he was soon his old self again. What was his old self? Much had happened over the last year or so. He had learnt a great deal about air fighting, but by the same token must have been only too aware that experience and luck were one thing, fate quite another. He realised the odds were as much against him as anyone. It only took a lucky shot, or a bit of structural failure in his aircraft, and all the experience gained was for nought. He had seen too much death to believe he was immune.

It appears that another visitor to the club was James McCudden VC DSO MC MM CdG. It hadn't seemed that long since Mannock was his aspiring pupil, and now here he was with the DSO & Bar, MC & Bar, and more than 50 kills to his name. McCudden was still an instructor at the School of Air Gunnery up at Ayr, and must have come down south for some well-earned leave. Then came the announcement of the award of a second bar to Mick's DSO, following another recommendation from Grid Caldwell for the upper echelons to reward his senior flight commander with an appropriate decoration. Was Caldwell hoping for something higher than a second bar – a VC perhaps? It must have been a close thing for not too many second bars were awarded. Perhaps the fact that all three DSOs had come within a period of just two months overshadowed a higher award!

Mick, seemingly taking this further recognition of his prowess in air combat in his stride, then travelled north to Birmingham to visit his mother. It was not an easy visit, Mrs Mannock having sunk deeper into an alcoholic state, and as soon as he was able, he was on his way to Wellingborough to visit Mr and Mrs Eyles – for the last time. They were quick to notice that Mick was not on good form. A few days earlier, when writing to them to tell them he would be coming to stay for a few days, he had noted:

> 'Just heard that I've been promoted (major) and am taking command of Bishop's squadron in France. I'm not sure that I'm glad of the transfer, as I don't like the idea of leaving the old squadron, but it can't be helped now ...'

Jim Eyles was to recall that Mick had broken down, shaking uncontrollably during the visit, while tears had streamed down his cheeks, and the older man was powerless to help or comfort his friend adequately. Mick later shrugged it off as merely nervous tension, but Jim Eyles could see than Mick was feeling the strain of recent weeks mingled with the prospect of returning to command a squadron. Mannock obviously kept up a strong demeanour in front of the men with whom he flew, and also the squadron doctor. While combat fatigue was finally being realised as a fact in this war, it still took a strong hand to suggest to anyone that they end operational duties. Then again, with a man like Mannock, with his record to date, who was going to deny him from carrying on? On the squadron he had masked much of his feelings with bravado and bluster, often carping on about people going down in flames and being keen himself to display a certain loudness when some of his victims had gone down burning. No doubt many of the youngsters had seen this as a wonderful warlike image but it obviously disguised his real state of mind.

Even the experienced Grid Caldwell saw no real signs that Mick was starting to crack up. He knew his senior flight commander had never reported sick, or had ever asked for time off, other than properly scheduled leave. Even when it was mooted that he was being considered for a command of his own, Mannock had pleaded that he be allowed to remain in action.

Not all COs were ace flyers, many not even flying, just leading from the ground. At various times, specially when experienced COs had flown and been killed, their active roles were positively discouraged, sometimes they were even ordered to remain on the ground. One could argue that being given a command of his own might provide Mannock with a reason not to be so operational, but it is a measure of the man that this possible escape route, even if it occurred to him, was not taken.

Mannock's 'gung-ho' nature as him having absolutely no fear was obvious, but in truth it was a mask, a mask that he could only lower with someone like Jim Eyles, who knew the real man behind the public war hero.

When he finally departed, Jim Eyles was very apprehensive. It certainly seemed to him that Mick was far from being that self-assured man he had known earlier, and in no real condition to return to the war. The manner of his departure showed signs that Mick was leaving for the last time. As it turned out, he was.

There was a party held for him just prior to his leaving for France. His sister-in-law, Dorothy Mannock, attended, and she later recalled that Mick seemed very much preoccupied with his thoughts, but when questioned was not forthcoming.

The date of departure, 3 July 1918, duly arrived. He returned by boat, again suffering from the seasickness that had plagued him on other trips. He no doubt felt weaker after his recent bout of influenza, and his overall physical condition was not good. All this made it a miserable return.

Once ashore, rather than make a beeline for 85 Squadron's airfield at St Omer, he dropped in on his old pals of 74, still at Clairmarais South. It was not far away, but he obviously felt happier to go there first rather than directly to St Omer. Surrounded by familiar faces, he broke down in front of them, but the next morning he seemed better. He had regrouped, and boarding a car, was driven the short distance to St Omer and his new command, with its new challenges.

One could argue that his return was too early. After all, his friend Jimmy McCudden had left 56 Squadron in February 1918, and was still in England awaiting his next operational posting, so why was it so imperative for Mannock to take over 85 so soon. After a long period with 40 Squadron, from April 1917 to the start of January 1918, then with 74 in France from April to June 1918, he was overdue for a long rest. On the other hand it was common knowledge 85 Squadron needed a boost and a strong hand at the tiller. Major Bishop VC had been a figure-head while commanding 85, and he had taken it to France in May 1918, but he had not been a leader in the same sense that Caldwell, Reggie Dallas or Mannock were leaders. Their first priority had been for their men. Bishop's was for Bishop.

Billy Bishop was a complex character who had built a fearsome reputation. A Canadian from Owen Sound, Ontario, he was 20 years old when the war started, having attended the Canadian Royal Military College in 1911. Once the war began he had become a second lieutenant with the Canadian Mounted Rifles but inactivity pushed him towards flying and he became an observer in France in 1915. After becoming a pilot he was sent to 60 Squadron, flying Nieuport Scouts, and where fellow pilot Keith Caldwell was a member. He soon began to score heavily, or at least, claim heavily, and by the end of May 1917, his total claims were 22.

He then went out early one morning and upon returning, claimed to have shot-up a German fighter airfield, and apart from hitting aircraft on the ground, maintained that he had shot down three Albatros Scouts that had taken off to engage him. Although there was nobody to corroborate or confirm his story, he received the Victoria Cross for this raid – the first and only time this decoration has ever been awarded just on the recipient's own say-so. His further claims with 60 Squadron, and later with 85 Squadron in the spring of 1918, again, mostly while out alone, without any confirmations by other people, raised his score to 72 – five of which he accounted for on his very last day of operational flying, and he'd known in advance it was his last day!

Air historians ever since have been trying to discover the name of the airfield he attacked on 2 June 1917, and which German unit he claimed against, but without finding any clues, which puts the whole thing in doubt. In later years there was even a Canadian senate enquiry into the matter, which did not come to any firm conclusions. Whatever the truth about the 2 June affair or Bishop's other claims, it must be said that he did at least survive flying over the Western Front at a time when many young men did not.

No doubt, with a VC DSO & Bar and MC, Major Bishop was an imposing figure to the young pilots of 85 Squadron when he was put in command of this unit. With that array of medals and the wartime newspaper coverage of his exploits, these pilots must have felt very privileged to have such a man leading them to the war in France.

Once 85 Squadron had settled in, Bishop was back to his old ways, going off on lone patrols and returning with claims of enemy aircraft shot down. There are many photographs of Bishop and his fledglings laughing and smiling for the camera, and no obvious disquiet about their leader. However, he led few patrols, leaving that to his flight commanders, which was, in any event, how things were usually done. Once Bishop left therefore, it seemed obvious to the 'powers that be' that an equally strong personality should follow, and lead this still embryo fighter squadron against the enemy. Mannock was the obvious choice, so that rather than a deserved rest, Mick Mannock was sent instead to command Bishop's old unit.

CHAPTER NINE

COMMANDING 85 SQUADRON

Following his visit to 74 Squadron, Major Mick Mannock drove from Clairmarais to St Omer on 5 July. Meeting his new command it seemed obvious to him that the pilots did not have the same level of morale as 74. Bishop had certainly been a figure-head but he had not developed into a patrol leader, nor had he encouraged a method of leadership that was now *de rigeur* in France. However, it has to be said that not everyone had doubts about Bishop. Lieutenant Elliott White Springs, one of his pilots, had recorded on his departure: 'So our Major has gone, but if ever a CO had the respect, admiration and love of his unit, 'twas him. The mechanics even are disconsolate.'

Springs was not to see the arrival of the new commanding officer, for he was brought down on 27 June and it was while he was in hospital that he was told he was being posted to the 148th Aero Squadron as a flight commander.

Since their arrival in France in May, 85 Squadron had claimed nearly 50 victories, half of which had been 'scored' by Bishop. The last ones had been claimed by Lieutenant A Cunningham-Reid, who had shot down a red and black Pfalz in flames between Bruges and Thielt, on 3 July, then drove down another out of control.

Captain G B A Baker MC, 85 Squadron flight commander. On the left is W H Longton, one of the few pilots in WW1 to win three DFCs.

Mannock's flight commanders were experienced men. Captain G B A Baker MC, had, like Young and Cairnes in 74, cut his teeth with 19 Squadron in 1916-17, flying BE12s, a fighter version of the BE2. His MC was awarded for leadership and for flying bombing raids. By the summer of 1917 he had been promoted to captain and sent to 23 Squadron, which flew French Spads. During his period with 23, he had scored a handful of victories, then been rested. In early 1918 he moved to 85 Squadron while they were still being 'worked up' as a

Mannock's senior flight commander in 85 Squadron was Captain S B Horn MC (left), seen here with Lieutenant J Dymond (centre) and W H 'Scruffy' Longton DFC.

Sopwith Dolphin squadron, then helped convert the pilots onto the SE5. He was Bishop's second in command and was just a couple of weeks away from his 24th birthday. He would become an air-vice marshal in WW2. In correspondence in 1967, George Baker said to me [NF] that as far as he was concerned: 'The outstanding fighter pilot of the 1918 period was, without any questions, Mannock.'

Captain Arthur Clunie Randall commanded B Flight, and was a Scot from Lanarkshire, aged 23. He had been with the Border Regiment before joining the RFC and his first combat tour had been as a DH2 pilot with 32 Squadron in late 1916, early 1917. He would gain another nine victories with 85 and win the DFC.

C Flight was led by Captain Spencer Bertram 'Nigger' Horn. Aged 23 too, he had actually been born in England the day after the ship that had brought his family

Captain M C McGregor DFC, 85 Squadron, a New Zealander.

and two brothers from Australia had docked. One brother, K K Horn, would win the MC with the RFC. Following service with the Dragoon Guards, Nigger Horn had trained as a pilot and flown with 60 Squadron in 1917, at the same time as Bishop had been there. He already had six victories and had also won the MC. When forming 85 Squadron, Bishop had asked Horn to become one of his flight commanders, and he had agreed. By the time Mannock arrived, Horn had claimed two more victories.

In Horn's Flight was another experienced pilot, Lieutenant Malcolm Charles McGregor who came from Hunterville, New Zealand. He was 22 years old and had earlier served with 54 Squadron flying Sopwith Pups in 1917, and had gained one victory. He would go on to become a flight commander with 85, and win the DFC.

According to McGregor, Mannock's appointment was a popular move. He was well known to all the pilots, who enjoyed debate and was never happier when discussing issues with a bunch of pilots. Unlike some leaders, he liked to share his thoughts and tactics with them, whereas some top aces tended to keep to themselves their secret of success. In his letters home, McGregor made frequent references to Mannock.

There had also been two Americans in the Flight, Elliott White Springs and Lawrence Kingsley Callahan. Both had been in 85 Squadron since May. Springs had later immortalised himself and Larry Callahan by editing and adding to the diary kept by a third American with the squadron, 25-year-old John McGavock Grider, from Arkansas. [1] Grider had been killed in action on 18 June, but the other two soldiered on, and both became decorated aces. Later, both moved to the United States Air Service, serving with the 148th Aero Squadron – Springs having left already, as mentioned earlier. Springs came from South Carolina and was approaching his 22nd birthday, while Callahan, from Chicago, was 24. According to Springs, it had been mooted that McCudden might be selected to command 85, but they had protested and instead asked for Mannock, as some of them had trained under him in England.

It is strange that when writing later about this change of commanding officer, Springs had noted that the squadron pilots were not keen on McCudden as: 'He gets Huns himself, but he doesn't give anybody else a chance at them.' This remark seems more in keeping with what some thought about Bishop, whereas McCudden, as well as being a tremendous stalker of German two-seaters, had always promoted the Flight system of fighting, and was an excellent patrol leader.

Others in the Squadron when Mannock arrived were again a mix of nationalities. Alec Stratford 'Bobby' Cunningham-Reid had been in the Royal Engineers and was another original pilot. He had lost a brother in the RFC back in 1915. He too would become an ace and survive the war.

Lancastrian, Walter Hunt 'Scruffy' Longton was 27, and had already been decorated with the Air Force Cross for his work as a test pilot. Finally getting away from test flying he had been posted to 85, and would be among a very few WW1 airmen to receive the DFC and two Bars. He gained 11 victories and remained with the RAF post-war, only to die while taking part in an air race in 1927.

Another experienced pilot was George Clapham Dixon, a Canadian from Vancouver. He was 22 and his army service had been with the Highland Light Infantry. George had then become an observer with the RFC, flying in the back seat of Sopwith 1½ Strutters with 43 Squadron, and with his rear gun had downed two German fighters. Following pilot training

---

[1] *War Birds; Diary of an Unknown Aviator*, George H Doran & Co, 1926.

Mick with some of his 85 Squadron pilots; (left to right): John Dymond, Mannock, -?-, Lawrence Callaghan, and Walter Longton.

he had been sent to 85 where he would score two more victories before becoming a flight commander with Mannock's old 40 Squadron, and raise his score to nine before being wounded in September.

John Davis Canning came from Waipukurau, New Zealand and had just celebrated his 21st birthday on 1 July. The son of a farmer he came to England and joined the 4th North Staffs Regiment, transferring to the RFC in March 1916. He had already seen much action, firstly with 19 Squadron, flying Spads, then 48 Squadron, Bristol Fighters, and then 85, which he joined on 27 June. He would become a flight commander before returning to England in October 1918.

Others were Lieutenants John Dymond, another American, J C Rorison, who had arrived in June, Arthur Hector Ross Daniel, from South Africa, aged 26, and C B R MacDonald, another Canadian. Charles Beverley Robinson MacDonald was the son of Lieutenant-Colonel A C M MacDonald DSO. After service with the Canadian REs, he moved to aviation and had actually been with 74 TS in February and March 1918, so had already met Mannock. He joined 85 in May 1918 and despite a slight wound the day before Mannock was killed, became a flight commander and remained with 85 till the Armistice.

Douglas Carruthers came from Kingston, Ontario and was 26. A student at Queen's University in his home town he had joined the RFC in June 1916, and flown as an observer briefly before training as a pilot. He had gone to 29 Squadron in April 1917 but was hospitalised before the month was out. Joining 85 in March 1918 he soldiered on until made a flight commander with 24 Squadron in October.

Edward Cecil Brown, 23, came from Dartford, Kent and had been an engineering student for three years before taking a commission into the Royal West Kent Regiment. Transferred to the RFC in August 1917 he joined 85 in March 1918. He did not survive the war (shot down by AA fire, 18 October 1918).

Gordon David Brewster MC, aged 21, hailed from Forest Hill, SE London. He had won his Military Cross with the 3rd Regiment of the Bedfordshire Regiment, and despite the rank of captain, had moved to the RFC in December 1917, dropping rank to second-lieutenant. He arrived on 85 in mid-June. Colin Frank Abbott from Palmers Green, north London, wouldn't celebrate his 21st birthday until a month after the Armistice. A junior draughtsman in London till late 1915 he had joined the RFC as 10410, air mechanic 2nd class. After service overseas he returned in August 1917 to learn to fly and came to 85 in February 1918. As noted in the Prologue, Donald C Inglis DCM, hailed from New Zealand, was 25 years old and had won his Distinguished Conduct Medal at Gallipoli with the NZ artillery.

Another recent newcomer to the Squadron was John Weston Warner, from Boston Spa, Yorkshire. He had claimed his first victory on 29 June and by mid-August was to achieve seven more and be awarded the DFC. He was still only 19 when he was shot down and killed by a Fokker DVII on 4 October.

William Edward Wittrick Cushing was the Squadron's recording officer. At 26 he had a wife in Swaffam, Norfolk, and had been a school master for the last year of peace. An officer with the 9th Battalion of the Norfolk Regiment, he became an observer in BE2c machines with 13 Squadron, completing his time at the front in May 1917. He had become an RO and joined 85 in May 1918. Peter Rosie was the squadron engineering officer. At 42 he was the oldest officer in the unit and had a wife in Upper Largo, Fifeshire, Scotland. For ten years before the war he had been branch secretary to the Scottish Provident Institution, Dundee. Despite his age he joined the colours and became an officer with the Leicester Yeomanry, attached to the 3rd Reserve Battalion of the Hussars. He had then joined the RFC in August 1917. His engineering experience is not known, but he held down the job from once posted to the embryo 85 Squadron in November 1917, till the war's end. He was responsible for taking numerous photographs of squadron pilots while with 85, for which historians are thankful.

** **

Once he had settled in, Mannock chose SE5a E1295 with a 200 h.p. Wolseley Viper engine. It had been brought from No.1 Air Issues Depot (AID) on 20 June 1918 and while it had been worked on by the mechanics to bring it up to 85's standard, it had only been test flown thus far and not operationally. Mannock would fly this machine for the whole of his short time with the Squadron. As far as we can tell, no photograph of this machine has ever been seen, so its markings are unknown, other than it no doubt had the white hexagon that identified 85 Squadron, on the fuselage sides aft of the roundel. Nigger Horn, who had done much to hold the Squadron together during Bishop's period and while awaiting Mannock's arrival (while George Baker did the paperwork), had taken over Bishop's SE5, No. C1904, and flew it for the rest of his time on the Squadron. This machine was declared unfit for further service by late September due to its long service, and flown back to England was struck off charge in October. It had been marked with the letter 'Z', painted both beneath the cockpit and on the upper starboard wing. One has to wonder if Mannock used the letter 'Z' on his machine too, and that Horn's C1904 was re-marked with the letter 'A', so as to denote the leader of A Flight. Squadrons that used letters on their aeroplanes generally tended to use

85 Squadron's SE5s just prior to Mannock's arrival as CO.

the letters A to F, for A Flight, G to N, B Flight, and M to R for C Flight. Letters after R would go to spare machines (at least one squadron used 'S' for its CO), or to fill in if a squadron's complement exceeded the normal number of 18.

** **

Whatever Mick Mannock's state of mind upon his arrival back in France, he showed little sign of having a problem as he arrived at 85 Squadron. Several pilots have recorded that soon after he took over he had all the pilots in his office and outlined what he thought they should do. Although Springs's book *War Birds*, referred to above, is a fictionalised account of Grider's diary, he remarked on this meeting:

> 'Mannock has arrived to take charge all rigged out as a major with some new barnacles on his ribbons, and he certainly is keen. He got us all together in the office and outlined his plans and told each one what he expected of them. He's going to lead one flight and act as a decoy. Nigger and Randy are going to lead the other two. We ought to be able to pay back these Fokkers a little we owe them.'

The Fokker DVIIs were now a force to be reckoned with and 85 and Mannock got amongst some on 7 July, in their first action together. The Squadron mounted an Offensive Patrol to the area around Doulieu, between Merville and Bailleul. Mick led three SE5s as the bottom section, with Randall's Flight above, and Horn giving top cover. At 08.15 Horn saw seven Fokker biplanes at 18,000 feet above them, and he led the patrol towards the lines in a climb, the Fokkers following. The leading two Germans started a dive as Horn turned into them, and the other Germans joined in.

As the dog-fight began, Horn spotted two DVIIs get behind 'Scruffy' Longton. Horn went after one, his fire sending it down in a spin. He then got on the tail of the other and after giving it good bursts, followed it down to 8,000 feet at which point the Fokker's wings ripped away and the wreckage crashed near Steenwerck. Heading back into the mêlée that was continuing to the west of him, he dived into it and saw Longton despatch another DVII, seeing it crash at position, Sheet 36A F.14.

Longton had earlier attacked a DVII that was closing in on another SE5 but moments later he had those two other Fokkers right behind him.

Major Edward Mannock DSO MC, Officer Commanding 85 Squadron 1918.

He saw Horn intervene and shoot down the first one, and as Horn tangled with the other, Longton got in behind another, firing half a drum of Lewis into it from close range.

The German machine went down in a slow spiral from 2,000 feet but then he had to pull out to engage another DVII. Horn, however, saw it hit the ground.

John Warner had a go at another DVII after the initial clash, climbing up beneath a Fokker that he saw 500 feet above him. He missed with his first burst and the German pilot shoved his nose down and dived. Chasing after it, Warner fired again from both guns but was unable to catch it nor see if the pilot survived the dive into some low ground mist.

Mannock meantime, still below Horn's Flight, observed the encounter, and began to let down as the battling aircraft drifted lower to around 7,000 feet. He was attacked by a red-bodied DVII, but its pilot seemed to lose control and fall away. Mannock followed, firing as his sights came to bear and watched until it went vertically into the ground about a mile east of Doulieu.

Down now to around 1,500 feet, Mannock climbed for about 1,000 feet and saw an SE5 being engaged by two enemy machines. Going after the one nearest the tail of the SE he fired some 30 rounds from each gun and the DVII went into a spin at about 1,000 feet and he lost sight of it but felt sure it must have crashed. Longton later confirmed seeing the first one go down.

In their first air action under the new 'boss' four DVIIs were claimed destroyed, two more out of control, and another driven down. Unfortunately there does not appear to be any losses in German personnel this date, even though one of the DVIIs was seen to shed its wings. Nevertheless it was a boost for the Squadron, and Mannock's tactics seem to have been successful, even though it appears to have worked in reverse, with Horn being attacked above while still covering Mannock's boys below.

**

On the 9th the great Jimmy McCudden was killed. This was a bitter blow to Mannock and undoubtedly made him think yet again of his own mortality. It was no consolation to learn that McCudden had not fallen in combat, although by the same token it was galling to know that a simple flying accident had robbed the RAF of one its greatest air fighters. Who knows what he might have achieved had he lived? A future career within the service seemed assured.

Had McCudden, if Springs remembered it correctly, been given command of 85 Squadron, he would not have been flying out to his new command, 60 Squadron, at Boffles, on this July day. If he had not become lost and landed at Auxi-le-Château to ask for directions, he wouldn't have crashed after he had taken off again and his engine packed up. He then made the fatal error of turning back towards the airfield, stalled, and crashed. He lies buried in nearby Wavens cemetery.

On 10 July Longton knocked down a Hannover two-seater, aided by Lieutenant Dymond. This occurred at 06.50 and after the initial attacks, the propeller stopped and the two-seater glided down to crash at Sheet 36A L.7.

On the 13th, George Dixon, now a flight commander as George Baker was tour-expired, led an evening patrol and ran into several Fokkers and Pfalz Scouts near Armentières. He was leading a top cover section of three SEs (himself, Callahan and McGregor) and he led them down onto four Pfalz and his opening burst of 50 rounds sent one down in a spin. As the engagement now commenced in earnest, he attacked another Pfalz and saw it turn onto its back and go down vertically to crash near the canal to the east of the town, confirmed by Larry Callahan.

Callahan himself dived into the German fighter formation and his fire also sent one of the enemy down out of control (a Fokker) and he saw it crash near the town, as well as seeing

Dixon's victim crash nearby. These machines may have been from Jasta 20, who had three pilots shot down this day, whilst claiming one SE5 down by the front lines. 85 Squadron lost Lieutenant William Scott Robertson south-east of Armentières, who was killed. Bill Robertson came from Middlesborough, Yorkshire. He was brought down by Carl Degelow, leader of Jasta 40s.

There was a big fight early on the 14th. Mannock, with Randall's Flight, was flying north-east of Merville at 08.35 and encountered a mixed bag of German fighters – Fokker biplanes, Pfalz and Albatros Scouts. Mannock dived from 10,000 feet on the leader of two fighters but disengaged as he observed a Fokker – marked with a white horizontal swastika on its fuselage (in those days a good luck symbol) and a black and white tailplane – on the tail of an SE. He fought this machine down to 1,000 feet and watched as it crashed. Randall was able to confirm this.

The SEs now began to split up, but Randall got into a favourable position on a Pfalz with a yellow tail

Group of 85 Squadron pilots. Dymond and Longton sit in the front, while behind them in the RFC 'maternity' jacket and pipe, is Donald Inglis DCM, who would accompany Mannock on his last flight. To his left is G C Dixon with Spencer Horn almost out of shot. Behind Dixon is E C Brown, while behind Inglis is Lt Carruthers.

and fuselage, firing several bursts from both guns until, just north of Armentières, it went down and crashed. Seeing then Mannock's Fokker crash, he began to regain lost height.

Scruffy Longton had also dived into the German formation, following one as it zoomed away. He got in two good bursts at close range before his Vickers gun jammed. With his Lewis drum now empty, he could not follow up on his attack, but he then saw Randall in his SE5 marked with the letter 'H', chasing it over Armentières.

Lieutenant Rorison was flying with Dixon's Flight nearby and initially got onto the tail of a Pfalz as it streamed away from the main fight. Despite several bursts, he lost it as the battle spread around him, then another German dived on him from above. He turned quickly and engaged this EA (a Fokker) firing several bursts from close range while having descended to around 1,000 feet. The Fokker dived earthwards and later he saw debris on the ground in a field south-west of Estaires. He also noted that he had seen Dixon attack a white-tailed Pfalz and thought it was starting to go down out of control.

Some minutes after this scrap broke up, Mannock spotted a green mottled two-seater and went into the attack. Both Mannock and the German crew opened fire at the same time, and bullets slashed into Mannock's machine. As they passed by each other, the German turned north, began to side-slip, then turned over about a mile east of Merville and went down. Mannock watched as this two-seater made a reasonable landing down wind on some rough ground, but noting that it did not break up, and assumed its engine had been damaged in their head-on encounter.

Longton meantime, had also spotted a two-seater, an Albatros C. He had cleared his jam by now and replaced his empty Lewis drum and together with Randall, dived on the German, getting in several good bursts at close range. At 200 feet this second drum was emptied so he zoomed up to replace it once more. Randall observed the two-seater continue down and crash.

Randall had already had a brief encounter with a Hannover CLIII after the fighter battle, but it quickly made off east, followed by a quick burst from the SE5's guns. Randall then saw the Albatros two-seater with Longton's 'K' attacking, but after a quick burst, both of his guns jammed, so had to follow Longton as he proceeded to despatch the Albatros on his own.

Some of the Germans encountered were once again from Jasta 40s. Carl Degelow claimed an SE5 in this fight and other pilots also made claims but 85 only lost one pilot, Second-Lieutenant H N Marshall, who was brought down and made a prisoner. It was Degelow's 10th victory and some minutes later he made it 11 by claiming an SE5 of 64 Squadron too.

This action resulted in another four claims, plus a two-seater forced to land. Once again there are no positive German personnel losses on the fighter side and it is often difficult to pinpoint two-seater crew casualties. Nevertheless, 85 were no doubt again well pleased with their efforts under Mannock's leadership.

There was a bit of a lull in activity after the 14th with a lot of low cloud over France, rain and even thunderstorms. When this cleared on the 18th, strong wind hindered operations, and on the 19th the Germans kept away from the front. Most of the land action was taking place further south on the French front, the Jastas in the north merely keeping a watch along the trench lines.

However, Mannock claimed a victory on the 19th during another early morning patrol to the Merville area. At 08.35 he spotted an Albatros two-seater flying well over the lines near Estaires but heading west. He led the patrol to the north-east in order to get between the German and his home territory, then swooped round and down to attack the German head-on. Once within an acceptable distance he began firing, blasting 80 rounds from both guns down to point-blank range, from the front and then, having shot below the two-seater, from below. Almost immediately the Albatros caught fire and dived leaving a flaming trail, and crashed, still burning, at map reference, Sheet 36A.K.34b – the feat being witnessed by all members of the patrol.

This was a machine from Flieger-abteilung Nr.7, who lost a crew at Merville this date. The two men were Unteroffizier Alfred Hartmann, from Castrop, north of Dortmund, aged 21, and Leutnant Eberhard von Sydow, 20, from Halberstadt, south-west of Magdeburg, the latter being buried at Seclin.

The maestro scored again the next morning on what is described as a special mission and Offensive Patrol. The patrol was over Salome, east of La Bassée at 11.15, exploding AA fire attracting Mannock's attention to an enemy machine. He was not sure of the type, although in fact it was another Albatros C XII, and again from FA7. The Albatros company had given their type C XII two-seater a rounded fuselage, much like that of their fighters, rather than the old flat-sided ones, which may be why Mannock thought it different.

In any event, the patrol dived from 10,000 feet from the east and again Mannock opened fire from head-on, his favourite position against two-seaters, so as to avoid detection and fire from the observer in the rear. Shedding pieces of torn fabric, the Albatros plummeted down, its pilot no doubt wounded. At 4,000 feet the machine seemed to flatten out, turned north, then vertically to the south and crashed near Illies, north-east of La Bassée, after some moments during which it seemed to float before finally crashing.

Continuing the patrol, an hour later, while south of Steenwerck, three Fokker DVIIs, with black fuselages, checkered wings and white tails, hove into view at 10,000 feet near Merville. Mannock led an attack from the east while others approached from the west. Following a close action combat, Mannock's fire sent one Fokker down out of control and trailing smoke, confirmed by Larry Callahan. More pressing encounters followed so nobody was able to see if the machine crashed. (While some German aircraft did have wings painted in a checkered fashion, it is more likely to have been lozenge fabric which they used on their aircraft increasingly in 1918.)

The FA7 crew, who both died in the first action, had been Unteroffizier Adolf Raths, aged 28, from Dalliendorf, and Leutnant Gross, who, if his name has been spelt correctly, has not yet been further identified.

**

Gwilym Lewis with 40 Squadron, had just been notified of the award of the DFC – the RAF's equivalent of the MC. He was about to go home on rest, and in his diary for 21 July he mentions a party in his honour that had occurred the previous evening:

'Last night I had my farewell dinner. Mick Mannock was there with two of his flight commanders, and also several members of the Brigade. It was a great binge. I feel awfully rotten leaving my priceless Flight. I am awfully pleased that I have had the luck not to lose a single fellow while I have been here, though two went down when I was on leave. Mac [McElroy] I believe thinks it is rather a bad sign, but I am truly thankful! Anyway, before he arrived B Flight led in the number of Huns from the new year. Now I tell Mac that while he counts the number he has shot down, I count the number I see. I believe he is still ahead! He has reached 47 now!' [1]

Gwylim Lewis DFC and George McElroy MC DFC, 40 Squadron in 1918. Mac was a particular friend of Mannock and was killed within a week of Mick's own demise.

[1] Actually 44 as at this date.

It was Mannock again who added to 85's laurels, on the 22nd. Shortly before 09.30 am, leading a patrol, he ran into five Fokker Triplanes near Steenwerck at 14,500 feet. These machines attempted to attack the SE5 patrol from behind, but Mannock's keen eyes had seen the danger, and pulled out of trouble. Part of the Flight now flew to the north-west, while the top three went to the north-east. This was another tactic introduced by Mannock, splitting the patrol in two in order to 'surround' the enemy, or at least, give him two groups of SE5s to watch out for, one on each side.

Mannock also began to climb towards Lille where the Triplanes were now headed, and intercepted them over Armentières. He fired tentatively at several of the three-winged fighters, following one into some clouds and on coming out the other side, and down to around 11,000 feet, shot the tail off it, confirmed by Lieutenant Dymond.

This seems like a certain victory, as Triplanes without a tail did not generally survive from a height of 11,000 feet! It was a day of heavy fighting and the Germans did lose a handful of fighter pilots. The most likely candidate for Mannock's victim would be Vizefeldwebel Emil Soltau of Jasta 20. He was reported lost over Gheluvelt, although this seems a bit too far north to be certain. Mannock noted the Dr.Is had brown and green mottling, and Jasta 20 were known to have brown fuselages. Soltau was 26 and came from Barsbüttel.

Ira Jones and Mannock often spoke to each other on the telephone. Jones had taken over Mick's A Flight after he had left. They would each try to pull the other's leg and Mick was becoming even more fatalistic about his future. In some ways he was masking this by over-emphasising men and machines going down in flames, as if obsessed by this terrible way to die. Generals and politicians at the top still doggedly kept to their decision not to supply parachutes to airmen – in case they became less aggressive and baled out if in trouble! Balloon observers had them, so why not pilots and observers in aeroplanes? It would make them more aggressive, not less, knowing that if things did go wrong, at least they had an escape route. Men like Jones and Mannock had seen many friends and comrades die a needless death in the fiery death-trap of a burning aeroplane. Jones wrote in his diary for the 24th, after having increased his own score to 26 with three DFW two-seaters shot down that day:

> 'I phoned Mick to pull his leg. He retaliated to my banter by asking me to have lunch and tea with him tomorrow to explain my methods. Silly ass!

> 'He told me he had shot a Tripe's tail off a couple of days ago over Lille. Some lad is our Mick. I often wonder whether he will live to get his century. Personally, I can't visualise a Hun getting him down, unless by accident, although it does look as if death cometh sooner or later to all the star fighters. Mine will come like the rest, I suppose. Well, I shall be quite ready. My only regret will be leaving my dear old mother behind to mourn me. Mothers have a tough time in wars.'

Mannock's boys had had a good day on the 24th, with another four fighters claimed as destroyed and another out of control. They were again out in two layers, the lower Flight acting as decoy. Once they found enemy aircraft, the top Flight attacked from the east, in Mannock fashion.

It was mid-morning, north-west of Armentières. Mac McGregor was leading the top Flight of four SE5s and manoeuvred east of the Fokker DVIIs they had spotted as they edged towards Randall's lower bunch. Mac dived and opened fire on one DVII from point blank range. The German, stung by the surprise attack, zoomed away and then began to go down in a wide spiral with its propeller stopped. Mac then saw another German behind the SE of Lieutenant D C Inglis, and attacking this at close range, saved the New Zealander, and was able to see his target go down and crash.

Lieutenant O A Ralston, another American with the Squadron, also went down on the six Fokkers as they began to head for Randall's men. He fired at close range at a DVII from one side, then attacked another from the rear. The second machine went down, diving over the vertical and Orville Ralston followed it to 4,000 feet then pulled round and watched it hit the ground.

Snowy Randall had seen the Fokkers above and had headed north towards Dickebusch, then south-east, losing height all the time. Meantime he could see McGregor's section coming round to attack from the east, then dive. One DVII started to fall, trailing smoke and Randall went after it, firing with both guns. It continued down to crash.

Longton was also in the lower section and saw the approaching Huns and as the attack developed, he turned and clamped himself onto the tail of a yellow-coloured Pfalz Scout. His fire caused it to go down and crash, followed quickly by another crash, the Fokker downed by McGregor.

Mannock was not on this patrol, but it is obvious his pilots had learnt this lessons and followed his doctrine to secure another victory over enemy fighters. His three flight commanders, Horn, Randall and McGregor were more than competent to lead the patrols and give Mick a rest. Whether he would take it would be another matter.

Jones accepted Mannock's offer of a visit on the 25th, a showery day with enemy activity down to a minimum. Down south the French front remained busy. Jones took Mick's old wingman, Clem Clements with him. Jones wrote in his diary:

Captain A C 'Snowy' Randall, 85 Squadron.

'On the afternoon of the 25th, Clements and I went over by car to St Omer Aerodrome to spend the afternoon and evening with our idol and friend. As ever, he was the personification of liveliness in the Mess. His pilots also were in high spirits; their successes over the enemy and their happiness as a family made them so. Whomsoever we spoke to, we heard little else but talk of their offensive patrols and of Mannock's wonderful leadership. The morale of the Squadron had reached its peak. The enemy was spoken of as so much dirt. Mannock was delighted.

'Whilst we were having tea on the grass outside the Mess, a couple of very pretty VAD nurses from the Duchess of Sutherland's hospital, located nearby, arrived to have tea with Mannock. This pleasant feminine touch added considerably to the enjoyment of the meal. The conversation naturally veered round to Hun-strafing, and as Mannock was explaining, amid roars of laughter, what it felt like to be shot down in flames, he suddenly said to a little New Zealander who was a comparatively new arrival: "Have you got a Hun yet, Inglis?" "No, Sir," was the shy and almost ashamed reply. "Well, come on out and we will get one."

'Rising and asking to be excused for "a few minutes", off he and his happy comrade went towards the aerodrome. With their machines ready to take off the leader gave the signal to taxi out, and in a few seconds he was in the air. His young companion, however, suddenly discovered to his dismay, that the elevator wheel of his machine was jammed tight, and on examination it was found that the machine would not be able to fly after all.

'Mannock circled once, then realised that Inglis was not going to join him, and set off alone for the lines. While he was away, the young pilot cursed, swore, worried, and walked up and down in front of the hangars impatiently waiting for the Master's return, secretly fearing he might not. Nearly two hours later an SE with a red streamer glided gently into the aerodrome, and young Inglis was happy once again. When he told Mannock what had happened, the mechanic was severely reproved for his carelessness, but as he was a good man, no disciplinary action was taken. The disappointed pilot was told not to worry, and that he would be taken out at dawn the following morning.'

Accompanying his friend to his hut, Jones continued:

'Once inside, I asked him how he felt; he then frankly told me that he thought that he would not last much longer. Suddenly he put his arms upon my shoulders, and looking me straight in the eyes with a suggestion of a tear in his, he said in a broken voice: "Old lad, if I am killed I shall be in good company. I feel I have done my duty."'

Clements, however, did not notice any problem with his friend, and amateur air historian Douglass Whetton, recorded in an article, that Clements had told him:

'I do not recall that he was depressed or in any way out of sorts. On the contrary he was quite cheerful, and did not mention in my hearing any morbid thoughts about being shot down.'

In the same article, Whetton quoted Keith Caldwell as saying that at this time Mannock was at the top of his form.

**

Mannock's victory score by a reasonable count on the morning of 26 July 1918 stood at approximately 60. According to most observers he was now living on his nerves, but to many others he was still the consummate fighter pilot, keen to get the war won, and although not what one might call a 'born killer', he had a burning hatred towards all Germans who had inflicted this mighty hurt and slaughter on civilisation.

Just as one might speculate what might have happened had McCudden not lost his way and made that extra landing, one can also wonder what might have occurred had Inglis's SE5 not have had that mechanical failure the previous afternoon. Would they have found a Hun for the New Zealander? If they had, Mannock would not be taking off at first light on this morning so as to escort the youngster out, and consequently, would not have met his end. At least, not on the fateful 26th.

The facts of this, Mannock's last sortie, are clear and well known. We will quote from Donald Inglis's combat report rather than paraphrase the events. The sortie was listed as a special mission, in other words, not an offensive patrol, or a line patrol, or an escort job, but a one-off operation. Mannock led off in his E1295, Inglis flying in E1294. They headed for the front line, hoping to catch either an early German recce machine, or a trench-strafer. Perhaps even an early fighter pilot having a stab at the British balloon lines. They came across a two-seater, and as far as Inglis was concerned, its actual type could not be defined. He later wrote in his report:

> 'While following Major Mannock in search of two-seater EA's we observed an EA two-seater coming towards the Line and turned away to gain height, and dived to get east of EA. EA saw us just too soon and turned east. Major Mannock turned and got in a good burst when he pulled away. I got in a good burst at very close range after which EA went into a slow left hand spiral with flames coming out of his right side. I watched him go straight into the ground and go up in a large cloud of black smoke and flame.

> 'I then turned and followed Major Mannock back at about 200 feet. About half way back I saw a flame come out of the right hand side of his machine after which he apparently went down out of control. I went into a spiral down to 50 feet and saw machine go straight into the ground and burn. I saw no one leave the machine and then started for the line climbing slightly; at about 150 feet there was a bang and I was smothered in petrol, my engine cut out so I switched off and made a landing 5 yards behind our front line.'

The action had taken place south of Lestrem, south-east of Merville, not far from Pacault Wood. The German machine was from Bavarian FA292(A), its crew perishing in the crash. They were Vizefeldwebel Josef Hein and his observer Leutnant Ludwig Schöpf. The Germans gave the crash position as La Croix Marmuse (some way east of the village of Pacault). Hein came from Dortmund and was 24 years old. Schöpf also was 24 and from Pfaffenhausen, south of Ulm. Fleiger-abteilung 292(A) made the following report on their loss:

> 'On 26 July 1918 the crew of Vfw Hein and Ltn Schöpf (DFW CV 2216/18) left at 5.45 am [04.45 British time] on an Artillery Observation Flight. Owing to low cloud they flew at low altitude. At 6.39 am [05.39 British time] they were attacked by an enemy scout which dived on them from the cover of clouds. During the combat the DFW was shot down in flames near Croix Marmuse [sic], south-west of Lestrem.'

A report by the 55th German Army Corps noted:

> 'At approximately 7 am a German aircraft was shot down by two British airmen in the area of Colonne [sic]. Both Englishmen were shot down by machine gun fire, the first aircraft, on fire, crashed in the locality of the 100th Infantry Regiment; the second aircraft fell between the lines. The pilot of the first aircraft is dead, the fate of the second pilot is unknown.'

The graves of Mannock's victims from his last air fight on 26 July 1918, Ltn Ludwig Schöpf and Vfw Josef Hein, of FA(A)/292. Billy-Berclau German cemetery, north of Lens.

Today both German airmen lie in Billy-Berclau cemetery, to the south-east of La Bassée, an extension to the town cemetery, at the rear of the German grave markers in the top left-hand corner, the crosses numbered 7/321 and 7/331.

* *

It has always been assumed that Mannock had been foolish in following down his last victim, thereby putting himself in range of ground fire. He invariably berated others for doing so, and continually warned against this stupidity. We shall, of course, never know why he did so on this occasion, but the fact remains that he did. But was there another motive? It may well be that he intended to shoot-up enemy trenches, or the German troops he knew to be in the northern half of Pacault Wood.

This had been done before, not the least by a Camel pilot with 4 Squadron, Australian Flying Corps. On 22 July – just four days earlier – Lieutenant R Moore had been part of a two-man patrol and at around 16.15 that afternoon, he had shot down a German two-seater near Pacault Wood, and had likewise pursued it earthwards. Meantime, Moore's companion, Lieutenant O B Ramsey had dived down and amused himself by firing into the Germans in the Pacault Wood trenches who were watching the incident.

Then, on the 28th, just two days after Mannock's fall, another 4 AFC Camel pilot, Lieutenant M T G Cottam, led five aircraft to low-bomb Lestrem. Returning to the lines, these pilots flew over Pacault Wood and loosed-off 1,400 rounds into the trenches there.

Meantime, 85 Squadron's equipment officer, Lieutenant Rosie, had been sent out to try and retrieve the SE5 flown by Inglis. This proved impossible as Rosie recorded in a memo to No.11 Wing HQ:

S.E.5A E.1294

I personally made an endeavour with a party of men to salve the above machine last night. I got to within 600 yards of its position, but owing to very heavy shell fire on the only available road, it was quite impossible to reach machine without serious loss of life. I am getting in touch with the O.C. Infantry Unit near the spot with a view to finding out present condition of machine.

In the Field
27.7.18.

P Rosie
Lieut.
Equipment Officer,
For O.C. No.85 Squadron, R.A.F.

Captain Randall had already sent off an Army Form W3347 for each missing machine to Wing Headquarters requesting the two missing SE5s be struck off squadron strength and with the agreement of the Wing CO, Brigadier-General T Webb Bowen, the brigade commander, duly concurred a couple of days later.

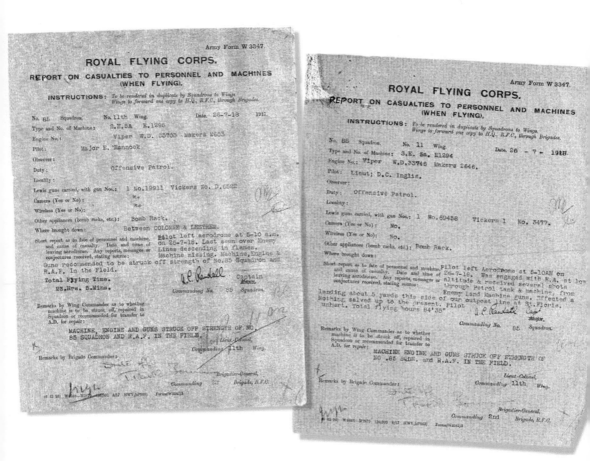

CHAPTER TEN

REGRET TO INFORM YOU…

The telegram sent to Mick's mother and addressed to 96 Ettington Road, Aston, Birmingham, was dated 29 July 1918. It was flat and formal, one of thousands just like it sent to parents, wives, brothers, or whatever next of kin was recorded in the dead man's file.

> 'Regret to inform you that Major E Mannock DSO MC RAF, is reported missing on July twenty-sixth. Letter follows.'

That same date a letter was sent to Mick's brother Patrick, at 13 Albert Road, Dover, giving him the same information. Patrick of course was in France, Private Mannock P, Tank Corps, BEF, so it was received and opened by his wife Dorothy. It did not take long for sister Jess to receive the news, living at 14 Rockview Street, Belfast.

Hope quickly faded that Mick might have survived although naturally the family members clung to that hope. As far as Donald Inglis had said, nobody had emerged from the burning crashed SE5 and everyone assumed the worst from the start.

Malcolm 'Mac' McGregor, one of his flight commanders, wrote at the time:

> 'We have lost our squadron commander. Went down in flames after getting over 70 Huns, and so the Royal Air Force has lost the best leader of patrols, and the best Hun getter it has had. In another month he would have had over 100. However, unlike other stars, he left behind all the knowledge he had, so it is up to the fellows he taught, to carry on.
>
> 'I was with him a few days ago when he shot down what turned out to be one of the crack Hun airmen [sic]. It all happened 25 miles across the lines, over a Hun aerodrome; and it was a pretty sight to see the way the Bosche handled his Triplane, pretty little thing, all black with a white tail. Although he put up a good fight he had somebody better after him, and it was not long before the Major got his position for a few seconds and, with both guns going, shot off his tail.'

Of interest is McGregor's assertion that Mannock's score was over 70.

Ira Jones too was shocked. Just the previous afternoon he and Clements had been laughing and joking with him at St Omer, whilst enjoying his company:

> 'July 26th – Mick is dead. Everyone is stunned. No one can believe it. I can write no more today. It is too terrible. Just off with Grid to 85 to try and cheer the lads up.
>
> 'July 27th – I can now realise how the Hun air force felt when they heard that Boelcke or Richthofen was killed. Mick's death is a terrible blow. We in 74 knew him better than

anyone. I have a deep aching void in my breast. I keep repeating to myself: "It can't be true. Mick cannot be dead." Yet dead I know he is.

'I flew over the charred remains of his machine yesterday morning. It lay between Estaires and Calonne. It got its position from Captain A G Randall, now in charge of 85.' [temporary – Captain Horn was on leave]

As far as Jones was concerned now it was up to him to seek revenge for Mick's death, writing: 'The apex of my desire for revenge has now been reached. To avenge Mick will be sweet. I shall never rest content now. "Kill or be killed" only can be my motto.'

Another letter survives, one written by 40 Squadron's padre, Bernard W Keymer, to Mannock's brother. It was dated 28 July, Keymer now being with Headquarters RAF, in France:

My dear Sir,

I feel I must write and tell you how grieved I am to hear of your brother's death. There are few men out here who I have known better and was more fond of then 'Edward' or 'Mick' as we called him.

I was padre with 40 Sq. when he joined it last year and have known him intimately during the whole of his wonderful career in France.

We were very close friends and I shall miss him more than words can say. I know him not only for the most dashing brave and clever pilot that the R.F.C. has ever produced, but also for 'one of the very best', and that is saying a good deal where the R.F.C. is concerned.

Only a week ago last night I sat next to him at dinner at 40 Sq. and we talked of the old days of '40' and of the future. And now he has gone, and I can scarcely believe it possible.

He was always so keenly interested in my work and used to attend my services very regularly. How we shall miss his kindly ways and irrepressible humour, but I trust we shall meet him again, and at least he has gone into wonderfully good company.

With most sincere sympathy,
Yours faithfully,
(Rev. Bernard W Keymer. C.F.)

There was also a letter to brother Patrick, from the Squadron recording officer, Lieutenant W E W Cushing:

Please accept the deepest sympathy from a whole squadron mourning a brave man and the best of comrades. There was no man or officer in the squadron but loved him for his bravery, for his cheerfulness, for his skill, for his patience in teaching others, and for his personality, which made him at once the most efficient and most popular Commanding Officer in France.

He was a friend to us all and had a great affection for the personnel of the squadron, which had he lived would have made the most famous flying squadron in the world, for he was endowed with the spirit of leadership, and any of his pilots would cheerfully follow him, no matter where he led.

I speak as if there was a spark of hope that he is alive; that is hardly true, but I am sorry to say the chance is one in a thousand. I will, however, inform you immediately we have any further news.

Again let me assure you of the real sympathy of all the officers and men of this squadron with whom he came in contact, for he was beloved by all.

Yours faithfully,
W E H Cushing, Lieutenant.

The following month, Mick's cousin Patrick had contacted 85 Squadron to ask for any further news. Lieutenant Cushing replied on 7 August:

Dear Sir,

I am in receipt of your letter dated August 3rd. I have already written to Major Mannock's brother, who has answered my letter.

I think I can tell you all you wish to know, but I was not an eye-witness. Only one officer was with him at the time, Lt. D.C.Inglis, who is at present on leave, and is due to return on the 14th August. You might be able to communicate with this officer at the following address (but I am not certain of this). Dr Lewis Hawkes, 2 Clifton Hall, St John's Wood, London, NW8.

At all events, this is what happened. At 5 am on July 26th Major Mannock left the ground in company with Lieut. Inglis; they drove down a hostile machine in flames, about 5.30 am, the fight finishing at a height of 200 feet over enemy territory. They then turned towards our own line, and had covered half the distance when Inglis noticed flame coming from Major Mannock's machine, which at once fell uncontrolled to the ground. Inglis spiralled down to fifty feet hoping that he would see Major Mannock climb out of his machine, but the S.E. was so completely obscured in smoke and flame as to render it impossible to see anything. Inglis then left for our lines and was himself shot down, but landed unhurt just inside our front line.

Under the circumstances it is useless to tell you that there is a chance of Mick being alive; it is such a remote hope that it would only raise false hopes. I should like to repeat what I wrote to his brother, that we all loved him; and no one of us but mourned him both as a friend and a chief. One could not wish for a more loveable, thoughtful or energetic leader. Please accept sincerest sympathy from 85 Squadron.

Yours faithfully,
W E H Cushing, Lieut.

* *

In due time, Mick Mannock's death was both assumed and presumed. Even before this his mother, now giving her address as 15 Witton Road, Near Sixways, Aston, Birmingham, wrote to Air Ministry at the end of August asking about a pension due to the loss of her son. Obviously reading about the death, a cousin, Charles M Mannock from Sheffield, also wrote to Air Ministry, requesting the address of Mick's mother.

Things moved on. The war ended, an Armistice was signed, signalling the close of hostilities at 11 am, November 11th, 1918. Peace came again to the world as it did to shattered France and Belgium. The men started to return home – those that were able. Mick Mannock, along with millions of others remained forever in a foreign field.

In February 1919, Mrs Mannock received a letter, but it did not carry any remuneration or even the suggestion of one. It was purely about an honour:

'I am directed to inform you that at the request of the RAC [1], London, a Diploma and Medal have today been despatched under separate cover to you, which have been awarded by the American Club to Major E Mannock DSO MC, of the RAF.'

Similar letters also went to the next of kin of Major J T B McCudden VC DSO MC MM CdG, and to Major R S Dallas DSO DSC.

One further honour awaited the man whom Ira Jones dubbed the 'King of Air Fighters'. Jones himself was one of the main agitators who began to make noises about Mannock being awarded a posthumous Victoria Cross. Finally the Air Minister of the time, the Right Honourable Winston Churchill ordered an investigation into the claims of these fellow airmen about their dead comrade.

On 20 June 1919, Air Ministry wrote to the General Officer Commanding the RAF, Army of the Rhine:

'Will you please let the Secretary of State have a full statement of service of late Major Edward Mannock including combat reports, *stop*. This is with special reference to services rendered subsequent to 16th June 1918, *stop*. Please state when forwarding report if such services merit consideration for award of Victoria Cross, *stop*.'

Obviously the GOC replied, and on 1 July 1919 a further telegram was on its way to him from Air Ministry:

'…. can you state the total number of enemy machines actually destroyed by him and also the total number driven down out of control, *stop*. According to *London Gazette* 3 August 1918 – Second Bar to DSO to 16 June = 48. According to combat reports received from you today, seven machines destroyed and four out of control after the fight of 16 June. It is important these figures are checked, *stop*.'

Considering that the Victoria Cross was sanctioned, and appeared in the *London Gazette* dated 18 July 1919, the matter had been quickly decided, the King given the recommendation to approve, and this, Britain's highest gallantry award, announced, in around two weeks. The victory total finally agreed for inclusion in the citation was 50. At the end of the *Gazette* announcement there was an attempt to clarify the position by noting that the total victories recorded in the citation for Mannock's second bar to his DSO, was incorrectly given as 48, instead of 41.

Just why this was changed is, of course at this stage, unclear. If 48 had not been adjusted, and Air Ministry had added the GOC's additional figure of 11 victories (i.e. seven destroyed and four out of control) the total would have been shown as 59, rather than 52, when the

[1] Royal Aero Club.

lower figure of 41, was added to the 11. Perhaps someone felt that a nice round figure of 50 seemed appropriate.

No sooner had this Victoria Cross been announced than Mannock's father, so long out of the picture since abandoning his family so many years previously, suddenly emerged (and from a bigamous marriage), writing to Air Ministry on 19 August 1919, from his home at 29 Siebert Road, Westcombe Park, Blackheath, south-east London, asking that if the death of his son Edward had now been officially presumed, was there a will or testament left by him or known to be in existence?

Air Ministry presumably replied with what information they had, namely that his son's death had now been officially presumed and that [if indeed there was a will as most soldiers were urged to leave] anything left by him would have gone to Major Mannock's mother. Not to be left totally empty-handed, the former corporal wrote again on 23 August:

> 'Please be good enough to inform me what steps are necessary for me – the above officer's father – to claim his Victoria Cross and 'tother decorations'?

** *

So, what sort of man was Major Edward Mannock. Many people and biographers have written of what they knew, or what they learnt, or in some cases, what they felt their readers might wish to read. Anyone can begin to think they understand someone they have never met, and take what those who did know him, as gospel. This is fine, that is the way of things. We prefer to leave it to the words of Keith Logan Caldwell, his wartime commanding officer in 74 Squadron, whose words, clear and precise on that 1964 tape recording, are good enough for us to understand Mick Mannock the air fighter. He as much as anybody would have been happy to say he knew what Mannock was like as a fighter pilot. Whether he or indeed anyone could really have known what was in Mick's heart is not so clear. We all hope to know ourselves, but do we truly let other people know what we think we are, or let them even think they know?

Mick found his niche in history in the cockpit of a fighter aeroplane in the first air war that started in 1914 and reached a certain pinnacle in 1918. In those four short years the aeroplane developed amazingly fast, and so did man's ability to use this third dimension. Men such as Mick Mannock could have had absolutely no idea in 1914 that within a very short space of time they could not only fly, but would have been able to learn about life and death in the air, adapt to and sometimes develop tactics in an equally short space of time. We read of these men today, and not only fighter pilots, but bomber pilots, reconnaissance pilots, etc. Sometimes one tends to forget at this distance, just how quickly events happened between 1914-18, and it is easy to see these men as vastly experienced, but if they lived long enough to gain this fleeting experience, it had been acquired in weeks, sometimes months. They lived by what they learnt and died if they made a mistake.

Keith Caldwell on Mannock:

> 'Mannock was said to be blind in one eye – I've read that quite often – and to be a fervent Hun-hater. Neither was quite true. Certainly the sight in one eye wasn't as strong as in the other, but there certainly wasn't blindness. This hatred attributed to him I don't believe was true. It was calculated, or assumed, to bolster up his own morale. Remember, Mannock was getting on for 33 [31 actually] and being a sensitive sort of chap, this calculated hatred for the Hun did boost up the morale of everyone in the Squadron. That

was the sort of war-going outlook it rather paid to have, one felt. Mannock was a very human chap, he didn't hate people or things at all really.

'Why was he so successful? It is very hard to shoot down an elusive aeroplane [whose pilot] is trying to avoid being hit; after all the target area is either the pilot or the petrol tank, but Mannock was an extraordinary good shot, and a very good strategist. I think his success came from these qualities, to make a good approach and when he got there to be a very good shot, in quickly and not to delay too long. Mannock didn't like being shot at more than anybody else did and he usually had the advantage when he went into a fight. After all, he was by this time [when he was with 74] a very, very experienced man and he very rarely had holes in his aeroplane – unlike others. He did not take un-necessary risks either.

'His friends could not imagine him falling to an enemy airman, and so it was to be. He was awarded the DSO and Bar while with 74 Squadron, and then of course his promotion, which was expected, which came, and our loss was 85 Squadron's gain, where he became CO. Again his influence was soon established with his new command, and up went the standards under his leadership and the example that he gave.

'What has often been written about Mannock is very true, that he did spare time and patience to build confidence in his new chaps. It was doing just this that brought about his end.'

Mannock had made a mistake. Against his own earnest doctrine, he had allowed himself to become distracted and paid the price he knew would be charged. Even if his intention had been to strafe German positions, he was still courting un-necessary danger. Shortly before his death, he had dined with his old friend George McElroy, himself by now a high-scoring ace, firstly with 40 Squadron, then with 24 Squadron, and finally back with 40 Squadron.

It was a farewell dinner for Gwilym Lewis who was going back to England for a rest. Both Mannock and McElroy attended and during the evening had chided each other for being too aggressive in 'their old age' and for going down too low after Huns, despite both of them admonishing others for doing so. Yet just six days after Mannock had died, Mac had made the same mistake and had been killed by ground fire following down what would have been his 47th victory. It had also been within a short distance of where Mannock had crashed. McCudden made a mistake too, and died in trying to make a turn back to an aerodrome when his engine cut. He knew he should not do so, but it only takes a moment to make the wrong decision. To believe one is invincible. The RAF lost three powerful air fighters and leaders during that month of July. They were sadly missed, but there were always others to follow their lead.

CHAPTER ELEVEN

HE MUST REMAIN MISSING

An inevitable consequence of the disappearance or death of famous personalities will be debate and controversy surrounding the circumstances of those events if they are not clear cut and final. We need to look no further, for example, than the assassination of John F Kennedy, the disappearance of Lord Lucan or the death of Princess Diana, to amply illustrate that point. The demise of famous aviators too has often led to intense speculation, and into this category the fate of the Red Baron is arguably the most notable example. What happened to Major Mick Mannock when he was brought down and killed has been no less hotly debated over the years.

View looking towards the La Bassée Canal (seen as a white line beyond the foreground trees). The building on the left was known as Hate Farm in WW1.

When Lieutenant Donald Inglis finally got back to the airfield at St Omer after that momentous dawn patrol of 26 July 1918, his testimony was clear and concise. Later, it became a matter of public record although he was not the only witness to Mannock's loss. Private Edward Naulls was a soldier in the front line between Mont Bernenchon and Pacault Wood from where he watched from his position on the ground somewhere near Hate Farm. He often spoke of the event, and in 1960, he wrote an account of what he had witnessed:

'On the 26 July 1918, I was with "D" Company, 2nd Battalion of the Essex Regiment, in the front line between Mont Bernenchon and Pacault Wood, on the Lys Sector of the Western Front. Stand-down was at 5 am. Shortly afterwards a Jerry monoplane (*sic*) appeared over no-man's-land, cruising to and fro. A little while later two British fighter planes from St Omer aerodrome, one piloted by Major Mannock, the other by Lieutenant Inglis, a New Zealander, arrived on the scene and engaged the Jerry in combat. A few bursts from their guns sent it crashing in flames behind Pacault Wood. Then Mannock dived to within forty feet of the ground. I think forty feet is a fair estimate because the trees in Pacault Wood were not more than thirty feet high and Mannock's plane cleared them by a few feet. Inglis circled at about a hundred feet.

'Suddenly there was a lot of rifle fire from the Jerry trenches, then a machine gun, using tracers, opened up and I saw tracers enter Mannock's engine on the port side. A bluish-white flame appeared and spread rapidly. Smoke and flames enveloped the engine and cockpit. The aircraft, engine still turning, making smoke rings, made a right –hand turn and came towards our lines, but just short of the line, it turned left over Pacault Wood and went down in a

The La Bassée Canal looking north towards Pacault Wood. It was from here that Edward Naulls saw Mannock fall on 26 July 1918.

This field, with the canal ahead and Pacault Wood beyond, was where Naulls's Regiment were positioned in July 1918.

long glide over the trees and beyond, gradually losing height until it [disappeared beyond the wood and] hit the ground in the direction of Merville. A column of black smoke shot up.

'Inglis started to climb away but his engine stalled – I distinctly heard it splutter twice before it stopped – and he force-landed just behind the front line held by a company of the Welsh Regiment near St Floris. We in the British front line had a grandstand view of the entire action and I would like to add that we knew the identities of the two airmen within an hour of the incident.'

Studying the war diary of the 2nd Battalion of the Essex Regiment, all appears routine and pretty quiet in the area where Naulls and his comrades saw the Mannock air action. Seeing aircraft in the sky was no longer a new and wonderful thing, so there was no reason to record an entry regarding this air fight however dramatic it had appeared.

The Regiment's situation had been very quiet for some days, although 'A' Company had made a night raid on enemy trenches on the 25th, but found no enemy soldiers to capture and bring back. The next day, Friday the 26th, the diary merely records:

'Situation unchanged. Casualties:- 3 other ranks reinforcements, 2 other ranks to FA. 5 other ranks wounded. 1 other rank to base for reporting. 1 other rank to England for commission.'

Naulls clearly believed he had seen a monoplane and maybe the angle and distance from which he viewed it made it appear so. In fact the German unit to which it belonged actually recorded the serial number of their aeroplane involved, 2216/18, which confirms it to be a two-seater DFW CV biplane, and this also corresponds to the two German graves of the lost crew.

It was difficult to change Naulls's belief in the aircraft type, although no one probably questioned him too closely. Frank Cheesman, an air historian, who as we shall read had much contact with Naulls, did show him a picture of a Junkers CL1 and Naulls confirmed this to be the type. Although the CL1 was put into production during the latter half of 1918 less than 50 had been built by the Armistice, and none appear to have been at the front. The highest serial number for the CL1 was 769/18.

In his account, Edward Naulls remained quite consistent over the next 25 years or so, neither over-embellishing nor amending his recollections. Frank Cheesman continued to put questions to him and his answers as to locations and the position from which he viewed the action hardly varied. By late 1971, Cheesman asked more questions, to which Naulls replied:

'The tail of Mannock's aircraft was towards us and we could see his port side. The nose was pointing in the direction of Merville and it was beginning to lift as Mannock was obviously beginning to rejoin Inglis when the tracers struck. The SE5 made two turns after it was hit and caught fire. It made a right-hand turn and came towards our lines, then it turned left and went down in a right-hand curve and then a long glide, gradually losing height until it [would have] hit the ground.' [NB. As it went lower it would have disappeared out of sight beyond Naulls's view, north of the wood. Ed.]

'Inglis's aircraft was broadside on to me, the nose pointing towards Lestrem. He was in the vicinity of Calonne-sur-la-Lys when Mannock's aircraft was hit. I did not actually see the Jerry machine gun that shot Mannock down, but did see the tracers. Searching my memory, the tracers came up over no-man's-land and just above eye level.'

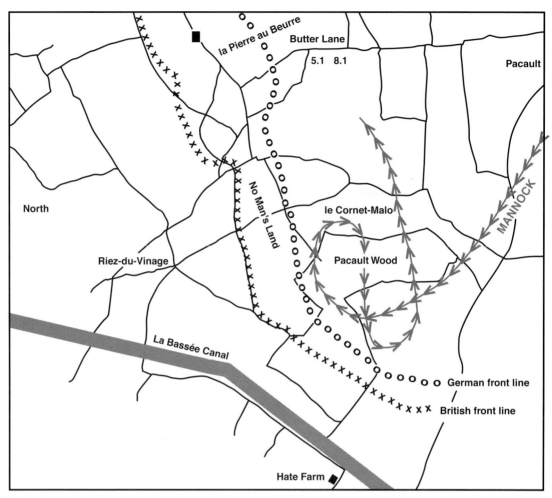

■ = Interpretation by WGC of German burial location of Major Mannock

Note how close 5.1 and 8.1 are together (just a few hundred yards). Very easy to confuse.

Where Mannock Came Down

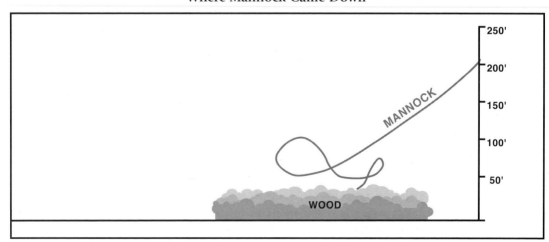

So, from the accounts of both Inglis and Naulls, we can see that Mannock certainly fell somewhere to the south of Calonne-sur-la-Lys, and, most probably from their evidence, in the triangle bounded by Calonne, St Floris and Le Cornet Malo, and apparently near to somewhere called La Pierre au Beurre. The clue to exactly where though, was provided by a German intelligence report (of which more later) that pinpointed his originally reported grave location. So, we can be sure exactly where Mannock was buried by the Germans in his original field grave. Or can we?

Certainly the general geographical location fits pretty neatly with that indicated by Inglis and Naulls although the reality is that we can now only be positive that the Germans confirmed his death and buried him. This is all. Unfortunately, the fog of war in 1918 has colluded with confusion throughout the intervening 90 years to draw a mysterious veil over what really became of his body and its subsequent burial place. In that time some have tried to make sense of the confusion, to examine the facts as they are known and to establish thereby the burial place of Major Mick Mannock VC DSO MC.

Mostly though, they have done so with incomplete information and this has sometimes led to heated debate, much of it speculative, about the possible location of his grave today. That said, and even with all known primary source material relating to the case being made available to the authors, it is still difficult to reach any absolute or definitive conclusion – although it is possible to reach one that is beyond reasonable doubt.

When examining the case of Major Mannock during the early 1980s, the Commonwealth War Graves Commission's chief records officer, Major T A Edwin Gibson MBE, wrote an internal report for CWGC suggesting the location of his grave to be in Laventie Military Cemetery, France, one marked as an 'Unknown British Airman'. This suggestion was later published by Gibson in the 1989 HMSO publication, *Courage Remembered*. This book had been written by him together with the Toronto-based military historian, G Kingsley Ward, and the Mannock story had thereby gained at least a quasi-official stamp of approval and credibility. That said, it is not the first time the theory of the Laventie grave had been aired as it had been previously published by another author in 1981. However, it is fair to say that some of those published details, including maps (which incidentally, put two significant locations in the wrong place), were a little wide of the mark factually and also in how they had been interpreted. Nevertheless, that author did actually lead his readers to the Laventie grave and publicly suggested for the first time a possible link with Mannock. Surely, though, the key to the whole story must lie within the CWGC files that were examined by and reported upon by Edwin Gibson? Generally, such files are not open to public scrutiny but in 1993 fate took a hand when one of Mannock's great-nephews, Mr Peter Burden, became involved though a chance meeting with Andy Saunders.

Fascinated by the suggestion that his famous great-uncle's grave might after all be identifiable, Peter Burden set out to enquire of the CWGC what further information they might have. The response was disappointing. Despite the previously published assertions of Major Gibson, who had by this time retired, the CWGC stated on 3 November 1993, that they were '… (unable) to identify the report which Edwin Gibson had compiled.' His report, or at least the archive material that had led to it, was obviously crucial in taking forward any further investigation of the matter. Consequently, Mr Burden wrote to his MP asking for the file on his great-uncle to be made available for inspection and, within a short space of time, the CWGC 'E' File ('E' for Enquiry) on Mannock was copied and sent to him.

Upon inspection, this file contained all relevant papers dating from 1919 through to 1993, although Gibson's report was not in it. It may not have been unreasonable to expect that Major Gibson's report and recommendations relative to the Laventie grave would be found within this large file. Sadly, it was not. However, all the documents apparently used and inspected by Edwin Gibson were now available and thus it was possible to follow, in detail, exactly the same paper trail he had taken in order to analyse that archive material and to reach an independent conclusion.

**

From the very outset of any study of this archive material it is clear that considerable confusion understandably reigned immediately after WW1, and it is important to realise that Mannock was but one of millions of Commonwealth war dead. Of these, the majority had fallen in France and Belgium and amongst them were many thousands who remained unidentified, and thousands more with simply no known graves at all, having simply disappeared in the mayhem and confusion of shell-torn battlefields. Therefore, and despite his 'hero' status, establishing the location of Major Mannock's grave was afforded no special prominence in the work of the Imperial War Grave Commission (IWGC) as it was known then, or of the Graves Registration Service in the massive amount of work they were then undertaking.

This work included locating and recording the graves of service personnel and in the examination, identification and then re-burial of the dead from field graves. In this respect, each man was dealt with on the basis of equality in death of all ranks from private to field-marshal – one of the tenets of War Graves Commission policy. In the case of Mannock, though, his long-time friend Jim Eyles became a constant correspondent and visitor to the War Graves Commission offices in the immediate post-war years. Tenaciously he harried the authorities for news as to the location of his friend's resting place, and it was the constant badgering of the commission by him that has enabled subsequent examination of the salient points surrounding the case and to re-appraise it in almost microscopic detail. Were it not for Eyles, then it is very likely that Mannock's place in War Graves Commission records might be restricted to a single entry on a casualty card and the bland recording of his name on the Arras Memorial to missing World War One flying personnel of the Commonwealth. Instead, a weighty E File now exists in the CWGC Maidenhead HQ, thus making it possible to take up Jim Eyles's long forgotten campaign. Significantly, it is correspondence from Eyles on 5 January 1919, that opens the Mannock E File.

**

At this stage, Eyles was simply enquiring as to the location of Mannock's grave and no doubt he expected a simple answer and to be told where it was. His request for information must have been but one of countless thousands received at that time from relatives and friends of war dead, but it sparked a paper chase that led to a more detailed examination of Mannock's loss than might otherwise have been the case.

Initially, though, the War Graves Commission wrote to him in March 1919 with what might be described as a holding letter, stating that the grave had not yet been found, and '… in the final clearing up of the battlefields it is expected that the identity of many unknown graves will be established, and in addition many graves will be found which to date have not been reported and registered by (my) Officers.' Thus some crumbs of comfort and hope were offered to Eyles who waited patiently until August of the following year before enquiring again if any news was yet to hand. In the event, it wasn't, but it did prompt the war graves service to write to the Air Ministry asking if they might have information as to the whereabouts of Mannock's grave.

They replied that they didn't have such information, though, and were only able to confirm the rough geographical location of his loss although for the first time it did spark enquiries to be made, on this occasion by the War Office, with the Directorate of War Graves Registration & Enquiries office in the German capital of Berlin. Crucially, the directorate were able to respond with what would be the first tangible clue to link Mannock with a positive field grave location, albeit that it then confused rather than helped to clarify the place of his actual burial.

Responding to the War Office in November 1920, Captain F G Wilson wrote saying that the information contained in a report of an intelligence officer of the German 6th Army, quoted the following, apparently translated directly from the German report:

> 'Flight Captain [sic] Mannock, 85th Squadron RAF, was shot down on 28 July 1918 [sic]. Machine crashed in flames. Body recovered and buried 300 metres NW of La-Pierre-au-Beurre on the road to Pacault.'

Aside from the two obvious discrepancies in these recorded details, concerning rank and date of death, here at long last was a crucial piece of evidence. Making sense of it though, both then and now, could be described as challenging to say the very least, and it certainly taxed the collective minds of registration officials in determining what had happened when they wrestled with the problem during the early 1920s.

They could not let it go, however. Eyles would simply not let them and refused to be fobbed-off with the simple expedient of being told that Mannock's grave could not be located. Besides, the posthumous award of the Victoria Cross (gazetted on 18 July 1919) had brought him very much into the public consciousness as an outstanding national hero. Just leaving the matter as it stood would simply not do. And so a concerted effort to unravel the convoluted train of events after Mick's death was embarked upon by the War Graves Commission during 1923/24 with the intention that he might at last be laid to rest, both in the physical and metaphorical sense.

Hopefully too, the tenaciously persistent and troublesome Jim Eyles could be given an answer that would finally satisfy him. As it would turn out, it seems that even when Captain F G Wilson had written his short note in November 1920, Mannock's original field grave had most likely already been unwittingly found, exhumed, and its then unidentified occupant buried elsewhere.

** **

Quite apart from the confusion of war and its aftermath that had seemingly conspired to cover up all traces of Mannock's grave site, it was simply map reading errors, first by the Germans and then by the Imperial War Graves Commission, that almost certainly lies at the root of this whole mystery. More accurately, it was not so much a map reading error – per se – that gave rise to incorrect grid references, but a simple misunderstanding as to what the Germans, and later the British, were reading, seeing, and interpreting on their respective maps and on the ground.

When the IWGC re-examined the case and their files in light of the 1920 revelation from Berlin about the burial having been carried out '300 metres NW of La Pierre au Beurre on the road to Pacault', they looked again at their maps. Those maps would have been standard trench maps in use by the British Army throughout the war and at once they spotted something very odd. If the Germans had buried Mannock where they said they had, then this made little or no sense to them. Looking at their maps they could see that 'NW of La Pierre au Beurre' was **not** on the road to Pacault – which was, in fact, due east of where La Pierre au Beurre was shown to be. However, things made a little more sense to them if one assumed the Germans had, perhaps, meant north-**east**. But did they really mean that? And in any event does it actually make any more sense?

It was a visit by the 41-year-old Jim Eyles to the offices of the War Graves Commission on 5 September 1923, that precipitated this much closer examination of the case. Writing an internal note after Eyles's visit, the commission's W H Bolton noted that he had looked and found an exhumation report that *might* well be linked. It reported, he said, an *Unknown British Airman exhumed from* [map reference] *36a Q22a 5.1* and that this was '... roughly about 1,000 yards from the reported location of Major Mannock's grave'. Bolton went on to say that: 'May this case be investigated and the grave of the Unknown Airman be considered with Major Mannock please?'

Thereafter, the train of events that Eyles had first put in place four years earlier was kick-started anew and given fresh impetus. At last, maybe, the answers to questions he had asked about for so long might finally be forthcoming.

**

At this point it is essential to examine *exactly* where La Pierre au Beurre lay. Or rather, where both the German army and, later, the IWGC evidently **thought** it lay. Herein lies the most important key to this conundrum. Clearly the German army believed La Pierre au Beurre to be the name of a settlement or hamlet, or at least, some fixed and tangible geographical location from where they had then been able to measure a point 300 metres to its north-west, and record this as the spot of Mannock's burial place. What maps they were using is unclear, but looking at the British trench maps then in use (and as later used by the WGC) it can be seen that the wording 'La Pierre au Beurre' lies adjacent to a small cluster of houses. This would not unreasonably cause anyone looking at a map to conclude that this was the *settlement* of La Pierre au Beurre. Not so.

The positioning of the wording on the map is purely coincidental, and La Pierre au Beurre is actually what the French might call an *arrondissment,* and which might be translated as a district, an area or a ward of a town. Indeed, La Pierre au Beurre is a parcel of land comprising many thousands of hectares, loosely bounded by Cornet Malot, Boheme, Quentin and Robecq. It lies just about a mile or so to the north of the La Bassée Canal and to the south of Calonne-sur-la-Lys. The trap the Germans had fallen into, as would the war graves service later, was a complete failure to realise that La Pierre au Beurre was not a specific geographical location but, rather, a very wide area of flat and spectacularly featureless farmland. Consequently, it would not have been possible to plot a 'fixed' location (i.e. a point 300 metres to its north-west) from such a loosely defined area. The Germans, therefore, had wrongly believed La Pierre au Beurre to be a fixed point just as the British would later. But where exactly did *they*, the Germans, believe this to be? And what maps were they using?

If one supposes that their maps had La Pierre au Beurre printed in, maybe, just a slightly different place relative to maps in use by the British, then their description of the field grave as being *'on the road to Pacault'* might make some sense after all, and especially if they took the few buildings as being the place. Then, the failure of the war graves service to later relate this described location with the situation on the ground, begins to add up. Indeed, the outcome of investigations during the 1920s might well have had a different ending and Major Mannock might no longer be missing. That though, is pure conjecture. We can only go with the documentary evidence we have and then interpret it accordingly. In that context, let us return chronologically to the next documents in the Commission's E File.

Responding to Mr Bolton's note following Jim Eyles's visit in September 1923, another IWGC officer, Mr J G Plummer, wrote a week later:

'Captain Mannock [sic], according to GB [German Burial] list, SSP4995/2231, died 28 July 1918 [sic] and was buried 300 metres NW of La Pierre au Beurre on the road to Pacault, approx, map reference 36a Q21a b.4. [NB: This latter plot is clearly an insertion by Plummer as his own calculation of the stated distance from La Pierre au Beurre, because no *actual* map reference was given in the original German report. Authors.] Pacault is 1,500 yards [937.5 m] East of La Pierre au Beurre, map ref. 36a Q23c b.4. The "unknown" being suggested [by Bolton] was exhumed from 36a Q23a 5.1 and roughly 1,000 yards [625 m] East of the spot mentioned in the GB list. The "unknown" was identified by a cross and wreck of a plane but *no date of death* is given nor were any effects forwarded to the Base. Exhumation reports for the area have been searched but no trace can be found of Captain Mannock. Should [illegible initials] be asked to make history sheet and forward a copy of the GB list to DC for investigations? Do you agree please?

[signed] J G Plummer, 12/9/23.'

The IWGC Burial Return showing that the body located at 5.1 was re-buried at Laventie in Row F, Grave 12, in 1920.

At last, or so it seemed, the pieces of the jigsaw were coming together despite the fundamental – and perpetual – errors in rank and date of death.

Perhaps given a glimmer of hope as a result of his last contact with the commission, Eyles again grew impatient and by December was pressing once more for further information. Those who needed prodding were prodded and, on 17 January 1924, a reply was received in London from the IWGC officer in France. In it, Mr E A S Gell, assistant director records, stated:

> 'A ground search has now been carried out at the map reference quoted which is given as 36a Q21. This locality is now reconstructed, and all fields are cultivated, there being no surface evidence of graves anywhere in the vicinity of the map reference.
>
> 'The remnants of an aeroplane were found at Q21.b.8.1, but unfortunately the condition of this plane is so bad that no markings could be traced – all woodwork being burnt away and metal rusted.[1] Local inhabitants differ as to whether it is British or German, some state that it is British, others that they saw the Iron Cross on a portion of the tail.
>
> 'According to the GB list the grave is situated at 300 metres NW of La Pierre au Beurre on the road to Pacault. In this connection a further search was deemed necessary at 36a Q20.d, which also proved unsuccessful.'

Butter Lane looking west, in 2007.

[1] Diligent and experienced WW1 air historians today would have had little difficulty in identifying the type of machine, but in 1923 .....!

Swinging the camera to the left, this is the field and approximate location where Mannock came down, with Pacault Wood beyond. The other side of the trees is the La Bassée Canal.

And so the misunderstanding as to where and what actually comprised La Pierre au Beurre was just compounded. Unwittingly, the war graves service were drawing ever tighter their blinkers and becoming increasingly unable to see the wood for the trees. As they tried to unravel the mystery, so they blindly deepened it through the basic failure to spot the La Pierre au Beurre anomaly. And yet, time and again they came so close – so tantalizingly close – to affording Mannock a marked grave and headstone.

Writing to the registrar in the spring of 1924, another IWGC officer, Mr A H Gosling, observed that: 'An unknown British aviator is shown in exhumation reports for Laventie Military Cemetery … and was exhumed from 36a Q22a 5.1, identified by a cross and wreck of a plane. No date of death is stated.' He went on to report the factual detail as set out earlier in Plummer's report of 12 September 1923 [see above] but his report is interesting in that it links directly to a specific burial at Laventie, with the exhumation at what we will now call 'the 5.1 location'. Mr Gosling goes on to comment upon the aeroplane wreckage reportedly seen at 36a Q21b 8.1 (which we shall now refer to as 8.1) and suggests that this was *probably* linked to the wrecked aeroplane beside which the unknown British airman was discovered and exhumed at 5.1.

Alternatively, although Gosling does not suggest this, it is entirely possible that 5.1 and 8.1 might well be one and the same. In the linear sense, both are closely related in grid squares that are side by side. Could it be that grid squares 21 and 22 have been confused or transposed, and that additionally, the numbers 5.1 had been misread as 8.1, or vice-versa, or even been due to a typographical error? It would not be the first time that map references have been misread or misunderstood, even by the most skilful of map readers, and it surely won't be the last time either.

Another possibility is that someone had simply misread a '5' for an '8' on some handwritten note. Easily done. Not only that, but both map references place the two locations at identical distances from the road to Pacault. British soldiers knew this road as Butter Lane, as shown on trench maps, although it is the Rue du Poncelet to the French. It crosses what is a bleak and utterly featureless landscape where even the most skilled of map readers might struggle to differentiate between positions 5.1 and 8.1. So much, though, for hypothesizing. The fact is that the War Graves Commission continued to be puzzled by the NW/NE bearings from La Pierre au Beurre, but realised that if the bearing was taken to mean *NE* from where **they** thought La Pierre au Beurre to be, then the unknown body of an airman at 5.1 could, at least loosely, be made to fit into where the Germans had reputedly buried Mannock. Once they realised this then things began to make more sense.

Inaccurate measurements of distance, though, are understandable when it was possible to only *estimate* due to the hostile nature of a wartime battlefield environment, with any observer being only able to approximate in round figures. Such estimates could, very easily be wildly inaccurate. So where does this take us? Very neatly it draws us to the penultimate chapter in the War Graves Commission's post-war quest to locate Major Mick Mannock's grave.

* *

In a memo dated 2 June 1924, Mr Gosling concludes, *inter-alia*, that: 'The unknown aviator in Laventie Cemetery from 36a. Q22.a.5.1 is the only unknown that can be considered. Had the location on the GB list have been 300 metres N.EAST of La Pierre au Beurre, then a provisional cross would probably have been justified, but as this discrepancy arises regarding the location then any cross action becomes rather difficult. Action please?'

With Gosling's work then passed further up the chain of command we subsequently see another officer, identified only by his initials of HGM, writing to the registrar of the IWGC on 4 June 1924 with some very definite statements. First, he makes the comment that: 'I know of no other Air Force casualties in this area.' Next, HGM makes an absolutely emphatic statement that: 'The location … confirmed by Berlin, is obviously incorrect. <u>North-East</u> of La Pierre au Beurre is meant, and not North-West.'

This second statement is clearly an attempt to make sense of the location reported by the Germans and explain away its apparent discrepancy. Ignorance of the geographical facts clearly continued to pervade the IWGC camp when it came to understanding what La Pierre au Beurre actually was. What HGM went on to say in the rest of his memo was, though, perhaps very significant in the overall picture: 'I should say that the Air Force casualties in the area in question were <u>few</u> as they must have occurred during the period April to about August 1918. Except for a short time in 1914, the area was in our hands until April 1918 when it was taken by the Germans in their big offensive.'

As far as the IWGC were concerned, they were now entering the end-game in terms of the quest for Mannock.

* *

From the report of 'HMG', the file progresses rapidly to a blow-by-blow account of the facts unravelled thus far by the IWGC, and summarising the salient points as follows:

> Assuming this to be the case [i.e. NE and not NW of La Pierre au Beurre] we have the following position:
>
> 1) Major Mannock buried 300 metres NE (?) of La Pierre au Beurre (approx 36a.Q21.b).

2) 'Unknown British Aviator' exhumed from 36a.Q22a.5.1 (no date of death) identified by wrecked aeroplane.

3) Remnants of aeroplane found by France [i.e. the IWGC French section] at 36a.Q21b.8.1.

No reference can be found of any other airman who might be considered as a candidate for the grave of the Unknown British Airman.'

The same report goes on to state:

'In the circumstances it is suggested that, in view of the close proximity of cases 1, 2 & 3 mentioned above, they be connected with Major Mannock and a provisional cross over Grave 12, Row F, Plot 3 (now marked Unknown British Airman) be erected. Is this justified please?'

Unfortunately, the response to this memo was in the negative.

Referred still further up the chain of command, an exchange of correspondence between the War Graves Commission director of records and registrar asked: 'Would you kindly read these notes and say if you think provisional cross is justified? WGR1 for identification purposes is an alternative.'

The reply was unequivocal and authoritative, and seemingly, final. 'I think the case is not quite strong enough for a provisional cross and WRG1 would not go through. He must be missing.' (i.e. – *he must remain missing!*) [Author's italics].

The large cemetery at Arras has the Flying Services Memorial, which is seen here under construction in 1931.

The finished memorial on which Edward Mannock's name is carved, along with all other airmen who have no known graves.

CHAPTER 12

BUTTER LANE AND THE GRAVE AT LAVENTIE

Notwithstanding the IWGC's understandable failure to appreciate the significance of the misunderstanding surrounding La Pierre au Beurre, they did at least recognise that something was not quite right with the recorded information they had available. Not only that, but some of its officers in the 1920s also believed there to be sufficiently strong evidence, circumstantial though much of it was, to link the field burial alongside Butter Lane with Mannock anyway – albeit that this link was ultimately vetoed when the report reached the top of the referral tree. That said, it is a matter of record that the Laventie grave has for a long time now been linked, if somewhat tenuously, with the famous aviator.

When, however, IWGC reached its final decision in the matter during the summer of 1924, it wrote to Jim Eyles and notified him of the ultimate conclusion that no grave for Major Mannock could be positively identified. Eyles was appraised in a letter from the IWGC on 25 July of the outline facts appertaining to the field grave and the associated aeroplane wreckage and was also told that a special search had been conducted for Mannock's body. The IWGC did not, though, make any mention of the unknown British airman being buried at Laventie. Indeed, there was no reason why they should. After all, that burial had now been officially excluded from any possibility that it was Mannock. Disappointing though the news must have been, Eyles seems to have accepted the outcome as final and no further correspondence from him appears in the E File. It was apparently not until the early 1980s that the War Graves Commission examined the circumstances surrounding the Laventie burial afresh.

Major T A Edwin Gibson MBE, RA Retd, was chief records officer for the Commonwealth War Graves Commission, having worked for them for 25 years from 1960. It was towards the end of his service, in the early 1980s, that Gibson initiated another look at the Mannock case. Unfortunately, and as mentioned in the previous chapter, the CWGC have thus far been unable to locate Edwin Gibson's internal report and it does not appear, as one might expect, in the Mannock E File, although papers and correspondence relating to Mannock right up to the present day are to be found there.

Whatever the report said exactly, we do know that Major Gibson was pressing for acceptance that the Laventie burial should be recognised in some way as Mannock's. Writing to one of the authors [Andy Saunders] in January 1994 Gibson had said: '… despite the case I put up, my findings were *not* accepted. I found the whole thing rather dispiriting, especially as exhumation was not allowed, although to be fair, an exhumation for identification in Cornwall of an unknown RCAF flyer (with positive results) was a "one off" in the 25 years I spent in the CWGC. I am convinced that the grave is Mannock's.'

So here we have a senior CWGC officer who was well placed to review all the available evidence and interpret every piece of relevant documentation – and, more importantly, to understand fully the systems, protocols and nuances therein – eventually coming to a pretty definite conclusion relative to the Laventie grave. It is unfortunate that so far the Edwin Gibson report has still not surfaced, although he did write a letter to the *Sunday Telegraph* in November 1993, suggesting exhumation of the Laventie grave for identification purposes and, if exhumation was either impossible or not conclusive, then a headstone should be erected over the Laventie grave with the superscription – *Believed to Be*. Such inscriptions are not without precedent in CWGC cemeteries. Anyone visiting the vast British cemetery at Tyne Cot near Ypres, will find at least one. In Tournai cemetery there is an airman's grave similarly marked. This is where Lieutenant H E Rath DFC, of 29 Squadron, is thought to be buried, brought down on 26 October 1918. Henry Rath, a Canadian from Toronto, was killed in what was understood to be a collision with another SE5 during a fight with Jasta 43.

The commission's own criteria for such inscriptions is stated as being '… where identification may be considered reasonable but not absolute.' More recently, in July 2007, Major Gibson has re-affirmed his view about the Laventie grave being linked to Mannock.

> 'Whilst I was Chief Records Officer of the CWGC (1977-85) I had the temerity to suggest the exhumation of the remains at Laventie. Mannock was a tall man and it might have been possible to identify (or not) the body. That course of action was turned down, as exhumations for identification were against CWGC general policy. So, I suggested the superscription "Believed to Be". This was also turned down by the Deputy Director General and so I spent no more time on the subject but always felt sorry for poor old Mannock.'

With the absence of Edwin Gibson's internal CWGC report we cannot be certain as to what detail he actually put across to support his conclusions. There are, however, a number of facts that were simply ignored and apparently not considered sufficiently and with due care during the original 1920s investigation of the matter. These issues can now be examined and are fundamental, if not crucial, in any overview of the case. First let us look again at the German perspective.

The report which came from out of Germany as a result of enquires to Berlin by the IWGC during the early 1920s pointed to a field grave location for a body that was certainly Mannock's and it was not an isolated German report so far as the incident itself was concerned. Indeed, a report by the German 55th Army Corps related the following for 26 July 1918:

> At approximately 7 am [German time] a German aeroplane was shot down by two British airmen in the area of Calonne. Both Englishmen were shot down by ground machine gun fire. The first aeroplane, on fire, crashed in the locality of the 100th Infantry Regiment; the second fell between the lines [*sic*]. The pilot of the first is dead; the fate of the second pilot is unknown.'

Despite the apparent time discrepancy it must be borne in mind that the Germans were operating one hour ahead of British time and thus the timing is, in fact, accurate for the Mannock loss.

This report, then, clearly refers to the Mannock/Inglis event and gives further confirmation that Mannock fell within – inside – German held territory. That confirmation is important given further 'evidence' that has been put forward since, and which might otherwise throw some doubt on the suggestion that Mannock was buried behind the German lines.

Evidently, and according to details published in *Cross & Cockade* (a quarterly journal for WW1 aviation historians) Volume No.2, 2004, a certain Sergeant Johns also witnessed the crash, as did an un-named intelligence officer. However, the substance of what they witnessed is not reported on and no indication made as to any primary source for this testimony. Further, no clue is given as to which units either men belonged, although an additional piece of information in this article states that the intelligence officer plotted a map reference for Mannock's crash. This is just beyond the German lines, NNE of Pacault Wood, and some distance south-east of the 5.1 and 8.1 map references.

Additionally, we are told of a 'J Macgregor Salter' who crawled out into no-man's-land and crudely buried Mannock. It was this man to whom journalist Bernard McElwaine referred to in the *Sunday Mirror* after he had reviewed the book *The Ace with One Eye* for this newspaper in 1963. Salter had written to McElwaine, and the journalist quoted the letter in the newspaper:

> 'I was just a mere boy when I joined up in World War 1, and Mick Mannock was my hero. I always knew his plane because he had two special long streamers trailing from his rudder and he would always give us a wave as he flew over our heads. He always did us a good turn by machine gunning German outposts but one day a few chance bullets from the ground set his plane on fire. He crashed in 'no-man's-land'. Late at night I crept out beyond our barbed wire and found the plane, a burnt wreck, nose down in a shell hole. I covered the charred remains of poor Mick, my hero, by scooping earth with my bare hands ...'

Clearly there are several points here – both in the *Cross & Cockade* article and in Salter's quoted remarks – that need critical examination. First we can dispense with Sergeant Johns. Nothing has been offered by way of what he might have observed to assist in the Mannock investigation. His introduction into the story seems to have been an irrelevance, and probably like scores of other soldiers on that part of the front, he simply observed the incident, or at least recalled seeing an incident that he later took to have taken place on or about 26 July 1918. Nothing more.

As for the intelligence officer and his plotting of the crash site, we have no idea of where he was standing – or in truth, crouching – although it is reasonable to assume he was somewhere along the La Bassée Canal area, and presumably somewhere to the west of Pacault Wood, otherwise his view north or north-east would be obstructed by the trees. It was certainly west of where Private Naulls was situated in order for him to have an open sight-line clear of the western tip of the wood. What is interesting about this map reference, and if it is to be given any credence, is that from what we might 'assume' the intelligence officer's position to have been, then the crash he reported must have been situated directly along his supposed line of sight, and importantly, looking almost straight towards the 5.1 and 8.1 positions! This must be just coincidental, or it could be that he was simply unable to make a totally accurate judgement of the true position of the burning wreck.

We should remember too that this whole area, apart from the wood, was a flat, featureless terrain not to mention a hostile battlefield environment. He would have had to have been exceptionally careful standing about taking bearings from a hand-held compass. Also, in order to get an accurate plot, he would have needed to have taken a cross-bearing from other positions as well. We don't know that he didn't do that, but we don't know that he did either. And was it worth noting some poor downed airman's position and endanger himself while wandering around in front of the enemy lines, in order to do so? He was either exceptionally foolhardy or terminally stupid. Either way, there must be some doubt as to the accuracy of his compass bearings and plotting.

As for Macgregor Salter's tale, it is full of holes. Quite apart from the inference he had Mannock as his hero – at the time, if not earlier – when even amongst his own air force he was not widely known outside his particular circle of friends within 40, 74 and 85 Squadrons, how can we believe he even knew his 'hero's' aeroplane, just because it carried streamers. Most flight and deputy flight leaders had streamers of various descriptions, and no self-respecting soldier is going to gaze admiringly up at some aeroplane in the sky and risk a sniper's bullet. At best this man may well have crawled out into no-man's-land on one occasion in order to scoop earth over a dead airman, but he was never going to creep not only across this danger area, but, as Mannock came down well inside German territory, continue on, without making a sound, and bury a body at this distance without either being heard, found, captured or shot. It's 'Boy's Own' stuff but hardly credible nor anything to do with 26 July 1918. Besides, if we accept in any way the intelligence officer's map reference then it is blatantly obvious the location is not in no-man's-land but some distance inside German lines. His is the only reference to the downed SE5 ending up in any sort of hole or ditch.

In any event we have factual and specifically documented records that Mannock was buried by the Germans. This is further substantiated by the subsequent return of identity discs and a singed notebook to the Mannock family after the war, via the International Red Cross, presumably forwarded on by the Germans who buried him. Edward Naulls too, had a view about J Macgregor Salter's testimony. Writing in 1963 he said:

> 'I have read Mr Salter's story several times and after considering it carefully I have come to the conclusion that it is too improbable for belief. Salter may have covered the charred remains of a British airman with earth scooped up in his bare hands but I am certain the remains were not those of Mannock. Mannock's plane certainly did not crash in no-man's-land. It went over Jerry trenches and beyond – a long way beyond. I did not take my eyes off it from the moment it caught fire, and it did not crash between the British and German trenches.
>
> 'Certainly there were nights so dark that Salter could have crept out into no-man's-land without his absence from the trench being noticed but I cannot understand how he managed to get beyond the barbed wire. There were gaps in the wire of course, and Jerry had the range of them to a yard and during the hours of darkness the Jerry machine gunners kept up an almost continuous fire so it is surprising he was not hit. I am sure that he would not have been ordered to crawl out into no-man's-land alone, even if there had been some military reason for it. Another weakness in Salter's story is that he does not mention where he was or give any place names.'

[In 1963 there had not yet been any published sources or information giving the locality of the incident. Authors.]

* *

The relative positions of the two front lines on 26 July 1918, though, is an absolutely crucial factor in the overall picture and when the IWGC were scratching their heads over the puzzling position '300 metres NW of La Pierre au Beurre', and the fact that this was obviously not 'on the road to Pacault' as the Germans had described, they seemingly overlooked this very important point.

A picture of the Army Graves Registration Unit at work before removing battlefield remains to the nearest military cemetery.

What we do know is that the 'NW of La Pierre au Beurre' location, and as understood and interpreted by the British authorities in the 1920s, would have placed that position slap bang in the middle of no-man's-land. In fact, almost exactly midway between the two trench lines! Clearly the Germans would not have sent a burial party out into such hostile territory merely to bury a British casualty. Not only that, but the described location cannot be accurate for the simple reason that the Germans are very precise and emphatic in their description, one aeroplane had fallen where the 100th Infantry Regiment were operating (its pilot dead) and the other (clearly Inglis) had come down between the lines (sic) with the condition of the pilot unknown.

If the machine whose pilot was dead – Mannock – had also fallen between the lines wouldn't they have said so? So, had the IWGC managed to understand this crucial factor then surely it would have more than reinforced their hunch that the position was wrong; i.e. to the NE and not the NW. The assertion, therefore, that a German party ventured out deep into open and exposed no-man's-land to identify and bury an enemy airman is just as implausible as is the suggestion that Salter ventured out to bury the airman, wherever the body was.

So, yet again, we are left with all pointers indicating Mannock's original burial place to be alongside Butter Lane at 5.1, which also *happens* to be the road to Pacault – just as the Germans had described. It is also well behind the German lines. And we know also that the unknown British airman found there post-war, at that map reference alongside Butter Lane, was exhumed and re-buried in Laventie Military Cemetery – Plot 3, Row F, Grave 12.

That the airman buried in this particular plot at Laventie originated from the field grave situated at 5.1 is beyond all doubt so far as the authors are concerned. As proof, there exists in the Mannock E File a 'Concentration of Graves (Exhumation and Reburials) Burial Return' form, for that specific Laventie grave, that came to light during W H Bolton's 1923 trawl for evidence as to the whereabouts of Mannock's resting place. On it is recorded that the body from 5.1 was that of an unknown British airman, identified by a cross and wreck of an aeroplane, and exhumed from it. No personal effects were found and presumably it was only identified as an airman by its uniform and badges or flying clothing.

Although no exact date of exhumation and re-burial is stated, the date '10 April 1920' has been written in pencil beneath the particulars given and there is a further rubber date stamp, apparently when the document was received or processed at an IWGC office, of 15 May 1920. Also, the *Cross & Cockade* article seemingly questioned the actual existence of any exhumation report for this casualty. Certainly, no actual exhumation report exists now, but documents in the E File confirm that the IWGC most certainly held and inspected the report in their original Mannock quest. It is impossible to ignore or discount this hard piece of evidence, although those who have challenged its merit, point amongst other things, to the lack of any chronological conformity when the Laventie burial is compared to the dates of death for those buried either side of Grave 12.

One of the arguments put forward about the grave in Laventie cemetery is the fact that this unknown British airman is buried almost exactly halfway along a row of soldiers, mostly of the West Yorkshire Regiment, and all of who died in 1917. This, say the doubters, must point to the unknown being a 1917 casualty and burial. The argument is, why would any

This grave lies between soldiers who died in 1917. To the left all are dated March while those to the right are dated April.

casualty brought in much later from a remote field grave be buried in the middle of a row of 1917 casualties?

The answer is quite simply, that there must have been an empty grave space there. Interestingly, those to one side of the unknown airman all died mostly during March 1917, while those on the other side died in April 1917, so there could easily have been a logical gap in the grave row that was quite simply filled when this unknown casualty was brought in from its battlefield grave. The argument that he is chronologically 'out of place' for a July 1918 death, and must have died in March or April 1917 (or his body found then) is entirely fatuous, especially in the face of incontrovertible evidence to the contrary within the burial return.

The 'unknown airman' grave is among the headstones on the far right, but this picture does show how many other gaps appear between graves in this cemetery.

On the subject of grave locations at Laventie, and rather than leave the reader still thinking that the 'unknown' grave has to be questioned due to its spot between rows of casualties from March and April 1917, let us consider other graves within this particular cemetery, and not take this one grave in isolation.

Mannock's great friend George McElroy, who it will be remembered was killed just a few days after Mick's death – 31 July 1918 – is also buried in Laventie. His named headstone is at the end of a row of dead soldiers from 1914! In Row 1C, there are 17 gravestones, all dated 1915, but there is one dated 1916. In Row 1A, of the 15 gravestones five are for 1917, one for 1918, then two more from 1917, another from 1918, followed by five more from 1917 before a final one from 1918. No consistency here.

Another row has March 1918 dead together with those of July 1917, plus a German grave for 1917 in their midst. In Row 1B there is a 1914, then a 1915 stone, then an Australian

Infantry private dated 6 March 1918. Next, an officer killed 12 January 1916, then a private from the East Lancs Regiment dated 2 September 1918. The sixth and seventh stones are for a Royal Flying Corps crew, killed on 17 February 1918, while the eighth is a private of the Duke of Wellington's Regiment, killed 28 April 1918. This is surely evidence enough to illustrate how burials could be, and often were, somewhat randomly situated. Most other WW1 cemeteries in France also have burials in no particular date order.

Again we return to the undeniable fact that there is ample official IWGC documentary evidence confirming both the exhumation from the field grave along Butter Lane *and* a re-burial from that field grave into a very specific Laventie grave. Not a shred of evidence exists to cause any doubt to be cast on this particular document and it is hard to understand why anyone should. Why on earth would the IWGC be recording the detailed specifics of an exhumation, tied to the discovery of aircraft wreckage, and then record the precise grave number into which that body had ultimately been placed if it were not the case? On the face of it, therefore, it is a convincing argument to identify this as the last resting place of Major Mick Mannock. There is, however, a fly in the ointment, or to be exact, there are two.

Notwithstanding the assertions by the IWGC in 1923 that there were '… no other air force casualties in the area who might be considered', we do need to ask the question: is Mannock really the only candidate who could have been buried in the field grave at map reference 36a Q22a 5.1? The answer has to be that there could be, in theory, two other contenders, also pointed out by CWGC:

1. Lieutenant W A Pell of 80 Squadron, killed on 12 April 1918 and last seen in combat over Paradis.

2. Lieutenant J Hollick, 210 Squadron, killed on 18 May 1918 and reported to have been shot down over Lestrem.

Both these Sopwith Camel pilots are missing with no known grave, both of them are reported to have fallen – or were last seen – in the general area of Mannock's disappearance and both of them had fallen in the period 12 April to 10 August 1918. This is the period 'HMG' referred to as that likely to have produced casualties in the area under review, and despite Mr Gosling's earlier assertion that he knew of no other air force casualties in this area.

Although Pell was last seen in combat, there are no obvious German claims for his demise. Hollick on the other hand, appears to have been shot down by Jasta 29, Unteroffizier Karl Pech claiming two Camels down north-west of Lestrem shortly before noon (German time) – shortly before 11 am British time. Both fell on the German side of the lines, so in theory Hollick would have been buried by the Germans, and his grave later lost during fighting over that area. North-west of Lestrem is, of course, some three miles to the north-east of the 5.1 grave location, so its seems very unlikely that his body would have been brought so far south-west for an isolated burial beside an equally isolated Butter Lane. The other 210 Squadron pilot survived as a prisoner of war.

Pell and 80 Squadron had left their base at around 3.30 on the afternoon of 12 April and he, along with two other pilots, had not returned. Their patrol area had been Merville-Radingham. Pell and one other had been killed, the third, although initially reported missing, later returned by road. Although Pell had been seen in combat with German aircraft it doesn't follow that he was shot down in the fight, and with no obvious victor among the Jasta pilots this day, the action over Paradis may have ended inconclusively. Or, he may have been in action with a two-seater, and there is a crew from Schutzstaffel 19 that claimed a

Sopwith Camel on the 12th, but the time and location is unknown. 80 Squadron were normally engaged in ground attack sorties, so Pell may well have been brought down by ground fire, and so might his companions lost this afternoon. Paradis is nearer to the 5.1 site, though perhaps a mile to the east of it. Again, if he did fall in the Paradis locality, there would be no reason to bury him alongside Butter Lane.

No Longer Missing?

During November 1993 the great nephew of Major Mannock, Peter Burden, visited the cemetery at Laventie and laid a poppy wreath at the grave that may well be the burial place of his illustrious ancestor. The event was covered by the *Sunday Telegraph* on Remembrance weekend. Whilst in France Peter also made a pilgrimage to Butter Lane, where, with one of the authors [Andy Saunders] he met Maria Betka-Dubois, widow of Gaston Dubois who had farmed the land at 5.1 and 8.1 in the immediate post-WW1 years. Maria clearly remembered the jumbled wreckage of an aeroplane being present alongside Butter Lane immediately after the war, thus bearing out what the IWGC field officer said he had found there. Her best recollection was that this debris was later tipped into one of the many shell craters as part of the battlefield clear-up. She was certain though, that she had been told it was of English origin but beyond that could add nothing useful. Suggestions have also surfaced elsewhere that the wreckage and field grave were located within an orchard. Madame Dubois was adamant the site had never been an orchard, either then or since, while those farming the area now, and who have knowledge of its agricultural history confirm that an orchard had never existed there.

Another Piece for the Jigsaw?

Interestingly, and somewhat tantalisingly, Brad King of the Imperial War Museum has located some glass plate negatives of a number of aerial photographs taken of the Butter Lane area by the RAF around the time Mannock was lost. One, taken from 5,500 feet, clearly shows Butter Lane and the terrain of La Pierre au Beurre, pock-marked with shell holes – and also, coincidentally, showing no orchard. This picture was taken at 12.30 pm on 31 July 1918 and the most intriguing feature is what Brad remains convinced is the upturned wreck of an aeroplane, very close to the 8.1 position, and just behind the clearly visible trenches of the German front line. Mannock's crash had been some days before and so it could be his machine.

This, however, was then discounted when a further aerial photo was found dated much earlier than the 26th, and showing the same feature, thus showing that it could not be anything to do with Mannock.

The question then is, always assuming we are looking at a wreck and not just a confusingly shaped shell crater, has this anything to do with the burial at 5.1? A wreck in itself does not necessarily suggest a dead airman, and war graves would only have been interested if its pilot had been killed. A pilot who survives as a prisoner would have nothing to do with them or their records. Although we acknowledge that this is a piece of 'evidence' that could be argued over interminably, it is not possible to ignore the hard facts that we <u>do</u> have; the documentary evidence held by the Commonwealth War Graves Commission, which forms the basis of our argument.

Conclusions

a. Major Mannock was shot down and killed by ground fire, crashing with his burning aeroplane behind the German lines north of Pacault Wood and in an area of land known as La Pierre au Beurre.

b. Mannock's body was found, identified and buried by the German army who recorded the field grave location beside the road to Pacault and returned identity discs and effects via the International Red Cross.

c. No credence can be attached to the statements by former British soldiers Johns and Macgregor-Salter; certainly without corroboration.

d. A good deal of credibility may be attached to the witness account of former Private Edward Naulls of the Essex Regiment.

e. A field grave marked by the wreckage of an aeroplane was found alongside the road to Pacault, known as Butter Lane, by the Imperial War Graves Service c.1920.

f. The occupant of this field grave was exhumed but could not be identified and was duly re-buried on or after March 1920, in Grave 12, Row F, Laventie Military Cemetery.

g Identification of Mannock's body, including papers and identity discs, had been removed by the Germans thus explaining a lack of identification on the exhumed remains.

h. On the almost certain assumption that the Germans had marked the grave with a cross in 1918, it had certainly disappeared by the war's end.
i. Suggestions that the occupant of the field grave at Butter Lane is not buried in Grave 12, Row F, Laventie cemetery, are dismissed.

j. No connection between the field grave exhumation at Butter Lane and Major Mannock was made until 1923, when the War Graves Commission re-examined its records at the behest of Jim Eyles.

k. The connection made with Mannock in the 1920s, although initially very convincing, was ultimately discounted when no sense could be made of the apparent anomaly between the reported position of the burial by the Germans (i.e. NW of La Pierre au Beurre) and the subsequent post-war discovery at Butter Lane.

l. Either an error in map reading by the Germans, quoting NW instead of NE, or a difference in the positioning of place names on equivalent British and German maps led to this confusion.

m. Butter Lane leads from the German front line towards Pacault and would thus have been known by the Germans as 'the road to Pacault' which is the location described for Mannock's original field grave.

n. No particular evidence, circumstantial or otherwise, exists to link Pell or Hollick, or any other aviator, with the Butter Lane field burial.

o. A great deal of factual and circumstantial evidence exists to link Mannock with a high degree of probability to the Butter Lane field grave.

p. On the foregoing basis, therefore, a robust case exists for the Commonwealth War Graves Commission to re-appraise its position relative to the Laventie burial and to erect a new headstone bearing the inscription:

Believed to Be
Major E Mannock VC DSO & 2 Bars, MC & Bar
Royal Air Force
Killed in Action 26 July 1918, aged 31

q. The criteria set by the CWGC for erection of such headstones, i.e. *"where identification may be considered reasonable but not absolute"* is fully met in respect of the Laventie burial.

r. Given the convincing case for re-appraisal it is essential to stress that no precedent is being set in the event of such a headstone being erected over the Laventie grave. In the unlikely event that subsequent evidence should come to light that either definitively proves or disproves the case then the headstone can be amended appropriately.

Finally, it is interesting to speculate, what if the IWGC had accurately interpreted the maps, the description of the field grave location and understood where the respective front lines were situated when they deliberated the matter back in the 1920s? What would they have then decided?

Had they looked at all those facts in light of the evidence offered here then it is surely a certainty that they would have marked the Laventie grave with a proper headstone to Mannock. In all probability it would have been an absolute identification rather than just a case of 'Believed to Be'. Consequently, it is unlikely that a debate would have ever surfaced to question whether it was his burial place or whether it was not. The fact is that the War Graves Commission didn't join up all the dots and complete the puzzle.

As a result of work carried out by the authors on the Butter Lane/Laventie burials, Air Chief Marshal Sir Peter Squire GCB DFC AFC DSc, Vice Chairman of the Commonwealth War Grave Commission, confirmed during February 2008 that the case would be submitted to the Ministry of Defence [1] for a ruling on whether or not the headstone should be replaced with one engraved 'Believed to be'. At the time of going to print an outcome from the MOD is awaited.

Maybe, after all, Mick Mannock is really no longer missing. Perhaps Jim Eyles's quest will one day bear the fruits of his earlier endeavours to find his good friend.

The grave to 'A British Airman of the Great Wa[r] Row F, Grave 12. 'Known unto God'. Believed [to] be???

[1] Up until 2000 the responsibility for the naming of unknown casualties already within the care of the Commonwealth War Graves Commission rested solely with the commission, the Ministry of Defence being solely responsible for the identification and naming of newly discovered casualties from WW1 and WW2. From 2000 that specific remit of the CWGC was transfered to the Ministry of Defence. This followed controversy surrounding the identification in 1992 of an unknown soldier of the First World War, named by the commission as Lt John Kipling of the Irish Guards, son of Rudyard Kipling. Doubt has since been thrown on the validity of that positive identification, thus highlighting the sensitivity of such decisions and impacting, surely, on the case of Major Mannock and the Laventie burial.

POSTSCRIPTS

Postscript One

Towards the end of the 1930s, Wellingborough Council, one imagines through the urging of Jim Eyles, was contemplating naming a road after Major Mannock. By this time many of the townsfolk must have begun to believe that Mannock was a native of the city, rather than someone who had merely been associated with it from just prior to WW1 until his death in 1918. Nevertheless, the town council had progressed the idea from wherever it came from and at the start of 1939, the suggestion was approved.

In a local newspaper for Friday 24 February 1939, the following headlines appeared above the article:

FAMOUS AIRMAN'S FRIEND ON
MANNOCK-ROAD DECISION
Better Late Than Never at Wellingborough
FORMER TALK OF MEMORIAL

Wellingborough's further move to commemorate the name of the late Major Mick Mannock VC DSO MC, most renowned of all wartime airmen, has the warm approval of his closest friend Mr A E Eyles, manager of the Highfield Foundry, Wellingborough.

When asked if he wished to comment on the Urban Council's decision to give the name 'Mannock-road' to a street on the new housing estate off Croyland-road, Mr Eyles said:

'The less I say the better, perhaps, at this date, although I really think something ought to have been done before this at Wellingborough in tribute to Major Mannock, as it is over 20 years since he died.

'The excuse was that Mannock did not happen to be a Wellingborough-born man but he was not a Canterbury-man either, and they have a tablet to his memory in the Cathedral.'

It was Coun. H C L Warwick who successfully introduced an amendment at last week's Urban Council meeting that the name Mannock-road should be given to the new street, in preference to Hayside-road.

Among those supporting him was Coun. J Peck CC, who commented that if Mannock had been in a higher social position he would have had a monument erected to him.

"King of Air Fighters"

Mannock was born at the Preston Cavalry Barracks, Brighton, on May 24th, 1887. His father was a corporal in the Royal Scots Greys, and his mother an Irishwomen of the maiden name Julia O'Sullivan. From her he inherited a 'strong streak of Irish'.

'I am glad Mr Peck thinks the same way as I do about it,' Mr Eyles said. 'If Mannock had been born higher in the world socially, I do think he would have been honoured rather differently.'

It was not until the publication of the book *King of Air Fighters* in 1934 by Flight-Lieut. Ira Jones DSO MC, a colleague, that the English public was put fully in possession of the facts about Mannock. The book established that he had the greatest number of aerial victories of any wartime airman – a total of 73 enemy planes destroyed.

Some mystery surrounds the circumstances of Mannock's death in the air, which is officially recorded as having taken place on July 26th, 1918. The Air Ministry subsequently informed Mr Eyles: 'It is regretted that no information is available as regards his place of burial.'

Meeting with Mr Eyles

'Mannock was at Wellingborough for about four years,' Mr Eyles said. He was transferred from the National Telephone Company's branch in Canterbury to a linesman's job at Wellingborough for which he applied. We first met when he came to apologise to me for "letting down" the Wesleyan cricket team. It was an away match and I could not turn out for the team, so they sent Mannock over in my place. He was soon out when he went in to bat, and when he got back to Wellingborough he came to me to apologise for being such a poor deputy.'

Subsequently Mannock went to lodge with Mr Eyles and his wife, and he used to spend much of his leave from the Front with them. At Christmas 1915 [sic] he flew to Wellingborough to stay with them, landing his plane in the School grounds.

Mannock's mother is still living in South London, now about 77, and Mr Eyles proposes to call on her again very soon to tell of the further move at Wellingborough to commemorate her famous son's name.

'A few years after the War, as a result of what appeared in your newspaper – I have the cuttings,' said Mr Eyles, 'there was talk of a committee being formed of members of the Council and townsmen to arrange a memorial for Mannock. I was given to understand that I would be on the committee, but I heard nothing more.'

Council Chamber Photograph

'All that was done was to hang the large coloured portrait of Mannock in the Council Chamber, and that was the gift of the late Ald. George Hensen.'

Mr Eyles related that the photograph was taken just before Mannock left Wellingborough to join No. 40 Squadron for the first time as a fighting pilot at the Front. 'He did not want to have it taken but Mrs Eyles persuaded him and one day he came in saying he had just been to the photographer as he promised,' Mr Eyles said.

Rejected Propeller

Mr N G Woodhead, the photographer of Midland-road, Wellingborough related: 'The photograph was actually taken by Mr Powell, whose business I took over in 1918. I made the large coloured portrait of Mannock and put it in the shop window, where it attracted a lot of interest. One day I said to Ald. Hensen, who was going by, "You know, that picture ought to be in the Council Chamber." He said he would see about it, and soon afterwards he purchased it for hanging in the Council Chamber.'

Mr Woodhead himself presented another large portrait to the YMCA, as Mannock had been an active member. He was also a leading light in the Labour Movement at Wellingborough.

Mr Eyes further said: 'Some years back I offered a propeller given me by Mannock from one of his planes, if the authorities at Wellingborough could find a suitable place for it. However, I heard no more about that. Eventually I presented it to the nation, and it is now displayed with a photograph in the Imperial War Museum.'[1]

Capt. Archie Reeves [2], of Wellingborough, a close wartime friend of Mannock's although they were in different flying squadrons at the Front, expressed his pleasure at the decision to give the town a 'Mannock-road'. He said:

'I am very glad indeed that something is being done, because Mannock deserved it – and more.'

Mr Eyles's concluding comment was: 'I only hope that Mannock-road will be worthy of the name it bears, and that it will produce men the equal of Mannock in their private lives.'

Mannock Road is situated off Henshaw Road, that leads into Croyland Road.

**

Canterbury Cathedral

By this time, however, another city had put up a memorial to Mannock, and that city was Canterbury. The memorial tablet was given by the citizens of the city and presented by the Canterbury War Memorial Committee, and a service to put it in place was held on 18 July 1925, not quite seven years after his death. It is the only plaque involving an RAF airman, and for many years there has been a wreath laying ceremony on the anniversary by the East Kent Branch of the Western Front Association, and the local Royal Air Force Association has been involved. The wording of the plaque is as follows:

[1] Jim Eyles presented the propeller to the IWM on 28 May 1936. However, while the date of acquisition is recorded, the actual whereabouts of the propeller are not known today. Nor were any marks on it recorded when it was received, so there is no way of knowing from what type of aeroplane it might have come from. It is difficult to believe that Mannock would have been able to bring either a Nieuport or an SE5 propeller back to England, by road, train and ship, so one has to consider that it was from an aircraft situated at one of the aerodromes from which he flew in England.

[2] Captain Archibald Charles Reeves was a Wellingborough man, and may well have come into contact with Mannock and Eyles before the war, as he was working as a contractor with the Wellingborough Iron Company prior to 1914. Reeves had flown with 55 Squadron in 1917 and had been awarded the Military Cross and been Mentioned in Despatches.

To the Honoured Memory of Major Edward Mannock VC DSO (2 Bars) MC (1 Bar), Royal Air Force who served with eminent distinction in the Great War and was killed July 18th 1918 while engaged in aerial combat. *Sic itur ad astra.*

He is one of the 517 men of Canterbury whose names are inscribed on The War Memorial by Christ Church Gate – The citizens of CANTEBURY place this tablet here.

It is unfortunate that the incorrect date was chiselled into this tablet, someone obviously confusing the date of his death with the date the tablet was to be erected, viz: 18 July 1925.

There is another memorial to Mannock at Broad Green, Wellingborough, so that town remembers him in addition to the road. Therefore it seems as though the town did eventually approve a memorial referred to in Jim Eyles's newspaper interview in 1939.

The Royal Air Force also named one of its fleet of VC10 transport aircraft after him, and it flew with No.10 Squadron in the latter half of the 20th century. It was a Mark C1K and its serial number was XV103. This aircraft was scrapped in November 2002. Other VC10s of this unit were also named after RAF Victoria Cross winners of both world wars.

**

Postscript Two

There is one final and very sad twist to that quest by Jim Eyles for the burial location of his airman friend Mick Mannock. Mention was made in chapter one of the young son Jim and his wife had at the time Mannock knew him. Jim's wife Mabel Annie 'May' (née Billingham) had died in January 1936, and with the coming of World War Two, this youngster had joined the Royal Air Force.

In due course Ernest Derek Eyles qualified as a navigator/radar operator and flew on operations as part of the two-man night-fighter crew of a Mosquito with 96 Squadron. His pilot was Flight Lieutenant Donald Leslie Ward from Warwickshire, who had earlier been with 68 Squadron. Ward and Eyles teamed up in early 1944 and enjoyed some success against the enemy. They had shot down two German Messerschmitt 410s and then in June, when the V-1 'doodlebug' menace began, they downed a number of these deadly flying bombs – Don Ward himself being credited with 12.

Both men were awarded the Distinguished Flying Cross, which must have given great pleasure to his father Jim. Ernest Eyles was also awarded the Czech Military Cross. Upon the disbandment of 96 Squadron both men were posted to 25 Squadron at Castle Camps.

The house at 183 Mill Road, Wellingborough, the home of Jim Eyles, as it is today and where Edward lodged before WW1.

In all, he had been involved in the destruction of four German aircraft, two with Ward, and two with other pilots. Eyles's citation (*London Gazette*, 17 April 1945) reads:

> Flight Lieutenant Eyles has completed two tours of operational duty. He is a highly skilled observer whose fine work has won much praise. He has assisted in the destruction of four enemy aircraft.

On 25 January 1945, during a practice interception sortie, Ward and Eyles collided with another aircraft and were killed instantly when their Mosquito (MT494) crashed at Camps Hill, Bartlow, Cambridgeshire. The other crew in MV529, Squadron Leader John Arnsby DFC and Flight Lieutenant Douglas M Reid DFC, also died, thus wiping out four DFC winners. The terrible blow to Jim can be imagined, but at least he had the satisfaction of knowing where his son would lay buried. Ernest was 31 years old and husband of Hilda Zoe Eyles of Northampton. He is buried in the Doddington Road cemetery, Wellingborough, Block Q, Grave 420. Today the grave is not in the best of conditions, but written along one of the stone edges is the name of May Eyles, and along the other is the commemoration to Mick Mannock, as if to say that although Jim Eyles's old friend could not be found by the authorities in France, then at least he could be remembered here, along with his son and wife.

There is one other 'memorial' to Mick Mannock, arranged by Jim Eyles. The Eyles family had moved from 64 Melton Road, Wellingborough to 183 Mill Road. Looking at the house today one can see a blue plaque with white lettering on the front wall. It is not the usual round blue and white plaque that adorns houses of well known people who have lived on the premises, but no doubt Jim had by-passed this official type with a rectangular metal one of his own.

The plaque Jim Eyles placed on the front of his home at 183 Mill Road, Wellingborough, to his great friend, Edward 'Mick' Mannock.

APPENDIX A

MAJOR EDWARD MANNOCK'S CITATIONS

The *London Gazette*, Monday 17 September 1917.
Military Cross – Second Lieutenant Edward Mannock, R.E. and R.F.C.

> *'For conspicuous gallantry and devotion to duty. In the course of many combats he has driven off a large number of enemy machines, and has forced down three balloons, showing a very fine offensive spirit and great fearlessness in attacking the enemy at close range and low altitudes under heavy fire from the ground.'*

NB. Due to the limited space within the *London Gazette* as each bravery award was given, the citations recorded were generally far smaller than the actual recommendations forwarded for consideration for an award. Each commanding officer could nominate one of his men for a decoration if he felt it warranted, either for some specific action, or for a period of prolonged activity in which the man in question had shown outstanding merit. Generally awards given for an act or acts of bravery within a small time-frame received Immediate Award status, while periods of good work were classed as Non-Immediate. These recommendations were regularly put forward for approval by 'higher authority'. In the RFC's case this higher authority was generally the brigade commander under whose command were the wings and squadrons within his brigade mandate. What follows each of Mannock's MC and DSO awards are the actual recommendations that passed through brigade. Although it did not apply to Mannock, awards that got as far as brigade had still to be approved, and any number of recommendations were either disallowed, or down-graded as far as the final decision on what medal was to be approved.

The recommendation for Mannock's MC, was noted as an Immediate Award and dated 14 July 1917:

For exceptional skill and daring in aerial combats:-
  On 13th July 1917, he attacked three Aviatiks East of LENS. Diving on one, he fired a whole drum at very close range, and the hostile machine fluttered down quite out of control.
  On 12th July 1917, he engaged a D.F.W., Aviatik and shot it down within our lines near LIEVEN. The German observer was killed and the pilot wounded and taken prisoner.
  On 7th June 1917, he attacked an Albatros Scout North of LILLE, and drove it down out of control.
  On 7th May 1917, he crossed the lines at 50 feet, under heavy fire from the ground, and brought down the hostile balloon at Quiéry-La-Motte in flames.
  In the course of many combats, this officer has driven off a large number of enemy machines, and has forced down three balloons.

Approved by Lieutenant-Colonel W R Freeman DSO MC, Commanding 1st Brigade, Royal Flying Corps.

**

The *London Gazette*, 18 October 1917 (Citation published in LG for 7 March 1918).
Bar to Military Cross – Captain Edward Mannock M.C., R.E. and R.F.C.

> *'For conspicuous gallantry and devotion to duty. He has destroyed several hostile machines and driven others down out of control. On one occasion he attacked a formation of five enemy machines single-handed and shot down one out of control. On another occasion, while engaged with an enemy machine, he was attacked by two others, one of which he forced to the ground. He has consistently shown great courage and initiative.'*

Recommendation which resulted in this Bar to his MC, dated 6 September 1917:

For consistent gallantry and devotion to duty on many occasions, notably the following:-
On 4th September 1917, he attacked and brought down in flames a D.F.W. two-seater, which fell just this side of the lines, North-East of VIMY.
On the same day, he attacked another D.F.W. over NOEUX LES MINES. The fight continued until he was well East of LENS, when the E.A. was forced down in a steep nose dive. The observer of the enemy machine was apparently hit as he was seen to be lying over the edge of the fuselage. On the same day he also attacked and apparently drove down out of control a D.F.W. just East of LENS. (Confirmed by AA observer.)
On August 17th 1917, he encountered a two-seater D.F.W. over LENS and fired a drum of ammunition into it at close range. The E.A. fell in a slow spinning dive and crashed near SALLAUMINES. (Confirmed by another Pilot who was flying very low at the time.)
On 12th August 1917, during an offensive patrol he saw an Albatros Scout attempting to attack one of our balloons; he climbed to meet the E.A. and attacked it at close range bringing it down this side of the lines near PETIT VIMY.
On 5th August 1917, he engaged one E.A. of a formation of five over [the] DROCOURT LINE and shot it down out of control. (Confirmed by other Pilots.)
On 6th September 1917, whilst attacking a D.F.W. he was attacked by two Albatros Scouts, one of which he forced to land near LENS. (Confirmed by A.A. observers.)

Approved as an Immediate Award by Brigadier-General G S Shepherd DSO MC, Officer Commanding 1st Brigade, Royal Flying Corps.

(It would seem that Major Tilney had already had this recommendation typed up and had to add the item referring to 6 September, at the end.)

**

The *London Gazette*, Monday 16 September 1918.
Distinguished Service Order – T/Captain Edward Mannock M.C., R.E., att'd R.A.F.

> *'For conspicuous gallantry and devotion to duty during recent operations. In seven days, while leading patrols and in general engagements, he destroyed seven enemy machines, bringing his total in all to thirty. His leadership, dash and courage were of the highest order.'*

Recommendation for his first DSO, dated 9 May 1918, reads:

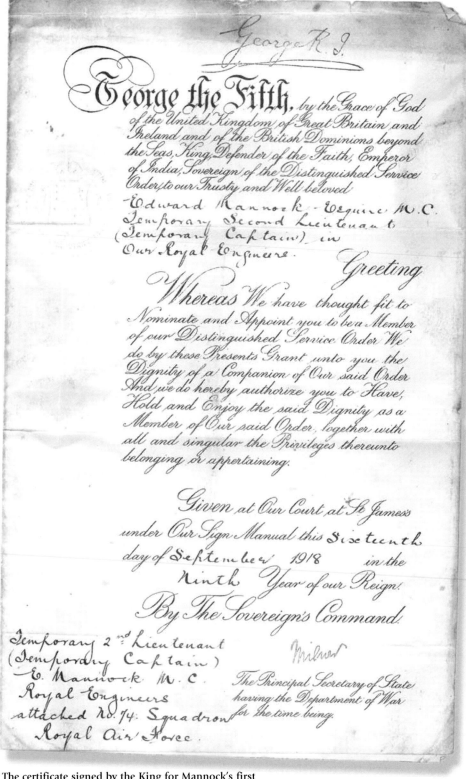

The certificate signed by the King for Mannock's first
DSO, dated almost two months after his death.

On 12-4-18, Captain Mannock, while leading his patrol, engaged a hostile formation over MERVILLE: two E.A. were destroyed, one by Captain Mannock. Later in the same day in a general engagement over BOIS DE PHALENPIN, Captain Mannock shot down an Albatros Scout.

On 22-4-18, a patrol led by Captain Mannock engaged several hostile Scouts. Captain Mannock destroyed one, a Pfalz Scout, which fell to earth at MOURILLON, East of MERVILLE.

On 29-4-18, ten enemy machines were engaged over DICKEBUSCH, one of them engaged by Captain Mannock fell in flames.

On 3-5-18, the whole of a patrol led by Captain Mannock engaged and destroyed an Albatros 2-seater S. of MERVILLE.

On 6-5-18, Captain Mannock engaged five hostile Scouts and destroyed one of them, a Triplane, which crashed at "The Bluff".

This officer has now accounted for 30 enemy machines, and is a wonderful asset to his Squadron. His leadership, dash and courage are beyond comparison.

Approved and forwarded on 9 May 1918, by Brigadier-General T I Webb-Bowen, Commanding 2nd Brigade, Royal Air Force.

* *

The *London Gazette*, Monday 16 September 1918.
Bar to the Distinguished Service Order – T/Captain Edward Mannock, D.S.O., M.C., R.E., and R.A.F.

> *'For conspicuous gallantry and devotion to duty. In company with one other scout this officer attacked eight enemy aeroplanes, shooting down one in flames. The next day, when leading his flight, he engaged eight enemy aeroplanes, shooting down the rear machine, which broke in pieces in the air. The following day he shot down an Albatros two-seater in flames, but later, meeting five Scouts, had great difficulty in getting back, his machine being much shot about, but he destroyed one. Two days later, he shot down another two-seater in flames. Eight machines in five days – a fine feat of marksmanship and determination to get to close quarters. As a patrol leader he is unequalled.'*

The recommendation for this Bar to DSO was again approved and forwarded by Brigadier-General T I Webb-Bowen, Commanding 2 Brigade, Royal Air Force.

On 11-6-18, in company with one other Scout, Captain Mannock attacked eight E.A. N.E. of ARMENTIÈRES and shot down one in flames.

On 12-5-18, when leading his Flight, Captain Mannock engaged eight E.A. near WULVERGHEM and destroyed three E.A. himself.

On 16-5-18, he led his patrol against six E.A. East of YPRES and shot down the rear machine, which broke in pieces in the air.

On the 17-5-18, when out looking for enemy balloons, he encountered an enemy two-seater Albatros N.E. of YPRES; this he shot down in flames. Later in the day he single-handed engaged five Albatros Scouts, one of which he destroyed near DOULIEU: being attacked by the remaining four, he had great difficulty in getting back, his machine being much shot about.

On the 18-5-18, when on patrol near STEENWERCKE, he encountered a Halberstadt two-seater at 14,000 feet and shot it down in flames.

In five days fighting Captain Mannock has destroyed eight enemy machines, bringing his total up to thirty-eight. He sets a wonderful example in marksmanship and determination to get to close quarters: as a Patrol leader he is unequalled.

**

The *London Gazette*, Saturday 3 August 1918.

Second Bar to Distinguished Service Order – T/Captain Edward Mannock, D.S.O., M.C., (formally Royal Engineers).

> *'This officer has now accounted for 48 enemy machines. His success is due to wonderful shooting and a determination to get to close quarters; to attain this he displays most skilful leadership and unfailing courage. These characteristics were markedly shown on a recent occasion when he attacked six hostile Scouts, three of which he brought down. Later on the same day he attacked a two-seater, which crashed into a tree.'*

(The announcement of award of Distinguished Service Order, and First Bar thereto, will be published in a later *Gazette*.)

The recommendation for this second Bar was approved and forwarded by Brigadier-General T I Webb-Bowen on 17 June 1918, Commanding 2nd Brigade, RAF. It was also annotated with the dates of his two previous DSO awards, together with a pencilled note to the General Officer Commanding: 'For information – he is recommended for a second Bar to the DSO' JF, 18/6/18.

On the 21-5-18, whilst on offensive patrol South of HOLLEBEKE, Captain Mannock attacked six hostile Scouts. The first fell to pieces in the air, the second went down in a spin and was seen to crash; the third put up a better fight and was followed down to 4,000 feet when it side-slipped and crashed. These machines were all seen to crash by other members of the Patrol.

During one patrol on the above date, Captain Mannock dived at 140 mph from above MONT DE CATS towards MERVILLE to cut off a two-seater. After firing 40 rounds the enemy machine, a Hannover, fell into a tree at LA COURONNE, S. of VIEUX BERQUIN.

On the 26-5-18, when leading his patrol about 1½ miles S. of BAILLEUL, four Albatros Scouts were encountered. Captain Mannock shot down one in flames.

On the 29-5-18, when engaged on a similar duty to the N.E. of ARMENTIÈRES, Captain Mannock attacked two Albatros Scouts at 17,000 feet. One fell and was observed to crash and burn on the ground.

On the 1-6-18, on Offensive Patrol over ESTAIRES, Captain Mannock's patrol engaged a formation of Pfalz Scouts. One engaged by the leader had a bottom wing shot away and fell E. of MERVILLE. A second was then attacked and burst into flames, falling in the same neighbourhood.

On the 9-6-18, when some two miles S. of KEMMEL, Captain Mannock observed two Albatros two-seaters at work; climbing into the sun to 10,000 feet, he dived on the enemy from the South and shot down one, which crashed close to one of the enemy balloons.

On the 16-6-18, when three miles S. of ZILLEBEKE LAKE, Captain Mannock's patrol attacked twelve Pfalz Scouts; the leader shot down one, which fell near KRUISEECK.

Captain Mannock has now accounted for 48 enemy machines. His success is due to wonderful shooting, and a determination to get to close quarters: to attain this he displays most skilful leadership and unfailing courage.

**

Mention in Despatches: 31 December 1918 (General Citation).

**

The *London Gazette*, Friday 18 July 1919.
VICTORIA CROSS

His majesty the KING has been graciously pleased to approve of the award of the Victoria Cross to the late Captain (acting Major) Edward Mannock, D.S.O., M.C., 85th Squadron Royal Air Force, in recognition of bravery of the first order in Aerial Combat:-

On the 17th June, 1918, he attacked a Halberstadt machine near Armentières and destroyed it from a height of 8,000 feet.

On the 7th July, 1918, near Doulieu, he attacked and destroyed one Fokker (red-bodied) machine, which went vertically into the ground from a height of 1,500 feet. Shortly afterwards he ascended to 1,000 feet and attacked another Fokker biplane, firing 60 rounds into it, which produced an immediate spin, resulting, it is believed, in a crash.

On the 14th July, 1918, near Merville, he attacked and crashed a Fokker from 7,000 feet, and brought a two-seater down damaged.

On the 19th July, 1918, near Merville, he fired 80 rounds into an Albatros two-seater, which went to the ground in flames.

On the 20th July, 1918, East of La Bassée, he attacked and crashed an enemy two-seater from a height of 10,000 feet.

About an hour afterwards he attacked at 8,000 feet a Fokker biplane near Steenwercke, and drove it down out of control, emitting smoke.

On the 22nd July, 1918, near Armentières, he destroyed an enemy Triplane from a height of 10,000 feet.

Major Mannock was awarded the under-mentioned distinctions for his previous combats in the air in France and Flanders:

Military Cross. Gazetted 17th September, 1917.

Bar to Military Cross. Gazetted 18th October, 1917.

Distinguished Service Order. Gazetted 16th September, 1918.

Bar to Distinguished Service Order (1st). Gazetted 16th September, 1918.

Bar to Distinguished Service Order (2nd). Gazetted 3rd August, 1918.

This highly distinguished officer, during the whole of his career in the Royal Air Force, was an outstanding example of fearless courage, remarkable skill, devotion to duty and self sacrifice, which has never been surpassed.

The total number of machines definitely accounted for by Major Mannock up to the date of his death in France (26th July, 1918) is 50 – the total specified in the *Gazette* of 3rd August, 1918, was incorrectly given as 48, instead of 41.

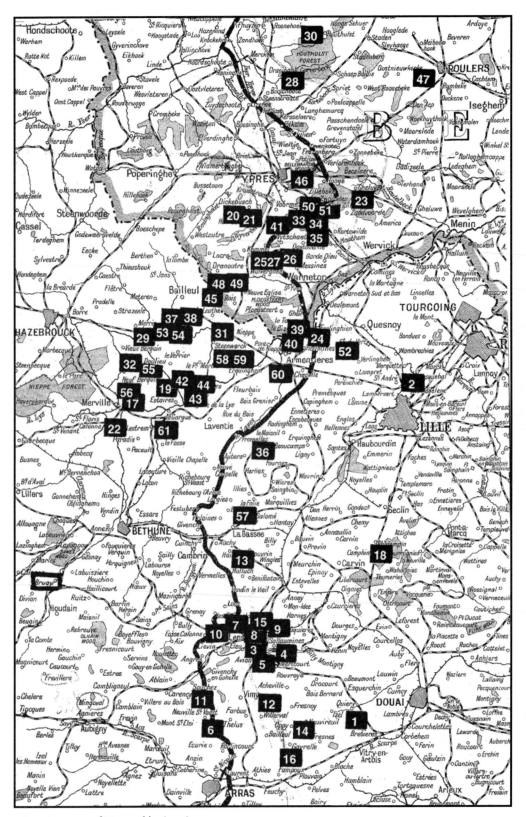

Location map of Mannock's victories.

Appendix B

Major Edward Mannock's
Combat Victories

The following compilation of Mannock's combat successes comes from basic sources, mainly his combat reports, or reports from other official records. After so many years it has to be said that some of these records have been lost or misplaced, even stolen, although at some stage they have been seen by various historians. There is also, fortunately, the late Air Commodore Keith Caldwell's personal diary in which, by all accounts, he maintained records of his 74 Squadron pilots' successes. He makes reference to these in his 1964 tape recording when talking to Edward Naulls. There is one obvious omission, but he may very well have merely missed speaking of it simply because he was scanning the page rather than making certain he did not miss anything. In any event, as Caldwell remarks, what does it really matter? That Mannock was a first-class WW1 fighter pilot, with more skills than merely the ability to shoot straight, is not in question. He still had a high score of victories, with many more confirmed than some other pilots. The fact is that Ira Jones, in making certain that his hero notched up more victories than Billy Bishop when he was writing his book on Mannock's life, merely muddied the water. What follows is an attempt at listing the victories known to have been attributed to Mannock with 40, 74 and 85 Squadrons in WW1.

Date	Type	Result	Time	Serial	Remarks
40 Squadron					
1917					
7 May	Balloon	Flames	09.35	B1552	SE of Souchez.
7 Jun	Albatros DIII	Out of control	07.17	B1552	N of Lille. Probably aircraft of Jasta 33.
12 Jul	DFW CV	Crashed	10.10	B1682	Nr Avion, British lines.From Schusta 12; – became G.53 of captured aircraft.
13 Jul	DFW CV	Out of control	09.20	B1682	N of Sallaumines. Possibly machine from FA(A)240.
28 Jul	Albatros DIII	Out of control	09.30	B3554	E of Lens. Possibly From Jasta 12.
5 Aug	Albatros DV	Out of control	16.00	B3554	Avion/Hénin Liétard.
12 Aug	Albatros DIII	Captured	15.15	B3554	SE Petit Vimy. Ltn von J Bertrab wounded & PoW.G.60 of captured aircraft.
15 Aug	Albatros DV	Out of control	12.25	B3554	Lens.
15 Aug	Albatros DV	Out of control	19.30	B3554	N of Lens. Jasta 30.
17 Aug	DFW C	Crashed	10.50	B3554	Lens.
4 Sep	DFW C	Driven down	09.45	B3607	Nouex Les Mines. Machine from FA(A)211. Obs hit.
4 Sep	DFW C	Out of control	11.30	B3607	E of Lens-Liéven.
4 Sep	DFW C	Flames/Capt	16.25	B3607	Souchez. FA(A)235. G.68 of captured aircraft.

Date	Type	Result	Time	Serial	Remarks
6 Sep	Albatros DV	Forced to land	08.45	B3607	Nr Lens.
11 Sep	DFW C	Out of control	11.15	B3607	Thelus-Oppy.
20 Sep	DFW C	Ooc/smoking	17.35	B3607	Hulluch. FA(A)240 ?
23 Sep	Two-seater	Crashed	16.45	B3541	E of Oppy.
25 Sep	Rumpler C	Crashed	15.10	B3607	Liéven-Lens. FA(A)224.
1918					
1 Jan	Hannover CLIII	Captured	11.30	B665	Fampoux. FA(A)288 G.121 of captured aircraft.

74 Squadron

Date	Type	Result	Time	Serial	Remarks
12 Apr	Albatros DVa	Crashed	08.25	D278	E of Merville.
12 Apr	Albatros DVa	Crashed	14.40	D278	E of Carvin.
22 Apr	Albatros DVa	Out of control	?	D278	E of Hazebrouck.(no C/R – noted in Caldwell's diary)
23 Apr	Pfalz DIII	Crashed	18.10	D278	Meurillon, E. of Merville. Jasta 7 ?
29 Apr	Fokker DVI	Flames	11.40	D278	S of Dickebusch Lake Jasta 'B' machine.
30 Apr	Halberstadt CLIII	Captured	14.40	D278	SE of Dickebusch Lake.Shared with H E Dolan, Schusta 12 – 'G/2nd Bgde 6.
3 May	LVG C	Crashed	18.55	D278	S of Merville. Shared with H E Dolan, A C Kiddie, and H G Clements. FA32.
6 May	Fokker Dr.I	Crashed	09.20	D278	Zillebecke Lake. Jasta 20.
11 May	Pfalz DIII	Flames	17.40	C1112	NE of Armentières. Jasta 47.
12 May	Albatros DVa	Crashed	18.20	C1112	Wulveghem. First two a/c
12 May	Albatros DVa	Crashed	18.20	C1112	collided and fell in pieces.
12 May	Pfalz DIII	Crashed	18.20	C1112	Wulveghem area.
16 May	Pfalz DIII	Crashed	11.00	?	SW of Houthulst Forest.Jasta 54.
17 May	Albatros DV	Flames	11.20	D278	Doulieu. Jasta 52 ?
17 May	Albatros CX	Flames	14.30	D278	NE of Ypres. FA(A)288b.
18 May	Albatros CX	Crashed	08.30	D278	Steenwercke. FA19.
20 May	Two-seater	Driven down	?	D278	Went down with centre-section tank on fire.
21 May	Hannover CL	Crashed	09.20	D278	S of Vieux Berquin. FA9w.
21 May	Pfalz DIII	Crashed	19.00	D278	S of Hollebeke. Fight with
21 May	Pfalz DIII	Crashed	19.00	D278	Jasta 16b. First EA fell
21 May	Pfalz DIII	Crashed	19.00	D278	to pieces in the air.
22 May	Pfalz DIII	Out of control	18.15?	D278	Fromelles.
26 May	Albatros DV	Flames	19.45	D278	S of Bailleul.
29 May	Albatros DV	Crashed	19.25	C6468	NE of Armentières.
29 May	Albatros DV	Out of control	20.05	C6468	-ditto-
29 May	Albatros DV	Driven down	20.05	C6468	-ditto-
31 May	Pfalz DIII	Out of control	19.40	C6468	N of Wytschaete.
1 Jun	Pfalz DIII	Crashed	16.25	C6468	Estaires – in pieces.
1 Jun	Pfalz DIII	Flames	16.35	C6468	-ditto- Jasta 52.
1 Jun	Pfalz DIII	Out of control	16.35	C6468	-ditto-
2 Jun	Pfalz DIII	Out of control	15.40	C6468	S of Mt Kemmel.
6 Jun	Fokker DVII	Crashed	15.40	C6468	E of Ypres.
6 Jun	Pfalz DIII	Crashed	19.45	C6468	W of Roulers. Shared with W E Young, Clements and Kiddie.
9 Jun	Albatros C	Out of control	08.05	?	S of Kemmel Hill. Shared with Kiddie and Clements.
9 Jun	Albatros C	Crashed	08.10	?	With Young. FA(A)254.
16 Jun	Pfalz DIII	Crashed	07.45	C8845	S of Zillebeke Lake

Date	Type	Result	Time	Serial	Remarks
16 Jun	Pfalz DIII	Out of control	07.45	C8845	
17 Jun	Halberstadt CLII	Crashed	09.45	C8845	Armentières. FA(A)205 ?

85 Squadron

Date	Type	Result	Time	Serial	Remarks
7 Jul	Fokker DVII	Crashed	20.20	E1295	Doulieu.
7 Jul	Fokker DVII	Out of control	20.20	E1295	
14 Jul	Fokker DVII	Crashed	08.35	E1295	NE of Merville.
14 Jul	Halberstadt CLII	Forced to land	09.05	E1295	" turned over on landing.
19 Jul	Albatros CXII	Flames	08.23	E1295	Merville. FA7.
20 Jul	Albatros CXII	Crashed	11.17	E1295	NE of Le Bassée. FA7.
20 Jul	Fokker DVII	Out of control	12.15	E1295	Steenwercke – smoking.
22 Jul	Fokker Dr.I	Crashed	09.52	E1295	Armentières. Lost tail.
26 Jul	DFW CV	Crashed	05.30	E1295	Lestrem. Shared with D C Inglis. FA(A)292.

A break-down of these claims shows 41 crashed, in flames or captured, 19 out of control, one balloon in flames, which makes a total of 61, which is around the total historians today generally agree is the more correct figure. Listed are two more recorded as forced to land and three others driven down – categories that by 1917-18 were not recognised as victories, as they might have been in 1915-16.

Appendix C

Major Caldwell's Diary Tally

Mick Mannock's CO when he was a flight commander in 74 Squadron, Major Keith 'Grid' Caldwell MC, kept a diary in France. In it he also recorded victories scored by his pilots. In the 1950s when he was contacted by Vernon Smyth, Caldwell had typed out his diary notes on Mannock. In 1964, when Edward Naulls had visited him in New Zealand, he also read out these entries for the tape recording. The sum of these entries are given here for reference to Mannock's claims while with 74 Squadron.

1918

12 Apr	Destroyed enemy scout .
"	With Flight was mainly responsible for shooting down 3 more (Capt Young and I each got one too, making 5 on our first day of action).
21 Apr	Helped Dolan in good scrap v two hot stuff Triplanes but no decision.
22 "	Got scout out of control.
23 "	Crashed enemy scout.
12-23 "	Still late getting off the ground with his Flight.
29 "	Got Hun in flames. Shot observer in 2-seater but Hun got away.
30 "	Led Glynn and Dolan against 9 Huns and crashed one – excellent show. Between 12/30 April, mainly responsible for all E.A. by A Flight.
3 May	Led patrol from 14,000 ft to 2,000 ft 1 mile east of Merville and crashed Hun 2-seater, with patrol to help. (I saw this and it was very neat work.)
6 "	With Dolan had running fight with Triplanes and crashed one.
11 "	Got scout in flames in fight with Dolan v 8 E.A.
12 "	With his Flight attacked larger formation from the sun and M got 3 of them (two in pieces and one crashed) – excellent show again.
13 "	Several indecisive scraps and some gun trouble through double feeds.
15 "	With Rox-Smith and Clements shot down a 2-seater.
16 "	Got scout in pieces.
17 "	Attacked 4 Pfalz alone and crashed one – (stout show). Later same day, 2-seater in flames. Recommended for D.S.O. a few days ago.
18 "	Got two 2-seaters, one in flames.
19 "	Missed three good chances with gun troubles. Awarded D.S.O.

20 "		Shot up centre section petrol tank – on fire – of 2-seater but could not confirm crash.
21 "		Got 2-seater and later in day got 3 scouts in big scrap. 4 in one day, great effort. Needs a rest, but won't take it yet.
22 "		[No entry in diary but both Mannock and Caldwell in fight against nine Pfalz Scouts, and Mannock shoots down one. Authors' brackets]
26 "		Scout crashed. Recommended for bar to D.S.O.
29 "		One scout ooc and one crashed.
30 "		Very fed up with gun trouble with easy Huns about.
31 "		One Pfalz ooc.
1 Jun		Awarded bar to D.S.O.
1 "		In dog-fight got Hun in flames and one in pieces – damn good show.
2 "		Got one of 4 Pfalz Scouts ooc.
7 "		Shared 2-seater with Young.
16 "		Crashed black Pfalz scout and one ooc.
17 "		Got 2-seater.

My diary entries end on Mannock's page by saying, 'Went on leave and took over 85 and killed a month later, shot down from the ground after getting 68 Huns.'

Edward Mannock's medals: VC, DSO with two Bars, MC and Bar.

BIBLIOGRAPHY

The following books and periodicals have been consulted:

King of Air Fighters by Ira Jones DSO MC DFC MM, Ivor Nicholson & Watson, (London 1934)

Tiger Squadron by Ira Jones DSO MC DFC MM, W H Allen, (London, 1954)

The Ace with One Eye, by Frederick Oughton & Commander Vernon Smyth, Frederick Muller, (London 1963)

The Personal Diary of 'Mick' Mannock, edited by Frederick Oughton, Spearman, (London 1966)

'Mick' The Story of Major Edward Mannock VC DSO MC RFC RAF by James M Dudgeon, Robert Hale, (London 1981)

Mick Mannock, Fighter Pilot, by Adrian Smith, Palgrave, (Hampshire and New York 2001)

Courage Remembered, by Major T A Edwin Gibson & G Kingsley Ward, (HMSO 1989)

For Valour, The Air VCs, by Chaz Bowyer, William Kimber, (London 1978)

Above the Trenches, by Chris Shores, Norman Franks & Russell Guest, Grub Street, (London 1990)

The Sky their Battlefield, by Trevor Henshaw, Grub Street, (London 1995)

Wings over the Somme 1916-18, by W/Cdr G H Lewis DFC, William Kimber, (London 1976)

Mac's Memoirs, by G H Cunningham, A H & A W Reed, (New Zealand 1937)

Popular Flying, editor W E Johns: various issues 1933-39

Cross & Cockade International Journal: various issues.

INDEX OF PERSONNEL

INDEX OF PERSONNEL

ERAU-PRESCOTT LIBRARY